"Imagine that apologetics wasn't so gladiatorial; it isn... luminous readings of the novels of George MacDon.... ....obinson, Justin Ariel Bailey offers a Christian witness for a secular age that is infused with blessing, hope, and grace. Everyone who teaches a course on apologetics should consider assigning this welcome, timely, and thoughtful book."

Timothy Larsen, McManis Chair of Christian Thought at Wheaton College, author of *George MacDonald in the Age of Miracles*

"Justin Bailey asks what apologetics would look like if the human creative imagination was in fact a response to the self-giving revelation of God. His answer involves a rich mixture of philosophical reflection, literary and aesthetic analysis, and biblical thinking. This important book should change not only the way apologetics is taught and practiced but also how worship and spirituality may be more deeply imagined. This is a book not only for the student or pastor but for any thoughtful Christian concerned about their secular neighbors."

William Dyrness, senior professor of theology and culture at Fuller Theological Seminary, author of *The Origin of Protestant Aesthetics in Early Modern Europe*

"In these pages Justin Bailey extends readers an enticing invitation to an expansive epistemology, one that weaves together truth, goodness, and beauty for a fresh vision of the gospel. Bailey locates this apologetic method at the intersection of theology, philosophy, and culture, shaping his innovative evangelistic approach through careful engagement with the work of Charles Taylor, George MacDonald, and Marilynne Robinson. What emerges is a volume as engaging as it is accessible, as historically informed as it is relevant, and as scholarly as it is practical. *Reimagining Apologetics* would be a fine fit for both college classroom and layperson's library alike."

Marybeth Baggett, professor of English at Houston Baptist University and coauthor of *The Morals of the Story: Good News About a Good God*

"Justin Ariel Bailey offers a significant and engaging contribution to theological studies of the imagination. Through both describing and demonstrating the imagination's integral relationship to the field of apologetics, he brings new vision, hope, and vitality to that field. Modeling the empathy he so aptly connects with the work of the inspired imagination, Bailey engages contemporary esteem for authenticity and reveals what a 'thick' view of authenticity entails. In this way he builds bridges of understanding and love toward neighbors who have yet to see the relevance of Christian faith in making their lives more authentic. This is a well-researched and carefully nuanced book that will be a gift to both academic and ecclesial contexts where people yearn to extend God's love in ways that are inviting and compelling."

Kerry Dearborn, professor emerita of theology at Seattle Pacific University and author of *Baptized Imagination: The Theology of George MacDonald*

"This is the latest horse to be added to the small but important new stable of works on the importance of the imagination for Christian apologetics. Instead of trying to fight our secular age on its own turf, Bailey shakes its modernist foundations and challenges its underlying social imaginary. *Reimagining Apologetics* takes up the unfinished task of George MacDonald, Marilynne Robinson, and other culture creatives to draw upon the resources of the imagination in order to help doubters gain a sense of what authentic Christian faith looks and feels like when it is embodied both in fictional characters (literature) and local communities (church). This is a vision-casting book about apologetic vision casting."

Kevin J. Vanhoozer, research professor of systematic theology at Trinity Evangelical Divinity School

"In *Reimagining Apologetics*, Justin Bailey makes a valuable contribution to the development of apologetics as an endeavor that does justice to the complexity of the human experience. Both his theoretical exploration of the functioning of imagination in the work of apologetics and his consideration of the work of George MacDonald and Marilynne Robinson show that there is much of value to be gained from an approach that takes seriously the role of literary and imaginative engagement in the presentation of the Christian faith."

Holly Ordway, the Fellow of Faith and Culture at the Word on Fire Institute

"This important book not only builds a case for an apologetics that takes 'the imaginative content of belief seriously,' but it is itself a marvelous exercise of the theological imagination. Drawing on poetry, novels, and our experiences of sunsets, Justin Bailey makes a convincing case for 'reimagining apologetics' that also speaks to our souls!"

Richard J. Mouw, president emeritus and professor of faith and public life, Fuller Theological Seminary

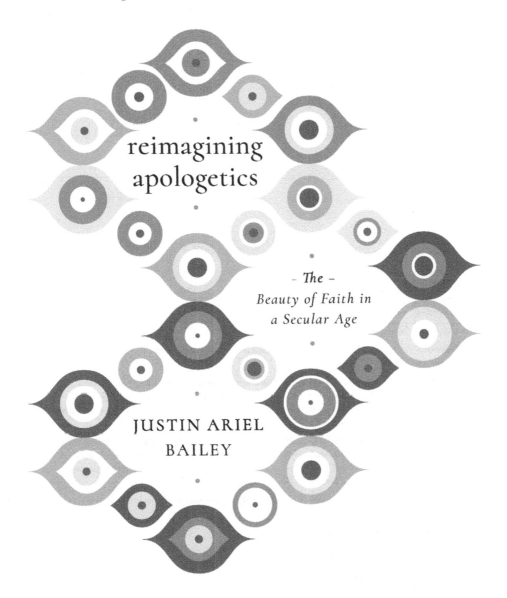

reimagining apologetics

- The -
Beauty of Faith in
a Secular Age

JUSTIN ARIEL BAILEY

Academic

An imprint of InterVarsity Press
Downers Grove, Illinois

InterVarsity Press
P.O. Box 1400, Downers Grove, IL 60515-1426
ivpress.com
email@ivpress.com

*InterVarsity Press® is the book-publishing division of InterVarsity Christian Fellowship/USA®, a movement
of students and faculty active on campus at hundreds of universities, colleges, and schools of nursing
in the United States of America, and a member movement of the International Fellowship of Evangelical Students.
For information about local and regional activities, visit intervarsity.org.*

*All Scripture quotations, unless otherwise indicated, are taken from The Holy Bible, New International Version®, NIV®.
Copyright © 1973, 1978, 1984, 2011 by Biblica, Inc.™ Used by permission of Zondervan. All rights reserved worldwide.
www.zondervan.com. The "NIV" and "New International Version" are trademarks registered in the United States
Patent and Trademark Office by Biblica, Inc.™*

*While any stories in this book are true, some names and identifying information may have been changed to protect
the privacy of individuals.*

Cover design and image composite: Faceout Studio
Interior design: Jeanna Wiggins
Image: © artskvortsova / Shutterstock

ISBN 978-0-8308-5328-1 (print)
ISBN 978-0-8308-5329-8 (digital)

Printed in the United States of America ♾

*InterVarsity Press is committed to ecological stewardship and to the conservation of natural resources
in all our operations. This book was printed using sustainably sourced paper.*

Library of Congress Cataloging-in-Publication Data
A catalog record for this book is available from the Library of Congress.

P	25	24	23	22	21	20	19	18	17	16	15	14	13	12	11	10	9	8	7	6	5	4	3	2	1
Y	37	36	35	34	33	32	31	30	29	28	27	26	25	24	23	22	21	20

TO MELISSA LEIGH BAILEY

Two thousand miles was far enough;

We found that tragedy does not discriminate

And yet where pain pierces, there grace abounds,

Overflows, overthrows the plans we make.

The world before us, hand in hand we stride

Into a future neither one controls;

Yet hope sustains when you are by my side,

Covenant covers, creates, and consoles.

But to love is to limit our wand'ring

And yet to find ourselves at liberty

Blown by winds and yet rooted in one thing

That in giving we find ourselves most free.

The years they run fast, and time's pace is swift.

Till the end you and I; each step a gift.

Table of Contents

Acknowledgments

THIS BOOK WOULD NOT EXIST WITHOUT THE LOVE, prayers, encouragement, energy, and attention from many mentors and friends who have enriched my life and my writing. It is impossible to list them all here, but I would like to acknowledge a few notable people.

I first want to thank my wise editor, David McNutt, who with his team at IVP guided me through the publishing process. I also want to thank my research assistant, Tom Oord, for his help in pulling together the indices at the end of this volume.

The ideas here, along with my academic imagination, have been shaped deeply by many sources, but three names must be mentioned. Bill Dyrness, Rich Mouw, and Kevin Vanhoozer are heroes who have not only inspired this project but also offered substantive reflections on it at various stages. Bill's poetic theology, Rich's generous Calvinism, and Kevin's spirited clarity have set a standard to which I can only aspire. I hope that they can see the ways I have tried to continue in the same way. Any missteps in the attempt are my own.

This book, of course, is more than a matter of academic formation. It emerges from my own journey of faith, which was birthed in the love and prayers of Warren and Tanya Bailey, together with my sisters Jennifer and Jacquelyn. Along the way, I have been shaped and shepherded by trustworthy friends who shared with me "not only the gospel but also their own souls": Cam South, Mark Tremaine, Steve Tremaine, Jim Capaldo, David Tae-Kyung Rim, Lito Guimary, Sung Ryong Kwak, Brannin Pitre, Joel Kok, Ben Thullen, Peter Pak, Davey Henreckson, Justin Hoskins, Joshua Jalandoon, James Lee, and Joshua Beckett. These fellow travelers have walked with me, answering my questions and questioning my answers.

When I write of the beauty of faith, I have in mind particular people in the various contexts where I have been privileged to serve: Christ Our Savior Church, Antioch Bible Church, Grace Pasadena, Madison Square, Covenant CRC, Fuller Seminary, and Dordt University. These ordinary, beautiful places have kept me grounded through all my flights of fancy. How beautiful is the body of Christ!

Lastly and most importantly, my children, Ben and Sophia, are unfathomable sources of inspiration and grace. And my wife, Melissa, has been my love, my friend, and my biggest fan for seventeen years. She has read this manuscript so many more times than duty requires. And so, it is with all my love that I dedicate this work of words to her.

Searching for Stronger Spells

The Apologetics of Hope

> *When we are in church and I'm listening to the preaching,*
> *it's like you are weaving a spell. I believe, and the world*
> *makes sense to me. But then I walk out the door*
> *of the church and the spell is broken.*

DANIEL, AGE TWENTY-ONE

WHAT DOES IT MEAN TO COMMEND the Christian faith in a secular age? This is one of the questions that sent me back to school. I was ministering to emerging adults in the Chicago suburbs and encountering a troubling fragility in their faith. They would speak of disconnection: Sunday was full of meaning, but God seemed distant outside the walls of the church. One student, whom I will call Daniel, described it to me this way: "When we are in church and I'm listening to the preaching, it's like you are weaving a spell. I believe, and the world makes sense to me. But then I walk out the door of the church, and it's like the spell is broken."[1]

---

[1] I originally published a version of this story (with a brief precis of my argument) as "In Search of Stronger Spells," *Inheritance Magazine* 53 (March 2017): 7-10.

As the one doing the preaching, I felt the fragility in my own faith too. Why did what felt so believable on Sunday not feel as believable on Monday? What had changed? Why did it seem as if everyday life existed in a different universe than the one we inhabited together on Sundays?

This experience is not unique in our contemporary context. Christian faith, which once enjoyed widespread cultural ascendancy in the Western world, is no longer taken for granted. Where it remains, belief is reckoned a lifestyle option. To the outside world, my faith may be an important identity marker but no more so than my preference for Kansas City Royals baseball rather than the St. Louis Cardinals. Students like Daniel may continue to believe, but they are in constant contact with others who seem to get along fine without formal religious faith. In place of a shared story we have a thousand micronarratives, which we are free to pick up or put down as we choose. There is the widespread sense that the only meaning to be had is the meaning that we ourselves must make. The existential burden is great: *choose your own way of being human*.[2] This prime directive, which philosopher Charles Taylor calls an *ethic of authenticity*, sets the parameters for faith and mission in much of the West.[3] How can we commend our faith within these new parameters? To continue with our analogy, where can we find "stronger spells"?

Answering these sorts of questions has traditionally been the province of Christian apologetics, the discipline associated with defending and commending the Christian faith. But depending on whom you ask, apologetics is either thriving or dying in the Western world. On the one hand, a perusal of bestselling Christian books reveals an ever-burgeoning market for new apologetic works, as well as the continued appeal of apologetic classics. Within conservative evangelicalism especially, apologetics enjoys popular practice and approval, whether as armor for clashes with "secular culture" or as a bulwark to bolster the belief of the faithful.

Within the broader world of Western Christianity, however, the discipline of apologetics has fallen out of favor. Courses on apologetics—still

---

[2]See this phrase in Robert Joustra and Alissa Wilkinson, *How to Survive the Apocalypse: Zombies, Cylons, Faith, and Politics at the End of the World* (Grand Rapids: Eerdmans, 2016).
[3]Charles Taylor, *The Ethics of Authenticity* (Cambridge: Harvard University Press, 1992).

required in many conservative schools—are no longer a part of the curriculum of mainline Protestant undergraduate and seminary programs. Already prior to the turn of the new millennium, Paul Griffiths reported the decline: "In almost all mainstream institutions in which theology is taught in the USA, apologetics as an intellectual discipline does not figure prominently in the curriculum."[4] Apologetics has been jettisoned as a relic of a bygone era.

Within broader evangelicalism, apologetics appears to be at a bit of a crossroads. A few years ago, I had the opportunity to teach a course in apologetics at Fuller Seminary, where the course (as of this writing) remains an elective. Many of my students expressed deep suspicion about the subject matter, uninterested in any sort of training in triumphalism. As one student put it: "If apologetics is about making arguments and hitting unbelievers over the head with the 'truth' I really want nothing to do with it." The students let me know that although they found the questions intriguing, they were put off by the aggressive posture manifested by apologetic practitioners. The students' suspicions manifest the complaint that traditional apologetic presentations are not effective in addressing contemporary crises of faith. They often serve only to confirm participants in what they already believe. This perceived impotence has led some academics to devalue the discipline as misguided at best and coercive at worst, and to call for "the end of apologetics" in light of our postmodern situation.[5] Indeed, at the end of *my* apologetics course, several of the students suggested that it be renamed ("Christian Witness") or at least given a modifier ("Pastoral Apologetics") so that other seminarians would not be scared away.

I feel the force of these concerns. It sometimes seems as if the apologetic project has simply run its course and that the word is too freighted with negative connotations to salvage. And yet the questions that apologetics has sought to address remain. Can we defend the faith without being defensive or contend for the faith without being contentious?

---

[4]Paul Griffiths, "An Apology for Apologetics," *Faith and Philosophy* 5, no. 4 (October 1998): 399.
[5]Myron B. Penner, *The End of Apologetics: Christian Witness in a Postmodern Context* (Grand Rapids: Baker Academic, 2013).

On what grounds may we appeal to those outside the walls of the church? Is there still hope for apologetics, especially in an age where people are more likely to construe faith in terms of internal resonance (authenticity) rather than external proof (authority)?

I believe the answer to this last question—whether there is hope for apologetics—is yes. I argue that apologetics remains an essential dimension of Christian witness in a secular age but that the discipline is in need of a fresh infusion of *imagination*. This is necessary because the dance of faith and doubt is experienced imaginatively and not just intellectually. Doubters require more than good arguments. They require an aesthetic sense, an imaginative vision, and a poetic embodiment of Christianity. If Christian faith can only be adequately grasped from the inside (from a position of commitment), how can we help those on the outside to experience its reorienting force? What is needed is a provocation of possibilities, a vicarious vision of what it *feels like* to live with Christian faith, a sense of the *beauty* of faith that is felt before fully embraced. For this, the imagination is essential.

WHAT DOES IT MEAN TO REIMAGINE APOLOGETICS?

By *reimagining apologetics*, I mean simply an approach that takes the imaginative context of belief seriously. Such an approach prepares the way for Christian faith by provoking desire, exploring possibility, and casting an inhabitable Christian vision. When successful, it enables outsiders to inhabit the Christian faith as if from the inside, feeling their way in before attempting to criticize it by foreign standards. Whether a person ultimately embraces the vision that is being portrayed, imaginative engagement cultivates empathy. It enables a glimpse, even if just for a moment, of the possibilities that Christian faith facilitates for our life in the world.

By *Christian faith* I mean a holistic pattern of life. This includes the embodied practices that make belief intelligible (prayer, worship, hospitality, peacemaking, creation care, etc.), as well as the felt sense of what belief means for everyday life. In other words, to be a Christian is not simply to believe a list of propositions but also to experience the world through the lens of a meaningful imaginative vision. This vision is a theodrama in which a world of meaning has been gifted to our perception, and ultimate reality is personal, revealed most fully in Jesus Christ.[6] Intellectual assent remains an essential part of the mix. The personal and relational nature of my faith does not exclude its propositional character. But beliefs should not be extracted from the imaginative context in which they become believable.[7] Indeed, it is impossible to separate my faith (what I believe and in whom I trust) from my desire (what I love and what I wish to be the case) and my imagination (what I feel is possible), as well as from my concrete, lived reality (the way that my faith is tested and maintained in the course of everyday life).[8]

UPPERCASE AND LOWERCASE APOLOGETICS

I want to make it clear that in proposing an imaginative approach I am not arguing that all other apologetic models be replaced. Still less am I calling for apologetics to end. I am offering what I hope will be a supplement to other forms of apologetics, or in Holly Ordway's words, "the return to an older, more integrated approach to apologetics."[9] Indeed, what most of the detractors are rejecting is a recent revision of the discipline. Let us call this Uppercase Apologetics (Apologetics-with-a capital A): an approach that seeks to ground the appeal of faith in unassailable proof. Uppercase Apologetics leverages "evidence that demands a verdict" to create epistemic *obligation*. In other words, it seeks to show that a person *should* believe on the basis of objective and universal grounds. In its harder forms, it defends not merely Christian claims but also a foundationalist theory of knowledge and a correspondence theory of truth.[10]

---

[6] I am using the phrase "theodrama" as developed in Kevin J. Vanhoozer, *The Drama of Doctrine: A Canonical-Linguistic Approach to Christian Theology* (Louisville: Westminster John Knox Press, 2005).

[7] "What makes belief believable?" is the methodological question pursued in Graham Ward, *Unbelievable: Why We Believe and Why We Don't* (London: I. B. Tauris, 2014).

[8] Belief is, as Anthony Thiselton writes, "action-orientated, situation-related, and embedded in the particularities and contingencies of everyday living." Anthony C. Thiselton, *The Hermeneutics of Doctrine* (Grand Rapids: Eerdmans, 2007), 21.

[9] Holly Ordway, *Apologetics and the Christian Imagination: An Integrated Approach to Defending the Faith* (Steubenville, OH: Emmaus Road, 2017), 5.

[10] In a foundationalist understanding every truth claim (proposition) must rest on indubitable foundations or be a part of the foundation itself. See the discussion in Alvin Plantinga, *Warranted Christian Belief* (Malden, MA: Oxford University Press, 1999). In a correspondence

Its first move is to establish an adequate test for truth and then to show how Christian claims pass the test.

My goal is not to refute either theory but rather to point out the way that Uppercase Apologetics shifts the conversation away from theological discernment of God's active presence toward tactical defense of Christian *truths*. It is for this reason that theologians like Karl Barth have alleged that apologetics betrays the faith it purports to defend.[11] I find this criticism largely convincing, so long as it is clear that what is being rejected is the revised agenda of Uppercase Apologetics and not the wider apologetic tradition. Uppercase Apologetics emerged in a particular historical context; if it had merely sought to work within the parameters of that context, it may have been one more contextual variety of the discipline. But insofar as it embraced Enlightenment parameters as the paradigm for Christian belief in all times and places,[12] it positioned apologists to speak to a diminished version of the human person: something like a brain on a stick. The insistence on starting with truth also prevented apologists from responding sensitively to the rising ethic of authenticity. It meant that the imagination, associated as it was with Romantic excess, became dangerous, a distraction from truth.

It is not for nothing that Uppercase Apologetics has fallen from favor.[13] But even where it fails, its failure does not rule out (to use Ordway's phrase) the "older and more integrated" way of doing apologetics, what

---

theory of truth, truth is what "corresponds" to empirical reality. See William Alston, *A Realist Conception of Truth*. (Ithaca: Cornell University Press, 1996). I am happy to work within both a modified foundationalist understanding and a chastened theory of correspondence. But I reject the methodological principle that either need be established before we can proceed with apologetics.

[11]Barth famously wrote: "There is no doubt that [Christianity] does not lack the necessary equipment, and can give a good account of itself alongside the other religions. But do not forget that if it does this it has renounced its birthright. It has renounced the unique power which it has as the religion of revelation." Karl Barth, *Church Dogmatics I.2* (London: T&T Clark, 2004), 333.

[12]I will explore this further in chapter one, but see the discussion in Charles Taylor, *A Secular Age* (Cambridge: Harvard University Press, 2007), 232ff.

[13]Penner's criticisms are representative: that contemporary apologetics is hopelessly wedded to the assumptions of modernity, impotent and unintelligible in a postmodern context, and even inclined toward violence and coercion rather than authentic Christian witness. For Penner, the postmodern turn is a blessing in that it exposes the fiction of objective, universally accessible reason and turns the apologetic enterprise back toward revelational, existential, and relational reasons for belief. Penner, *End of Apologetics*, 7.

we might call *lowercase apologetics*. Lowercase apologetics (apologetics-with-a-small-a) is the conversation that becomes necessary whenever Christianity meets a world outside itself. As a sort of public theology, lowercase apologetics always varies based on the challenges encountered in different contexts.[14] Nevertheless, it does not seek to create a single approach that obtains for all times and places.

I feel no desire or need to defend the magisterial claims of Uppercase Apologetics. But lowercase apologetics is a ministerial necessity. It is an unavoidable part of the Christian mission: it is concerned with attending to the particular questions that are being asked in our context, with a view to the ways that those concerns allow the gospel to flower forth in new ways. We see this wider tradition throughout church history: in Justin's *Apology*, Augustine's *City of God*, Aquinas' *Against the Pagans*, and Pascal's *Pensées*, to name a few outstanding examples. Apologetics in the ministerial sense is concerned with the question of intelligibility. It responds organically to how Christian claims are understood and received by the context in which believing communities are embedded. The wider tradition begins in faith, seeks understanding in hope, and commends the gospel in love. It does not secure epistemic *obligation*. The possibility always remains that the gospel may be rejected. Nevertheless, the apologist seeks to grant epistemic *permission*, to show how a person may believe and how faith makes sense. Lowercase apologetics seeks to give outsiders a maximally hospitable

---

[14]The task of theology is always shaped by, responsive to, and in an ongoing process of negotiation with its context. This means that all theological discourse, insofar as it desires to be intelligible to its various publics, has an implicitly apologetic thrust. It is intriguing that apologetics has fallen out of favor during a time when "public theology" has risen in esteem. Public theology seeks to engage conversation outside the walls of the church without losing its distinctively Christian voice. Yet, proponents of public theology such as Max Stackhouse and Elaine Graham identify their discipline as a kind of apologetics. So Graham: "In a post-secular context, public theology must claim an identity as a form of *Christian apologetics*." Elaine Graham, *Between a Rock and a Hard Place: Public Theology in a Post-Secular Age* (London: SCM, 2013), 179. Quoted in Christoph Hübenthal, "Apologetic Communication," *International Journal of Public Theology* 10 (2016): 8. Even ethicist Stanley Hauerwas, who has questioned whether believers and nonbelievers even have a shared vocabulary, has self-identified his theological project as apologetic, going so far as to say: "You really could say that everything I've ever written is apologetics." The citation is from Jeremiah Gibbs, who reports Hauerwas's answer. Jeremiah Gibbs, *Apologetics After Lindbeck: Faith, Reason, and the Cultural-Linguistic Turn* (Eugene, OR: Pickwick, 2015), ix.

space to consider the invitation of faith. It proceeds by removing whatever barriers can be removed and framing the good news with a force that can be *felt*.

THE APOLOGETICS OF AUTHENTICITY

The approach pursued in this book is a lowercase apologetic for the age of authenticity. Authenticity is difficult to define because it is a qualitative rather than quantitative value, like beauty. Nevertheless, by authenticity I mean *the internal call to compose an original life*, a life that makes sense. Rather than conforming blindly to the expectations of society, I "follow my heart" and "choose my own adventure." If this framing of things raises a red flag, consider that there are both thick and thin versions of this. Thin versions might lead to narcissism and sociopathy. But thicker versions could result in a more examined, creative, and self-responsible life.

As an example, perhaps no company pushes authenticity as pervasively as the Walt Disney Corporation. In its many movies we find ballads of self-discovery and self-expression, counseling each viewer to "follow your heart." But within these cinematic universes, authenticity is *not* self-justifying. Villains like Ursula (the sea witch) and heroes like Moana (the seafarer) both follow their hearts. But only the latter's pursuit is meant to be exemplary. This is because authenticity requires a moral horizon, one that takes seriously the nature of the world and our place in it. Thin versions of authenticity become self-defeating, because they fail to find resonance outside our narrow pursuits. This means that the question is not *whether* authenticity is a worthy pursuit, but *what kind of* authenticity will lead us to the good ending we so desire.

My argument, following Charles Taylor, is that authenticity is a key—and often *the* key—factor in what makes belief believable in secular settings. Addressing authenticity means accounting for a person's embodied, aesthetic experience of the world, their *felt* sense of their place in the world, and the possibilities that are available. This quest for authenticity is fundamentally an imaginative quest, and for many people it takes place without explicit reference to God. But I will argue that God may be more present in the quest for authenticity than we think.

The conviction of God's active presence calls for an apologetic that meets people where they are, with confidence that God's Spirit is already at work as well. It means that winsome believers are called to join our neighbors in the quest for authenticity, offering a larger horizon in which God's active presence can be named as it is felt. For faith begins, as Marilynne Robinson reminds us, as an intuitive response to "the feeling of an overplus of meaning in reality, a sense that the world cannot at all be accounted for on its own terms."[15] It is in moments of imaginative excess, when Reality breaks through—perhaps summoning unlooked-for tears to our eyes—that we are especially open to the provocations of belief.

As a value, authenticity is not uniformly distributed. Its gravity is felt to a greater degree in metropolitan Los Angeles, for example, than in rural Iowa, to cite two very different places I have lived. But while the ethic of authenticity may vary by degrees, the need for imaginative provocation should not be underestimated in any case. To ignore the aesthetic context of belief is to miss the reasons why particular problems matter to those who doubt. This would be necessary even if we did not live in the age of authenticity.[16]

Thus, in arguing for a reimagined approach, I am trying to demonstrate both a missional sensitivity to authenticity in my own context as well as a theological rationale for taking the imagination seriously in all contexts. I do not seek to pit the imagination against the intellect; my model supplements rather than replaces more analytic approaches. Rather, I want to correct an imbalance and to draw attention to the way that the imagination already plays a substantial role in the way that beliefs are formed. It remains the case that contemporary apologetic method consistently discounts aesthetic concerns in favor of the rational ones. If the aesthetic dimension is taken into account, it is often in terms of making the truth

---

[15]Marilynne Robinson, *What Are We Doing Here? Essays* (New York: Farrar, Straus and Giroux, 2018), 206.

[16]The irony is that as culture has moved toward giving the imagination its due, apologetic method among evangelicals has often moved in the opposite direction, insisting that authenticity is no more than expressive individualism run amok. Authenticity must be undone. For many conservative apologists the way to resist the slippery subjectivism of authenticity is to double down on defense of the truth. This has led to a narrower scope for apologetics and sometimes the triumphalism of Uppercase Apologetics.

claims of Christianity more attractive or of supplying an "extra push" into belief.

But if my argument is correct, this works upside down: it demonstrates faith's rationality without making clear why someone should care about the demonstration. Rationality and truth are essential, but in our context the prior necessity is a demonstration of faith's generativity and beauty. Indeed, in our postromantic context the aesthetic cannot be bracketed until we adjudicate the truth. The aesthetic dimension is the space in which beliefs become believable. This does not mean that questions of truth are no longer relevant but that they should be situated in terms of the larger imaginative frame. As Kant argued, the questions What can I know? and What ought I to do? are inextricably connected to the question What may I hope?[17]

THE APOLOGETICS OF HOPE

Indeed, imaginative apologetics is not new; it predates modern secularity. Recall Pascal's famous prescription: "Men despise religion. They hate it and are afraid it may be true. The cure for this is first to show that religion is not contrary to reason, but worthy of reverence and respect. Next make it attractive, make good men wish it were true, and then show that it is."[18] For Pascal, the demonstration of faith's beauty precedes the demonstration of faith's verity, even if the demonstration of faith's rationality precedes both. But what has changed with our current situation is that the aesthetic dimension has become "the way into" rationality.[19] The two obstacles are related: part of the unattractiveness of Christianity is the (often-warranted) caricature that it is irrational and anti-intellectual. But caricatures are imaginative construals, and pictures have incredible power to hold us captive. Freedom may be found in painting a better and more beautiful picture. If a person can picture a resonant life of faith, she can begin to entertain the possibility of its rationality and its connection to reality.

---

[17]Immanuel Kant, *Critique of Pure Reason*, ed. Paul Guyer and Allen W. Wood (Cambridge: Cambridge University Press, 1999), A804-805/B832-833.

[18]Blaise Pascal, *Pensées*, trans. A. J. Krailsheimer (London: Penguin, 1995), 4.

[19]Indeed, the provenance of "rationality" gives us reasons to be suspicious. See Alasdair MacIntyre, *Whose Justice? Which Rationality?* (London: Bloomsbury, 2013).

Pascal's example remains instructive. Pascal's strategy was to make people "wish it were true" by attention to the negative space, the vacuum created by alienation from God. This has been called "the apologetics of despair." According to Lee Hardy, it seeks to "push the assumptions of the secular worldview to the point where that worldview becomes untenable, to trace out the logic of atheism to its bitter and presumably unacceptable conclusions, thereby creating a new openness to the hope of the Gospel."[20] Despair, of course, is not the ultimate goal. The ultimate goal is to puncture human hubris, creating space for a humility that is open to divine address.

My proposal operates in a similar register as the apologetics of despair. It is sensitive to existential implications—the *felt* sense of a worldview—and it seeks to provoke rather than to prove. But rather than seeking to surface the weaknesses of a rival worldview, I want to move in the opposite direction. I want to explore aesthetic sensibilities and to situate desire within a broader theodramatic context. I want to water the best imaginative impulses and to provide them a more fertile, transcendent ground.

Thus, the project of reimagining apologetics is a move toward the apologetics of hope rather than despair. The two apologetic strategies are not necessarily in competition. For some skeptics, an apologetic of despair may be necessary to clear the way for hope. Despair can expose pretensions of objectivity, deflate narratives of enlightened maturity, and undermine humanistic confidence. But without corresponding engagement with hopes

---

[20]Lee Hardy sees this strategy at work in Pascal's *Pensées* and Kierkegaard's *Sickness unto Death*. Lee Hardy, "The Apologetics of Despair," unpublished syllabus, Calvin Theological Seminary, Fall 2007. Building on this foundation, Willem de Wit outlines three primary criteria for the apologetics of despair: (1) the address of a worldview that excludes God; (2) the use of a *reductio ad absurdum* argument that shows the absurdity of unbelief; and (3) the sensitivity to the existential implications of belief, especially whether the worldview is satisfying on its own terms. Willem J. De Wit, *On the Way to the Living God* (Amsterdam: VU University Press, 2011), 62-64. Bavinck also described Pascal's apologetic in similar terms, highlighting the latter's emphasis on the aesthetic and existential elements of belief: "[Pascal's] apologia is anthropological; it proceeds from humanity's misery and seeks to arouse in people a felt need for redemption. It then shows that those needs remain unmet in pagan religions and philosophical systems and find satisfaction only in the Christian religion as based on the faith of Israel." Herman Bavinck, *Reformed Dogmatics, Vol. 1: Prolegomena*, ed. John Bolt and John Vriend (Grand Rapids: Baker Academic, 2003), 1:527. I am indebted to my friend Brandon Jones, who participated in Hardy's seminar and first helped me draw a connection between strategies of despair and hope.

and desires, an apologetic of despair runs the risk of leveling in order to build, rather than attending to the ways that God is already at work. Instead of starting with our existential angst caused by our finitude and fallenness, hope moves forward on the conviction of the original goodness of creation and human creativity. It does not ignore fallenness but seeks the renewing power of the Spirit to heal creation.

When I speak of the apologetics of hope, I mean it in at least three ways. First, hope identifies the *existential register* of my argument. To explore a person's hopes and imaginings is to place the conversation in the realm of desire, the aesthetic realm, where the felt experience of meaning is most important. Second, hope signifies the *scope* of my apologetic aims. What I have proposed in this book is an imaginatively inflected exploration of the argument from desire: that our desires are not delusions but are responsive to the provocations of God's active presence.[21] As Robinson writes, "We are a part of this ultimate reality and by nature we participate in eternal things—justice, truth, compassion, love. We have a vision of these things we have not arrived at by reason, have rarely learned from experience, have not found in history. We feel the lack. Hope leads us toward them."[22] Similarly, Avery Dulles notes that the very idea of hope compels us to inquire as to its ground: "An apologetics of hope might be expected to establish two propositions: first, that it is fitting and proper for man always to hope and never to despair, and secondly, that Christianity sustains the type of hope that it is good for man to have. Of itself this argument does not prove that Christianity is true, but it provides strong reasons for taking the Christian message seriously."[23] My aim is not to prove Christianity's truth but to provide a provocation for its ground of hope seriously, appealing to the gospel's resonance, beauty, and generativity.

---

[21]C. S. Lewis, *Mere Christianity* (New York: Harper Collins, 2009), 135-36. One nuance I want to emphasize with respect to Lewis's classic argument is that the desire does not merely linger as a trace of God's past action (i.e., my having been made for another world), but as evidence of God's continuing engagement.

[22]Robinson, *What Are We Doing Here?*, 232.

[23]Avery Cardinal Dulles, *The Survival of Dogma* (New York: Crossroad, 1982), 64. Cited in James G. Mellon, "The Secular and the Sacred: Reflections on Charles Taylor's a Secular Age," *Religion, State and Society* 44, no. 1 (January 2, 2016): 75-91.

Finally, hope identifies the orienting *posture* of the Christian apologist: full of hope that God is present and active in the world, that God was in Christ reconciling the world to himself, and that the Holy Spirit is bringing creation to consummation. Apologetics, after all, has to do with speaking about hope (1 Peter 3:15). In our contemporary situation it means doing so in response to the particular questions that are being asked.

A well-known example of an apologetic of hope can be seen in J. R. R. Tolkien's poem *Mythopoeia*, which addressed then-atheist C. S. Lewis's contention that "myths were lies and therefore worthless, even though 'breathed through silver.'" Tolkien responded that although the desires of the human heart may be disordered, and the creative impulse misused, the power to dream, desire, and create is itself good. As part of our created structure, the right of subcreation "has not decayed. We make still by the law in which we're made."[24] It is the goodness of creation and human creativity that God seeks to renew through Son and Spirit. We should expect human desire, drawn out by the imagination, as well as the products and practices that desire produces to be sites of God's active presence. The apologetics of hope seeks to explore the experience of presence in creation and creativity, inviting seekers to consider whether the presence might have a transcendent source and a personal name. It seeks the source of our imaginative longings as well as a larger context in which these musings can be explored, deepened, negotiated, and fulfilled.

A map of my argument. I will make my argument in two parts. Part one (chapters one through three) deals directly with the relationship of apologetics and the imagination. Chapter one draws from Charles Taylor to sketch the missiological context for my argument. In this chapter I seek to demonstrate that secularity is an *imaginative* crisis. In other words, the apologetic challenge is not just that particular beliefs have been contested, raising new questions that require new answers. Rather it is that the underlying conditions of belief have changed, and with them the felt experience of faith and doubt. Beyond well-reasoned arguments, finding faith requires an invigorated imagination, in which we "feel our way in."

---

[24]John Ronald Reuel Tolkien, *Tree and Leaf; Smith of Wootton Major; the Homecoming of Beorht-noth, Beorhthelm's Son* (London: Unwin, 1975), 56-57.

That is to say, in an age of authenticity, faith and doubt are first navigated imaginatively and affectively, and the felt dimension of faith is most decisive in belief. Apologists can either resist the framework of authenticity—seeking to turn back the clock—or accept authenticity as a fact on the ground, seeking to cultivate a deeper authenticity with the resources of Christian faith. Those who are most interested in the historical conditions that led to the ascendancy of authenticity may benefit from this chapter.

Chapter two is concerned with testing apologetic methodologies in light of our diagnosis. I orient the discussion around Friedrich Schleiermacher's attempt at an apologetic of feeling, drawing attention to Schleiermacher's followers as well as to his critics. These critics allege that Schleiermacher's apologetic loses its connection to the truth and its embeddedness in the church. The goal is to carry forward Schleiermacher's basic impulse to account for "deeply felt personal insight," but to do so with broader theological horizons, which can sustain a more substantial, or "thick" version of authenticity. This chapter will interact most fully with the other apologetic schools and those whose primary interest is the relationship of imaginative apologetics to these other approaches may wish to start with chapter two.

Chapter three seeks to reflect on the faculty of the imagination itself. This chapter gives a threefold account of imagination as seeing, sensing, and shaping. Here I seek to develop the interplay between imagination, embodied experience, desire, meaning making, and faith. In conversation with other philosophical and theological thinkers, I offer an account of how God engages, how sin impairs, and how grace renews the human imagination. Those seeking a concrete description of something so slippery as "imagination" may enjoy my wholehearted attempt to provide a constructive account.

Whereas part one seeks to lay a historical, methodological, and theological foundation for reimagining apologetics, part two (chapters four through six) offers generative models: George MacDonald (chapter four) and Marilynne Robinson (chapter five). Although separated by nearly a century, the similarity between these two writers is compelling. Both emerge from similar theological contexts.[25] Both have produced imaginative as well as didactic literary works that tackle contemporary issues. Both write fiction forged in the fire of well-publicized challenges to Christian faith: for MacDonald the "Victorian crisis of belief," for Robinson the "new atheism." Both are widely read across the spectrum of faith and doubt.

Yet beyond these biographical similarities is a far deeper similarity of apologetic method. Neither MacDonald nor Robinson are apologists in the contemporary sense of "public defender of the faith." Yet both bodies of work have an implicitly apologetic thrust, especially in novels that utilize ministers as their main characters. Writing with the pastoral voice and persona of churchmen, a strain emerges that is sensitive to expressions of doubt in their respective eras. MacDonald and Robinson rarely make direct arguments. Rather, they thrust the reader into the midst of stories that breathe with the Spirit, embodying the Christian vision. They offer a more robust conception of faith's appeal to the human person, exploring the dynamics of faith and doubt, fraught with the messiness of human loves, longings, and laments. They demonstrate that in such matters, it is the imagination that is engaged first, as desire is drawn out through aesthetic experience.

MacDonald's work is instructive for several reasons.[26] First, he lived and wrote amid the burgeoning secularity of the Victorian "crisis of faith." MacDonald's personal and literary engagement with the Victorian fragilization of belief is an instructive example of apologetics within Taylor's

---

[25]MacDonald was raised in (and fired from) the Congregationalist Church; Robinson was raised in the Presbyterian Church and moved to the Congregational Church.

[26]The irony in MacDonald's popular reputation is that although many readers come to MacDonald through the praise of better-known writers (G. K. Chesterton and C. S. Lewis), these writers do not position us adequately to understand MacDonald's project. Their assessments result in two problematic lenses for viewing MacDonald's work: one that denies his Calvinist upbringing any source of his imaginative vision, and one that denigrates his "realistic novels" as unworthy of serious attention. I hope to show that both portraits are misleading. MacDonald's imaginative universe remains shaped by a broader Protestant imagination, and it is therefore fitting that his principal mode of writing is the "realistic novel." Indeed, the descriptors *Calvinist* and *realistic* are part of the problem. MacDonald's example problematizes both terms. See Chesterton's introduction in Greville MacDonald, *George MacDonald and His Wife* (Whitethorn, CA: Johannesen, 1998), 14; C. S. Lewis, *George MacDonald: An Anthology* (New York: Macmillan, 1947), xxiv.

immanent frame.[27] As an early postromantic, MacDonald was deeply influenced by Romanticism, yet his Calvinist sensibilities allowed him to resist its more subjective tendencies. Second, MacDonald developed and displayed a theological account of the imagination that worked itself out consistently in his fiction. Finally, insofar as MacDonald's writing has a pastoral thrust, it serves as an ideal model of a reimagined apologetic. My ultimate goal is to show that MacDonald's aim in all his writing is to wake his reader's imagination, to start a vital process of wrestling with reality in which virtue opens the way to vision. In particular, virtues like humility prepare the heart to inhabit an ever-expanding view of God and the world. Chapter four situates MacDonald within the Victorian crisis in which doubters sought a more generative and generous view of the world. Here I will explore the aesthetic dimension of the crisis and show how MacDonald's response is to sketch an imaginative approach resonant with Victorian sensibilities, especially in his Wingfold trilogy. I will show how the trilogy engages three different types of doubters, grounding MacDonald's apologetic in terms of his friendship to the deconverted Victorian luminary John Ruskin.

Marilynne Robinson occupies a somewhat different position with respect to secularity than George MacDonald. When MacDonald worked, the new option of unbelief was just beginning to gain social respectability. Victorian thinkers were navigating between empiricism and expressivism, and space for the new aesthetic faith of Carlyle and Arnold was still being cleared. By contrast, Robinson is writing on this side of the emergence of the masters of suspicion (Nietzsche, Marx, and Freud) as well as the triumph of authenticity. On the surface, Robinson seems far more interested in offering an alternative to suspicion than in engaging authenticity; indeed, all four of her fictional works are set prior to the upheavals of the 1960s. Yet I want to show how the defense of human consciousness in her nonfiction work, as well as the celebration of the same in her fiction, offers

---

[27]So Taylor: "The deeper, more anchored forms of unbelief arising in the nineteenth century are basically the same as those which are held today. We can see the Victorians as our contemporaries in a way which we cannot easily extend to the men of the Enlightenment." Taylor, *Secular Age,* 369.

a promising resource for the thick version of the apologetics of authenticity sought in chapter three. Chapter five will explore Robinson's imaginative art by highlighting the apologetic logic of her fiction. Robinson's novels invite her readers to experience a capacious Christian imagination, to see the world through the eyes of faith, and perhaps to feel "the shock of revelatory perception," all of which may open the door for faith, and thus for understanding.

Chapter six brings MacDonald and Robinson into conversation. Two common threads will become clear: a posture of blessing toward the world as a place drenched with divine presence and a Calvinist epistemology that fuels this posture. I will also raise the questions of the limits of the imagination with respect to apologetics, in search of both theological and aesthetic integrity. Rather than shrinking the literary to fit a narrow vision of apologetics, assigning an apologetic label to literary art means rethinking what we mean by apologetics. As Alison Milbank argues, an apologetics of the imagination has two primary aims: "The first is to awaken what one might call the religious sense, that homesickness for the absolute. . . . And it is to help those with whom we come in contact to recognize their own assumption of a religious depth to experience. . . . We want non-believers to understand that Christianity is not narrow but a vision that includes everything, restoring the lost beauty of the world."[28]

Here are the two aims: to awaken the religious sense and to reveal the religious depth of experience. MacDonald excels at the first of these aims, Robinson at the second. Both unite to demonstrate that the Christian faith offers a wider vision and a beautiful God. Looking to these writers as our teachers in what it might mean to give a reason for our hope invites a renewed conversation for what an imaginative approach could look like in the age of authenticity. The contribution of these authors to apologetics comes not primarily in terms of a particular literary style (their styles are very different) but in terms of a shared theological vision.[29] For both

---

[28]Alison Milbank, "Apologetics and the Imagination: Making Strange," in *Imaginative Apologetics* (Grand Rapids: Baker Academic, 2012), 44.

[29]I should make it clear that I am not seeking to encompass either author's literary project, or even to provide an adequate description of their body of work. My focus here is narrowly on their imaginative approach to commending the Christian faith. My goal is to discern MacDonald's

thinkers, a theology of divine address works itself out in novels that look for God amid the mundane, especially in the most ordinary experiences of life. Part of the burden of this section is to demonstrate how imaginative apologetics taps into an entirely other dimension of revelation than its intellectual counterparts. My goal is to discern MacDonald's and Robinson's apologetic method not primarily as a rhetorical strategy but as the organic outworking of their theology.

I should say that I have endeavored to write part two so that it could stand on its own. Those readers who begin with part one will see my working categories more clearly, but I have restricted most of the explicit connections to the first three chapters to the footnotes. Readers who are most interested in MacDonald and Robinson, or who simply want to see imaginative apologetics at work, may desire to begin with part two.

In the concluding chapter I draw together the strands of the argument to sketch the contours of a reimagined approach.[30] Here I will offer a working model and three essential elements of reimagining apologetics. Although I have not endeavored to write a handbook on apologetics ("if *they* say that, *you* say this"), I will also offer a few examples of imaginative apologetics in action.

This brings me back to the beginning: the existential impulse for this book. The struggle to experience God in the midst of a secular age is one I resonate with both on a personal and a pastoral level. I have been deeply affected by the disenchantment that I have encountered in the churches where I have ministered, in the college students I now teach, and in my own experience of faith and doubt. I find myself increasingly dissatisfied

---

and Robinson's apologetic method not primarily as a rhetorical strategy, but as the organic outworking of their theology.

[30]I would be remiss to neglect mentioning two other projects with a family resemblance to my own. First, "imaginative apologetics" is the name taken up by Michael Ward and Holly Ordway to denote their method at Houston Baptist University. See Ordway, *Apologetics and Christian Imagination.* My understanding of imaginative apologetics overlaps with these authors, but my primary criterion is postromantic rather than classical: authenticity. Second, a recent collection of essays also takes "Imaginative Apologetics" as its title: the approach of the volume is both to consider the apologetic value of imaginative works as well as to consider reason itself as imaginative. I will cite several of these essays throughout the course of the book. Andrew Davison, ed., *Imaginative Apologetics: Theology, Philosophy, and the Catholic Tradition* (Grand Rapids: Baker Academic, 2012).

with traditional apologetic strategies and have long been convinced that the imagination is in some way the missing piece. My professional work in general, and this book in particular, is guided by this conviction of the centrality of the imagination, even as I seek to establish with greater clarity what that might mean. In some ways, this book is my attempt to work out my own sense of hope in Christ, for the church, and for the world.

As long as there is faith, traditional apologetic argumentation will continue. But what is really needed in secular settings is the willingness to engage imaginations and not just intellects. The possibilities are exciting: what might it mean—for theologians, for pastors, and for the people in the pews—to reimagine apologetics?

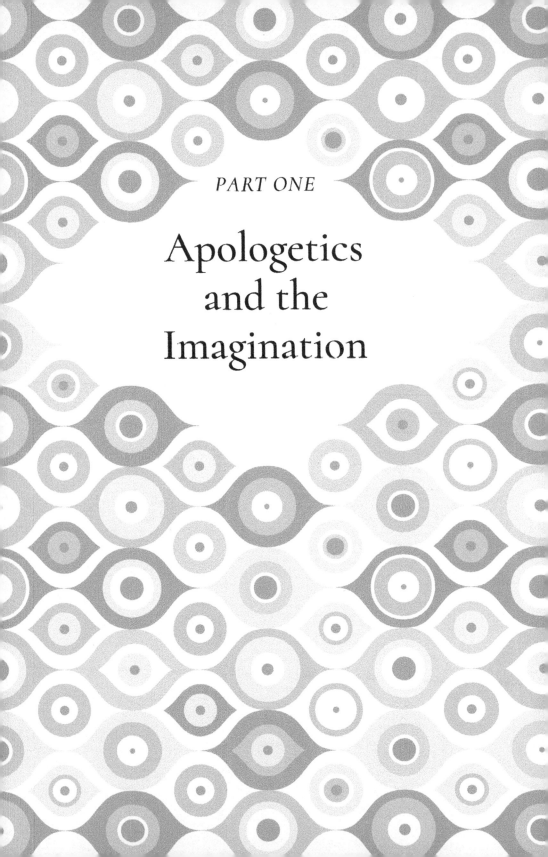

PART ONE

Apologetics
and the
Imagination

one

Eclipsing Enchantment

Charles Taylor and Our Imaginative Crisis

There is a certain way of being human that is my way. I am called upon to live my life in this way, and not in imitation of anyone else's. But this gives a new importance to being true to myself. If I am not, I miss the point of my life, I miss what being human is for me.

CHARLES TAYLOR, *THE ETHICS OF AUTHENTICITY*

"WHY DOES THIS MATTER?"

It was my first solo flight as a seminary instructor. I had just finished a lecture comparing Plato and Aristotle and asked the class if there were any questions. After a pause, a student raised his hand and asked the question dreaded by humanities professors everywhere: "Why does any of this matter?" It was a fine question, and I was relatively prepared to answer it, even if I was annoyed by the pragmatic overtones. "I am telling a story," I said. "And this part of the story matters because it has shaped so much of the way that we think in the Western world. If we want to understand how we got to where we are, we have to understand what has changed in the way we imagine the world." That answer seemed to satisfy the student, but I'm not sure he was convinced. I knew I needed a fuller explanation.

I feel something of a similar impulse as I situate my argument historically. Some of my readers may wonder why such a deep dive into the work of Canadian philosopher Charles Taylor (my primary conversation partner in this chapter) is necessary. So, by way of introduction, I will begin with the longer answer that I gave to the class the next time we met.

There is a passage in John 12 that places Jesus in Jerusalem just days before the crucifixion. As Jesus stands before the crowd, something happens—a noise from heaven—and it immediately generates three different descriptions. For one group, the phenomenon is an entirely natural one: "It's just thunder," they say. Another group believes that something mystical has occurred: "An angel spoke to him." But Jesus and the gospel author identify the sound as nothing less than the voice of God (John 12:27-33).

Thunder, an angel, and the voice of God. These are not just three different interpretations but three fundamentally different experiences.[1] This is because the act of interpretation is never detached from life; it is a continual, lived reality. Our experiences are composed of countless simultaneous interpretations, suspended in webs of significance within which the world takes shape.[2] Every person's power of perception has been cultivated in a particular imaginative field, and in different sorts of soil, different sorts of ideas more readily take root, grow and flourish. Randolph Richards tells a story from his time working as a missionary in Indonesia. He was praying with some Indonesian believers who were deciding whether they should proceed on a serious matter. On an otherwise clear day there came a sudden boom of thunder. "I scarcely noticed and continued praying," he writes. "My friends all stood up to leave. Clearly God had spoken (Psalm 18:13)."[3]

---

[1] See the discussion in Graham Ward, *Unbelievable: Why We Believe and Why We Don't* (London: I. B. Tauris, 2014), 179-80.

[2] See Clifford Geertz, *The Interpretation of Cultures* (New York: Basic Books, 2017), 5.

[3] E. Randolph Richards and Brandon J. O'Brien, *Misreading Scripture with Western Eyes: Removing Cultural Blinders to Better Understand the Bible* (Downers Grove, IL: InterVarsity Press, 2012), 158.

We have all been trained to perceive the world in a particular way, and it can be very difficult to get outside that way of seeing. Our life experiences are located inside conversation circles that can become echo chambers if we are not careful. Personal growth often means deliberately engaging unfamiliar perspectives and listening to voices that you might not normally choose, if for no other reason than to call our default understanding of the world into question. When it comes to faith formation, we need to discern the unconscious currents that have shaped our ability to hear the thunder or the voice of God.[4] Why do different people at different times and in different places experience the world in such different ways? Why have some people experienced the world as bursting with God's presence, while others perceive nothing more than noise?

This riddle of perception is one of the central preoccupations of Taylor's monumental work *A Secular Age*. Early in the book Taylor raises this question: "Why was it virtually impossible not to believe in God in, say, 1500 in our Western society, while in 2000 many of us find this not only easy, but even inescapable?"[5] When it comes to belief, what society takes for granted has changed. Explicit faith commitments are now considered private preferences rather than fundamental frameworks. But how did such a dramatic shift occur, and what does it mean for faith after the shift has occurred? This is the story that Taylor helps us tell, and this is why he is such an important conversation partner for our project of reimagining apologetics.

This chapter is an exercise in imaginative soil science, and Taylor is our lead researcher. As we follow behind him, we will see that the modern condition of secularity is an imaginative crisis, calling for a reimagined apologetic. It is a crisis of the imagination because the imagination is being tasked with the burden of finding meaning in a flattened world. One of the great achievements of the secular age has been the ability of culture makers (those who provide us with the stories we live by) to forge "subtler

---

[4]I am aware the modern social imaginaries are not monolithic. Throughout this chapter I use the pronouns like "we" and "our" to refer to background features shared by those who live in the modern West, the foremost of which is Taylor's "the immanent frame." There are gaps in this frame, and in various social and cultural locations, the gaps are expansive.

[5]Taylor, *Secular Age*, 25.

languages" of meaning to stand in for traditional religious commitment. This means that the crisis is also an opportunity for the imagination because the aesthetic dimension is a primary realm in which faith and doubt are negotiated. This aesthetic dimension, I argue, is integral in making belief believable. This is because the ethic of authenticity—the internal call to compose an original life—has become the very air we breathe.

My contention is that apologetic engagement in a secular age means making sense of the ethic of authenticity. Although there are certainly shallow versions of authenticity that tend toward narcissism, the solution is not to reject authenticity but to seek better expressions of it.[6] Such expressions of authenticity are possible—a faith that is deeply "resonant," for example—and I believe that the good news of Jesus Christ can be communicated in the logic of authenticity without compromising its integrity. Expressive individualism requires a critique, but we must feel its inadequacy from the inside. The thinness of narcissism pushes us to look for something more, even as the sheer gratuity of being—what Marilynne Robinson calls the "givenness of things"—pulls us from fascination with ourselves.[7] It is in this space, caught between these cross pressures, that apologetic witness must be reimagined.

TAYLOR'S STORY OF THE SECULAR SHIFT

Disenchantment or enchantment? Against subtraction stories. What, then, is the story that Taylor is trying to tell? Taylor is seeking an account of how life without God became not just imaginable but often inescapable, in his words: how we moved "from a condition in which belief was the default option . . . to a condition in which for more and more people

---

[6]This perspective diverges somewhat from recent appropriations of Taylor's work. James K. A. Smith has offered a cogent synopsis of *A Secular Age*, Andrew Root has developed Taylor's themes in service of faith formation, and Alan Noble has leveraged Taylor's diagnosis for the sake of cultivating a "disruptive witness." All three otherwise excellent books major on giving a critique of authenticity as expressive individualism run amok. They seek to show how the push for authenticity quickly becomes a slippery slope to narcissism. The critique is fine as far as it goes, but it underestimates the positive possibilities of the shift in sensibility. See James K. A. Smith, *How (Not) to Be Secular: Reading Charles Taylor* (Grand Rapids: Eerdmans, 2014); Alan Noble, *Disruptive Witness: Speaking Truth in a Distracted Age* (Downers Grove, IL: InterVarsity Press, 2018); Andrew Root, *Faith Formation in a Secular Age: Responding to the Church's Obsession with Youthfulness* (Grand Rapids: Baker Academic, 2017).
[7]Marilynne Robinson, *The Givenness of Things: Essays* (New York: Farrar, Straus and Giroux, 2015).

unbelieving construals seem at first blush the only plausible ones."[8] Taylor's story is significant because he is not primarily interested in the content of belief but in its conditions, the imaginative soil in which belief withers or flourishes.[9] How did God's presence, once as unavoidable as the sun, suffer an eclipse?

Here we might outline two different possibilities. The first option is what Taylor calls a subtraction story. Such an account assumes that the world was never really enchanted in the first place. What we call enchantment was actually superstition, and now that superstition has been scraped away by science, we have begun to live in the real world. We have, as it were, emerged from the cave of artificial light into the real sun of scientific certainty. This story pictures human persons as buffered individuals who use reason to control and manage the world rather than persons embedded in an intrinsically meaning-filled cosmos, beholden to a transcendent reality not of their making. Subtraction stories take a disenchanted world as the default setting and the diminishing of religious belief as the restoration of factory settings.[10]

Reports of faith's demise, of course, have been greatly exaggerated. In stubborn defiance, religion has demonstrated remarkable staying power.[11]

---

[8] Taylor, *Secular Age*, 12.

[9] In his words, the "whole context of understanding in which our moral, spiritual, and religious experience and search takes place." Following Wittgenstein, Heidegger, or Polanyi, for Taylor an imaginary is the "background" of belief, that which is taken-for-granted, which usually remains tacit, and may even be as yet unacknowledged by the agent, because never formulated. Taylor, *Secular Age*, 13. See also Charles Taylor, *Modern Social Imaginaries* (Durham: Duke University Press, 2004).

[10] For many years, the subtraction story formed the core of the secularization thesis: modernization leads to the decline of religion. For the classic articulation see Auguste Comte, *A General View of Positivism*, trans. J. H. Bridges (Ithaca: Cornell University Library, 2009); Émile Durkheim, *The Elementary Forms of Religious Life*, trans. Karen E. Fields (New York: Free Press, 1995).

[11] This has brought the secularization thesis under strong scrutiny. Critics point out several problematic assumptions: first, religion is conceived solely in terms of intellectual beliefs that are presumed to be either false (in light of science) or irrelevant (in light of technological advance), rather than as robust form of life composed of meaningful practices and imaginative vision. Second, religion is too often conceived as a static and dependent variable, underestimating the power of religious systems to adapt, change, and to produce new forms of expression commensurate with new situations. Only an ideological commitment requires a fundamental conflict between religion and modernity, such that replacement of the latter by the former is the only possible outcome. Finally, both religion and modernity are often essentialized in accounts of secularization. These are not simple wholes in conflict; both are a collocation of many moving parts that are combined in unique configurations dependent on each context.

And yet it is also clear that a shift has occurred. Religious faith has not been abolished in the Western world. But for increasing numbers of people (and this is especially the case with younger generations), it has been rendered *optional* and *customizable*. The emergence of the self-described "spiritual but not religious," and the rise of the "nones" (those who do not identify with any faith tradition), are both signs of a profound change in the conditions of belief.[12]

All of this encourages us to consider another possibility: not subtraction, but addition. Taylor wants to show that our secular age is not the result of triumphant elimination but rather a long process of construction.[13] Rather than the result of myth busting, Taylor wants to consider secularity as an imaginative accomplishment, a creative composition forged from diverse cultural processes, products, and practices. While many in the majority world still inhabit an enchanted world, in the West we have enclosed our experience in an insulating "immanent frame." This frame shuts out the transcendent, making possible life in a world "no longer under heaven."[14] If the construction story is correct, the journey from enchantment to disenchantment is less like emerging from a cave and more like building an immense stone castle and then forgetting that there is anything outside the castle.

Such an account calls to mind C. S. Lewis's classic story *The Silver Chair*. Two children, Jill Pole and Eustace Scrubb, are sent to an underground realm. The realm is ruled by a sorceress, and she bewitches them to

---

See Jeffrey K Hadden, "Toward Desacralizing Secularization Theory," *Social Forces* 65, no. 3 (1987): 587-611; Rodney Stark, "Secularization, RIP," *Sociology of Religion* 60, no. 3 (September 1999): 249-73; Shmuel N. Eisenstadt, ed., *Multiple Modernities* (New Brunswick: Transaction, 2002); Philip S. Gorski and Ates Altinordu, "After Secularization?," *Annual Review of Sociology* 34 (2008): 55-85.

[12]Revised secularization theories take religion much more seriously but highlight the fact that modernity has created profound new challenges for belief. See Karel Dobbelaere, "The Meaning and Scope of Secularization," ed. Peter B. Clarke, *The Oxford Handbook of the Sociology of Religion* (Oxford: Oxford University Press, February 2011). Such "do it yourself" spiritualities are representative of the ethic of authenticity, of which I will have much to say below.

[13]Nevertheless, we are dealing with "long processes which no one oversees or controls." Charles Taylor, "Afterword: Apologia pro Libro Suo," in *Varieties of Secularism in a Secular Age*, ed. Michael Warner, Jonathan VanAntwerpen, and Craig Calhoun (Cambridge: Harvard University Press, 2010), 302.

[14]A. J Conyers, *The Eclipse of Heaven: The Loss of Transcendence and Its Effect on Modern Life* (South Bend, IN: St. Augustine's Press, 1999), 14.

believe that the above-ground world does not exist. What they believe to be their memories of the surface are no more than imaginative projections. They look at a lamp and imagine a much bigger lamp, which they call the sun. They look at a cat and imagine a much bigger cat, which they call the lion Aslan. These daydreams are lovely, the witch grants them. But it is time to wake up and acclimate to life in the real world—her world. Here's how the conversation goes:

[Jill:] "I suppose that other world must be all a dream."

"Yes. It is all a dream," said the Witch.

"Yes, all a dream," said Jill.

"There never was such a world," said the Witch.

"No," said Jill and Scrubb, "never was such a world."

"There never was any world but mine," said the Witch.

"There never was any world but yours," said they.[15]

The Witch's disenchanting spell—which aims to strip away the children's superstition—is actually an active enchantment. When the spell works, the heroes are in danger of denying a reality that has been rendered remote. Cut off from the above-the-surface world of sun, sky, and Aslan, all that remains is the immanent underground.

Once again, we are in search of stronger spells! Lewis would explicitly use this language in his famous sermon *The Weight of Glory*:

Do you think I am trying to weave a spell? Perhaps I am; but remember your fairy tales. Spells are used for breaking enchantments as well as for inducing them. And you and I have need of the strongest spell that can be found to wake us from the evil enchantment of worldliness which has been laid upon us for nearly a hundred years. Almost our whole education has been directed to silencing this shy, persistent, inner voice; almost all our modern philosophies have been devised to convince us that the good of man is to be found on this earth.[16]

---

[15]C. S. Lewis, *The Silver Chair* (New York: HarperCollins, 2002), 184.
[16]C. S. Lewis, *The Weight of Glory* (New York: Macmillan, 1949), 31.

Like Lewis, Taylor wants us to consider that our immanent experience of the world—in which we seek no goals beyond ordinary human flourishing—is a stunning enchantment, a remarkable feat of human imagination. Re-enchanting the immanent frame will not be simple and may not even be entirely possible.[17]

Taylor's project is significant not simply because of his diagnosis but also because of his bedside manner. His method of narrating the secular shift shows his Romantic sensibilities; he is disenchanting us! For its force to be felt the story must be sketched; the narrative mode enables us to inhabit it aesthetically. Accordingly, I will follow Taylor's story in four movements (the alliteration is my own): enchanted *traces*, Reformation *trajectories*, Enlightenment *transitions*, and Romantic *transformations*. After sketching the story, I will finish with a discussion of the new ethic of authenticity, and what it means for apologetic witness in a secular age.

Enchanted traces: A threefold cord. Our story begins near the end of the Middle Ages, when the world was still enchanted. By "enchanted" I mean that individuals understood themselves to be vitally embedded in a world full of good and evil powers. These powers could interfere with life at any time: acting on, inspiring, and even possessing. Particular objects and places were similarly "charged" with good or evil magic, instantiated in holy relics and holy sites. Life in such a world is inherently less *manageable*: I am either at the mercy of these elements or in the mercy of God. But an enchanted world is also more *meaningful*, because I participate in a world which impresses itself upon me rather than bearing the burden of making meaning by expressing myself. Owen Barfield, one of the Oxford Inklings, called this rich experience of connection "original participation."[18] The term refers to the way that pre-modern people felt a

---

[17]Even if something like re-enchantment is possible, Taylor writes, it will always be re-enchantment *after* disenchantment, that is, in the awareness that the former apprehension of the world is no longer sensible. Charles Taylor, "Disenchantment-Reenchantment," in *Dilemmas and Connections: Selected Essays* (Cambridge, MA: Harvard University Press, 2011), 287-302. See also Robert Lundin's argument that we no longer merely believe; our believing is always "believing again." Roger Lundin, *Believing Again: Doubt and Faith in a Secular Age* (Grand Rapids: Eerdmans, 2009).

[18]Owen Barfield, *The Rediscovery of Meaning, and Other Essays* (Middletown, CT: Wesleyan University Press, 1977), 16. Even though this enchanted participation has been lost, our words remain haunted by this older way of seeing—words like *panic, erotic, music*—recall the specter of Pan, Eros, and the muses. Consciousness, Barfield argues, was mythological before it was purely

conceptual unity between nature and their inner feelings. The possibility that outside forces—stars, spirits, and spells—can exert their gravity on me, impress meaning upon me, implies that the boundary between my mind and the world is quite porous.[19]

In an enchanted world, atheism is nearly unimaginable, and certainly unlivable. This is because in an enchanted world God is the only thing that guarantees that the good powers will triumph over the evil ones. To turn away from God is to face the "frightening field of forces" alone.[20] Furthermore, inasmuch as society's stability depends on divine favor, to turn away from God is to undermine its very foundations. This is why heretics had to be put to death. Just as the "atheism" of the earliest Christians was seen as endangering the Roman order, so too under enchanted Christendom heretics tore the social fabric. As Taylor writes, "As long as the common weal was bound up in collective rites, devotions, allegiances, it couldn't be seen just as an individual's own business that he breaks ranks, even less that he blaspheme or try to desecrate the rite. . . . The deviancy of some would call down punishment on all. At a certain point, God even owes it to himself, as it were, to his honor, we might say, to strike."[21]

This sense of corporate solidarity is foreign to contemporary sensibilities, but it is critical to grasp in the pre-modern world. A person living in the fifteenth century would not have seen herself as an autonomous individual. Rather, human agents exercised faith as those deeply embedded in society, incorporated in the cosmos, and impinged upon by the divine.[22]

---

concrete or purely abstract, and while this mythological consciousness has been lost, metaphor and myth continue to "haunt" our language. We still use the word *panic* but no longer have the sense of Pan acting upon us; we feel the wind but no longer sense the breath of a god. Nevertheless, it is through *words*, especially older words, we catch glimpses of other and older *worlds*. This is one of the reasons, Barfield believed, that poetry, metaphor, and myth can still shift the consciousness of its readers. This capacity of literature to shift consciousness is important, since both of my models for reimagining apologetics are known primarily as writers of fiction. Owen Barfield, *Poetic Diction: A Study in Meaning* (Middletown, CT: Wesleyan University Press, 1973), 80.

[19]In the enchanted world, certain [modern] boundaries/dichotomies are not as pronounced: *subject/object* and *mind/world*. Taylor, *Secular Age*, 35.

[20]Taylor, *Secular Age*, 41.

[21]Taylor, *Secular Age*, 42.

[22]Taylor, *Secular Age*, 152.

Society, cosmos, the divine: this was a threefold cord not easily broken. One could no more escape this sense of embeddedness than modern people can escape electricity or the internet. And yet, the miracle of modernity is precisely the short-circuiting of this threefold connection so that the disenchantment, disengagement, and disbelief became thinkable.[23] Once again, it is not just a matter of discarded beliefs but a "change in sensibility; one is open to different things."[24] A large part of the imaginative crisis that constitutes secularity is that this embeddedness has been lost, and something is needed to fill the vacuum. It has resulted in a situation that gives tremendous power to and places incredible pressure on the imagination to supply new connections.

Reformation trajectories: A shift in gravity. How then did the conditions begin to change? Taylor demonstrates that secular space opened up not from movements outside of Christianity but from reform movements within. These reform movements anticipated and coalesced into the Protestant Reformation. Dissatisfied with the dichotomy between the "natural" and "supernatural" in medieval life, the Reformers sought to disciple the whole of society, giving new dignity to ordinary life.[25] Quite inadvertently, this emphasis on remaking the world began to carve out the possibility of a humanist alternative to the Christian faith.

Indeed, the iconoclasm of the Reformers demonstrated a new strategy for dealing with the magic of the pagan world. The medieval church had provided protection from evil magic through good magic, instantiated in saints and relics and centered in the Mass. By contrast, the Reformers emphasized the need to "leap out of the field of magic altogether, and throw yourself on the power of God alone."[26] In order to purify the demands of individual devotion, collective rituals were abolished as "superstitious." The mediatory ministry of the saints was similarly rejected, with veneration reframed as the imitation of saintly virtue. The theocentric

---

[23]Taylor calls this "the great disembedding." Taylor, *Secular Age*, 146.

[24]Taylor, "Afterword: Apologia pro Libro Suo," 303.

[25]Taylor describes the Reformation a theocentric shift, an "attempt to recover and impose on everyone a more individually committed and Christocentric religion of devotion and action." Taylor, *Secular Age*, 305.

[26]Taylor, *Secular Age*, 74.

shift had a disenchanting edge toward the world at large: magic was ille-gitimate because God alone was to be adored and feared. With grace be-stowed through faith alone, the sacred could no longer be located in people, places, or things of intrinsic power. To do so would undermine divine freedom, suggesting that "there is something of saving efficacy out there in the world at the mercy of human action."[27] Instead of insisting on medieval distinctions, all people were reimagined as equidistant from grace. All places could be holy places. All honest vocations could advance God's kingdom. Ordinary life took on a new significance.

This meant a profound shift in the center of gravity. If medieval worship was *centripetal*, drawing worshipers toward the liturgical event of the Mass, Protestant worship was *centrifugal*, directing its energy outward into the lives of believers and the wider world. Calvin famously locked the door of the Genevan church during the week. This was both to avoid superstition and to remind his congregation that the wider world—the theater of God's glory—was the site of the real action, as believers sought to live out their vocations before the face of God.[28]

With the negative energy of iconoclasm came the positive energy of reform. Freed from fear of hostile powers—because they have been de feated by Christ—the gospel included a call to reorder all of life.[29] The inward orientation of Protestant worship (in which we hear and inter-nalize the Word) was designed to generate an outward thrust in terms of moral transformation and mission, in order to remake the whole of so-ciety in accordance with Christian standards. Comprehensive devotion was not just for monks but for everyone.[30]

---

[27]Taylor, *Secular Age*, 79.

[28]William Dyrness writes that the Reformation gave believers a dramatic-historical sensitivity, and the sense that the theodrama was being played out not primarily in the events of worship but in everyday life. William A. Dyrness, "Is There a Reformed Aesthetic?" (Presented at The Reformed Institute of Metropolitan Washington, Washington, DC, January 25, 2014).

[29]Taylor writes: "We feel a new freedom in a world shorn of the sacred, and the limits it set for us, to re-order things as seem best." Taylor, "Disenchantment-Reenchantment," 80.

[30]This disciplinary impulse predates the Reformation, and Taylor locates the starting point here as the Renaissance notion of "civility," which focused on human life at its best and defined itself in opposition to the "savages" who live outside of the city. What was remarkable in the sixteenth century (during the Reform period) is the intensity and scope of the attempts to make over the lower orders. This was driven in part by fear (more civilized societies have more effective

Perhaps we can begin to see some of the emerging tensions in this profound gravitational shift. Let us call this the Syndrome Paradox, named after the villain of the 2004 film *The Incredibles*. Syndrome's scheme is to eliminate superheroes by giving ordinary people the ability to be "super." Why? Because when everyone is super, no one will be. Similarly, if all places can be holy, are any places holy? Have all vocations been elevated by the priesthood of all believers, or have the distinctions simply been leveled? If all spheres of life matter, then what truly matters? Clearly the Reformers—who still moved in a God-entranced world—intended to broaden the scope of the sacred, to signal that God was sanctifying God's people everywhere. But the shift also made it possible for the scope of sanctification to be stretched thin and for superficial versions—like civil religion—to emerge. Thus, one of the great paradoxes of history is that the possibility of disenchantment came about through heightened attention to God's presence in ordinary life.

This all-too-brief account scarcely does justice to the complexities of Reformation movements.[31] I want to make it clear that disenchantment is not the necessary destination of Reformed theology. As I will argue throughout the rest of this book, a Protestant imagination retains profound resources for recovering a God-entranced world, even if those resources have not been taken up so readily. I am retelling Taylor's story to indicate that the Reformed corrective to late medieval Christianity privileged certain currents without determining them in the direction of a disenchanted world.

What currents do I have in mind? The first is *inwardness*: the impulse to turn inward before moving outward. There is of course a long tradition of inwardness—particularly as it relates to Christian piety—that predates the Reformation. But whereas in the past the inner journey was taken by a select few, the Reformers made it an expectation for all of society. The fruit of this move is that when we look for meaning, depth, or God, we

---

armies), ambition, but also by the desire to make certain norms universal, to keep society on the right track. Taylor, *Secular Age,* 100-101.

[31]As I will argue in part two, the Protestant imagination retains profound resources for recovering a God-entranced world, even if those resources have not been taken up so readily.

start by looking within (e.g., we "ask Jesus into our hearts"). A second and related trajectory is the celebration of *ordinary life*.[32] The inward turn—internalizing the Word to orient the inner life—was meant to produce a corresponding outward organization of everyday life. Spheres of ordinary life—especially work and the family—became sites in which the world would be reordered, remade, and restored, as it were, "to its edenic purity."[33] Yet both of these currents would take unexpected new directions during the transitional age of Enlightenment.

Enlightenment transitions: The shrinking of scope. The Reformation mission to reorder society, Taylor argues, was successful beyond "what its originators could have hoped for."[34] This prompted even greater dreams of a colonizing Christian civilization, one so self-contained that it could take on a life of its own outside of the theological soil in which it had grown. Confidence in human ability to achieve this order became the driving engine of humanism. All that was required, as the project of re-organization took on ever greater aspirations, was that the goal be narrowed to ordinary flourishing, and the power to pursue it rendered an innate human capacity rather than a divine gift.[35] These transitional moves would take place during the Enlightenment period.[36]

---

[32]These two impulses would intensify as modernity gained steam, and unsurprisingly, they are two of the three features identified by Taylor as central to modern identity. The third feature, expressive authenticity, would be the special contribution of Romanticism. Charles Taylor, *Sources of the Self: The Making of the Modern Identity* (Cambridge: Harvard University Press, 1992).

[33]Dyrness speaks of these impulses in terms of an "inward turn" and a "longing to see the world remade, restored to its edenic purity," which better captures the theocentric nature of the turn to "ordinary life." William A. Dyrness, *Reformed Theology and Visual Culture: The Protestant Imagination from Calvin to Edwards* (Cambridge: Cambridge University Press, 2004), 304-9.

[34]Taylor, "Afterword: Apologia pro Libro Suo," 305. Here Taylor makes an overstatement, neglecting the much darker "underside" of the Enlightenment. Though the Age of Reason was not global phenomena, it had global repercussions. The enlightened used "scientific" and "rational" methods to prove the deficiency (and undermine the humanity) of other "races" and to justify the military and economic imperialism of European nations. Europe, as the most supremely rational, had a mission to civilize the world. It is a tragic reality this was almost always combined with the religious sanction of Christian theology, and that apologetics became not just about defending Christian faith but also about defending particular forms of Eurocentric culture. See Willie James Jennings, *The Christian Imagination: Theology and the Origins of Race* (New Haven: Yale University Press, 2010).

[35]Taylor, *Secular Age*, 85.

[36]"Enlightenment" is a misnomer, insofar as it represents a complex set of phenomena that varied by geographical location. Yet I am following the standard heuristic use of the term to refer to

Once again, the motivations of Reform were theocentric, but in the centuries that followed, the secondary goal of understanding and reforming the world in accordance with the primary goal of conforming to God's Word began to become an end in itself. Interest in this world (the immanent) grew large enough to eclipse concerns about the next (the transcendent). An immanent frame was constructed to enclose the world in a space that entertains no ends beyond ordinary human flourishing.[37]

Taylor makes plain that the construction of the immanent frame could not have occurred without theological revisions. An important example is the construal of the doctrine of divine providence. For the Reformers providence designated God's active guidance and governance of creation toward consummation; it meant God's moment-by-moment presence and action. In the eighteenth century, however, providence was revised to emphasize the order itself rather than the ordering. The singular goal of this ordering was clear: the realization of human happiness.[38] With a truncated target, divine involvement became less important and less expected. Indeed, for many thinkers the idea of interventions in the divine order seemed irresponsible if not downright offensive. Providence was thus affirmed but flattened and emptied of mystery; "particular providences" (miracles) were unforeseeable, and thus were disallowed.[39]

Here we begin to see signs of a significant shift in the discipline of apologetics: from a discernment of divine presence to a defense of

---

the period between the publication of Newton's *Principia Mathematica* (1686) and the French Revolution of 1789.

[37]James K. A. Smith notes that Taylor (perhaps owing to his Roman Catholicism) posits something of a dichotomy between ordinary human flourishing and God's higher purposes for creation. The Reformed tradition, as Smith notes, emphasizes a fundamental continuity between nature and grace, such that ascetic disciplines "are not repressions of flourishing but rather constraints for flourishing." James K. A. Smith, *How (Not) to Be Secular: Reading Charles Taylor* (Grand Rapids: Eerdmans, 2014), 48n1.

[38]Matthew Tindal's popular *Christianity as Old as Creation* (published in 1710), a sort of handbook for deism, argued that God's purpose for humanity consisted in the "mutual Happiness of his rational Creatures." Taylor, *Secular Age*, 222. This pruning of providence complemented the empiricism of Francis Bacon, who similarly argued that the goal of science was not to understand the world in a global sense but rather to "improve the condition of mankind." Taylor, *Secular Age*, 543

[39]As Taylor writes, "If God is relying on our reason to grasp the laws of his universe, and hence carry out his plan, it would be irresponsible of him and defeat his purpose to be intervening miraculously." Taylor, *Secular Age*, 223-24.

disembodied truth. Taylor himself highlights the changing shape of apologetics within these new parameters. Sheer unbelief was rare, understood as an achievement of rationality rather than an element of popular consciousness. Yet it was during this time that apologists like Joseph Butler—responding to a decline in zeal rather than disbelief—began to narrow the scope of apologetic defense to the origin and orderliness of creation. Butler's apologetics, Taylor notes, "barely invoked the saving action of Christ, nor did it dwell on the life of devotion and prayer, although the seventeenth century was rich in this."[40] Neither popular apologists nor Christianity's enlightened despisers made much space for divine intervention, with "no place at all for communion with God as a transforming relation."[41] It was as if the order apparent in the natural world was sufficient to compel people to order their lives in accordance with the expectations of Christian civilization.

Furthermore, apologists sought to show how the evidences of Christianity were clear to human reason without appeal to special revelation, church tradition, or denominational distinctive. Apologists adopted the Enlightenment stance of the disengaged scientist, taking a step back to see the whole of reality. Here the inwardness of the Reformation has been intensified, taking on a new "buffered identity," calling all things outside itself into question.[42] Luther's question, "How can I find a gracious God?" was contracted to Descartes's inability to find solid ground outside his own act of searching.

Correspondingly, the scope of theology was readjusted to what was intelligible to the human intellect, God's gift for discerning the order of the world. This meant an allergy to the miraculous and the mysterious. To leave spaces unexplored, after all, would be a failure to realize God's plan for humanity. Thus, the other apologetic preoccupation became theodicy, the attempt to solve the problem of evil. But the endeavor to unravel evil assumes that they are in a position to see all the evidence, that "we have all the elements we need to carry out a trial of God (and triumphantly

---

[40]Taylor, *Secular Age*, 225.
[41]Taylor, *Secular Age*, 280.
[42]Taylor, *Secular Age*, 262.

acquit him by our apologetic)." Taylor's discussion of the divine trial recalls a similar framing by Lewis:

> The ancient man approached God (or even the gods) as the accused person approaches his judge. For the modern man, the roles are quite reversed. He is the judge: God is in the dock. He is quite a kindly judge; if God should have a reasonable defense for being the god who permits war, poverty, and disease, he is ready to listen to it. The trial may even end in God's acquittal. But the important thing is that man is on the bench and God is in the dock.[43]

Believers have always wrestled with faith in the face of suffering—Scripture is full of examples—but only during this period of growing confidence in human reason did the expectation arise that the problem could be resolved to our satisfaction. As we will see below, the apologetic picture that emerged during this period still continues to exert imaginative force today.

We should note that piety remains within the parameters of Enlightenment deism: "God remains our Creator, and hence our benefactor, to whom we owe gratitude beyond all measure." We are also "grateful for his Providence, which has designed our good." We can anticipate "an afterlife, with rewards and punishments" that direct human virtue. But insofar as our orderly, ordinary lives are now absent of divine address, and are no longer dependent on grace to restore nature, our faith is no longer thick enough "to block exclusive humanism."[44] In the space created by these shifts, exclusive humanism began to gain plausibility.

The redirection of the Reformation revisions corresponded to political shifts as well. The splintering of the church in the sixteenth century, the religious wars of the seventeenth century, and the intraconfessional divisions of the eighteenth century would necessitate new political options.[45] A more uniform basis for toleration and dissent was sought, and the result was the formation of "polite society, in which civil religion

---

[43]C. S. Lewis, *God in the Dock: Essays on Theology and Ethics* (Grand Rapids: Eerdmans, 1972), 244. Lewis's point is not to question the legitimacy of attempts at theodicy; he offered one himself in *The Problem of Pain*. The point is rather that in the modern picture God is always the one on trial.

[44]Taylor, *Secular Age*, 233.

[45]James E. Bradley and Dale Van Kley, eds., *Religion and Politics in Enlightenment Europe* (Notre Dame: University of Notre Dame Press, 2001).

plays an important role in giving legitimacy to the order, but it is no longer able radically to call the status quo into question."[46] This led to three possible options, which are still with us today. We can identify Christianity with the civil religion of law and order (where Christian faith props up the social order); we can reject the civil religion in favor of an intensified piety (where Christian faith leads us to critique the status quo but also to circle the wagons); and, most significant, we can come to reject Christianity altogether as an enemy of the civil religion (where Christian faith is seen as morally deficient, backwards, and even barbaric).[47] In this way, Christianity supplies the moral force and framework for its own rejection.

The flattened faith of deism, along with the politics of polite society, became essential pieces for constructing the immanent frame. It was a tremendous imaginative achievement. The enchanted cosmos was evacuated, first of hostile powers, then of divine intervention. It was reimagined as a "universe ruled by causal laws . . . unresponsive, or indifferent, like a machine, even if we held that it was designed as a machine for our benefit."[48] Modern society was also reimagined, from a web of relationships rooted in God to a confederation of voluntary associations (groups I choose to join).[49] Finally, human consciousness was buffered—radically disengaged—and given the right to call everything into question apart from its own disengagement. Taylor's summary is powerful:

> Fed by the powerful presence of impersonal orders, cosmic, social, and moral; drawn by the power of the disengaged stance, and its ethical prestige, and ratified by a sense of what the alternative was, based on an elite's derogatory and somewhat fearful portrait of popular religion, an unshakeable sense could arise of our inhabiting an immanent, impersonal order, which screened out, for those who inhabited it, all phenomena which failed to fit this framework.[50]

---

[46]Taylor, *Secular Age*, 238.
[47]Taylor, *Secular Age*, 263.
[48]Taylor, *Secular Age*, 280.
[49]Taylor, *Secular Age*, 281.
[50]Taylor, *Secular Age*, 288.

This is the immanent frame: a society constructed with a ceiling to block out the transcendent. But such a building would still need to provide its own lights. Indeed, without the transformations of Romanticism, it would be unlivable for most people. Yet unbelief—with its own system of morality drawn from Christian sources—had begun to be a live option. It was finally in the nineteenth century that a society emerged which "managed to experience its world entirely as immanent."[51] This option would become an expansive and colonizing force in the Western world. But once again the story of its ascendancy is not so simple.

Romantic transformations: The making of meaning. The story is not straightforward because the loss of widely shared meaning created a major imaginative crisis. Against common readings that understand Romanticism as a nostalgic stopgap against Enlightenment rationalism, Taylor tells a more careful story.[52] The Romantic impulse, Taylor argues, is a response to an encroaching feeling of emptiness: the sense that in an immanent world, "our actions, goals, achievements . . . have a lack of weight, gravity, thickness, substance."[53] This existential anxiety is the crisis to which Romanticism seeks to respond. Radically aware that the world has changed, a self-conscious search for new ways of finding fullness must begin.

The malaise of modernity can be characterized in terms of three interconnected crises, which relate to individualism, instrumentalism, and

---

[51]Taylor, *Secular Age*, 376.

[52]Romanticism is a slippery term: Lovejoy's famous aphorism that we should speak of Romanticisms is surely correct. Arthur O. Lovejoy, "On the Discrimination of Romanticisms," *PMLA* 39, no. 2 (1924): 235-36. While there is a certain family resemblance, differences are profound. Yet we can say that Romanticism is marked by a consciousness of revolution and represented strategies of dealing with the revolutionary ethos and its effects. Taylor's understanding of Romanticism as the recognition of radical reflexivity and the response of expressivism certainly fits within this revolutionary ethos.

Taylor argues that Romanticism produces not just a reactionary movement to undo the Enlightenment but an attempt to carry the Enlightenment project forward in a new way; countercurrents of the Enlightenment become the driving currents of Romanticism. Jager argues that Taylor at times perpetuates the Enlightenment vs. Romanticism binary, but also problematizes it in his methodology. Even the phrase counter-Enlightenment is misleading, since it seems to assume chronological succession. But Jager emphasizes that the Romantic strain developed not after the Enlightenment, but at the very "moment of its inception" in the seventeenth century, arising not in reaction to the Enlightenment but within it. Colin Jager, "This Detail, This History: Charles Taylor's Romanticism," in *Varieties of Secularism in a Secular Age*, ed. Michael Warner, Jonathan VanAntwerpen, and Craig Calhoun (Cambridge: Harvard University Press, 2010), 188.

[53]Taylor, *Secular Age*, 307.

institutionalism.[54] The first crisis results from the individual's disembeddedness from her place in any higher order and the responsibility to make sense of the world within a wholly immanent frame. The second crisis is the triumph of instrumentality: reason's goal is no longer to know the world but to control, dominate, and manage it through economic calculations and technological solutions. This results in innovation and progress, but it also carries the sense that we are ourselves no more than cogs in a machine, constrained by powers (especially the market and the state) that pull the strings. This leads to a third crisis, one of institutional participation. Knowing that our decisions are situated by sociopolitical powers, it is difficult to feel any real sense of agency (e.g. "My vote doesn't matter!"). Institutional affiliation declines as people consistently prefer the distractions of private life to public activism.[55] When public participation occurs, it often has more to do with personal meaning than meaningful change: activism merges with brand management.

Religious faith is also affected. As it is reduced from transformative communion to transactional affiliation, faith becomes one more battle of the brands. What happens in a world where the former anchors of personal and institutional identity have been called into question, where "publicly available orders of meaning" are no longer available, and reason itself has been instrumentalized? The answer is that "subtler languages" must be developed; new ways to find fullness must be forged.

This was the call the Romantics sought to answer. Whereas Enlightenment thinkers privileged reason, Romantic thinkers delegated the responsibility to remake the world to the imagination.[56] Here we find a

---

[54]While consistent with Taylor's organization, the alliteration is my own.

[55]Research indicates that the religiously unaffiliated in the United States reflect a suspicion toward institutions in general, not just to institutional religion. They are, for example, less likely to vote or to be affiliated with other voluntary or civic institutions. See Tim Clydesdale and Kathleen Garces-Foley, *The Twentysomething Soul: Understanding the Religious and Secular Lives of American Young Adults* (New York: Oxford University Press, 2019).

[56]This has led some to identify an aesthetic "will to power" at work in Romanticism, highlighting trajectories that could and would be taken in a Nietzschean direction. William Desmond articulates a popular critique of Romanticism when he writes that after Kant, there was a new "apotheosis of imagination." Desmond argues that rather than being "the antithesis of rationalistic enlightenment," the Romantic imagination actually came from the same source: a culture of autonomy. He writes, "There can be an aesthetic will to power in Romantic imagination, as there can be a rationalistic will to power in Enlightenment reason." William Desmond, *Is There a*

parallel between Enlightenment instrumentalism and Romantic imagination; both assume the loss of absolute purpose and place the burden of making wholly into human hands. As Taylor writes, "We are alone in the universe, and this is frightening; but it can also be exhilarating."[57] Taylor sees Romantic poets as attempting to articulate an "original vision of the cosmos" developing subtler languages that "enabled people to explore these meanings with their ontological commitments as it were in suspense."[58] On this account, it is not just the push of rationalism but also the pull of these subtler languages that made the middle space between belief and unbelief livable.

The Romantics believed that poets and artists would midwife a faith for the new world through literature and the arts. Beauty is truth, wrote Keats; truth, beauty. And beauty will save the world.[59] As literary historian Philip Davis notes, "Writers were to be the world's new priests, a literary faith replacing a dogmatic one. In an age of mechanical materialism, it was writers who insisted on the world's spiritual reality, with or without the formal support of religion as such."[60] The aesthetic visionaries were instrumental in forging artistic orders of meaning and a "free and neutral space, between religious commitment and materialism . . . neither explicitly believing, but not atheistic either, a kind of undefined spirituality."[61] The sense that existential depth can be found, and fullness forged—transcending materialism without a transcendent referent—this is the Romantic legacy.

Here we arrive at another significant point. The Romantic achievement that made the immanent frame habitable was the opening of an aesthetic realm "in which people can wander between and around all these options

---

Sabbath for Thought? Between Religion and Philosophy (New York: Fordham University Press, 2005), 137.

[57]Taylor, *Secular Age*, 367.

[58]Taylor, *Secular Age*, 356, 351.

[59]Taylor, *Secular Age*, 359.

[60]Philip Davis, *The Oxford English Literary History, 1830-1880: The Victorians* (Oxford: Oxford University Press, 2002), 100.

[61]Taylor, *Secular Age*, 360. The space is neutral not in terms of objectivity but in terms of explicit commitment. In this neutral zone, a person can engage in meaning making while holding ontological commitments—about God or the universe—in suspense.

without having to land clearly and definitively in any one."[62] This province would remain sparsely occupied for at least another century, but already in the early nineteenth century a space was being cleared where doubt and disbelief could approximate religious feeling without necessarily returning to religion. For Taylor, the key feature of Romanticism is the privileging of the aesthetic realm, which supplemented the "felt inadequacy of moralism" with a new goal of aesthetic fullness, the experience of beauty.[63]

The aesthetic space carved out by the Romantics was the province of artistic elites and bohemians in the nineteenth and early twentieth century, but in the 1960s authenticity reached a tipping point.[64] In the decade immediately following the Second World War, mass society had encouraged duty, obligation, and conformity. But the 1960s began to see a revolt against duty in favor of desire. The malaise of modernity struck back with a vengeance.

Taylor sees the revolts of the 1960s as quintessentially Romantic, "directed against a 'system' which smothered creativity, individuality and imagination."[65] It was during this period that advertisers took up the language of expressive individualism, that "the limits on the pursuit of individual happiness" were set aside, and the Romantic project was translated into the aspirations of everyday people.[66] Consider a recent poll that

---

[62]Taylor, *Secular Age*, 351. On the opening of the space, Taylor writes, "It is largely thanks to the languages of art that our relation to nature can so often remain in this middle realm, this free and neutral space, between religious commitment and materialism. This too has helped create a kind of middle space, neither explicitly believing, but not atheistic either, a kind of undefined spirituality." Taylor, *Secular Age*, 360.

[63]Taylor, *Secular Age*, 358.

[64]Taylor is representative of theorists who see the 1960s as the climax of a long process, while others, like Callum Brown are suspicious of master historical narratives and see the 1960s as a decisive break with religion, which begins the secular age. Callum Brown, "The Secularisation Decade: What the 1960s Have Done to the Study of Religious History," in *The Decline of Christendom in Western Europe, 1750-2000*, ed. Hugh McLeod and Werner Ustorf (Cambridge: Cambridge University Press, 2011), 29-46. Hugh McLeod takes a mediating position, distinguishing between "long-term preconditions for and the short-term precipitants of the 1960s crisis." Hugh McLeod, *The Religious Crisis of the 1960s* (Oxford: Oxford University Press, 2010).

[65]Taylor, *Secular Age*, 476. For a fuller discussion of this shift in the United States see part one of Root, *Faith Formation in a Secular Age*.

[66]Taylor, *Secular Age*, 485. Taylor notes that in the developed world, where the "disciplines of deferred gratification" have long held sway, people find it easier to "relax many of the traditional disciplines in their lives, while keeping them in their work life. . . . This feat of selective assumption of disciplines, which supposes a long, often multi-generational interiorization, is a crucial

asked respondents which aspirations were extremely important in their vision of the American Dream. Although 75% of those surveyed expressed the desire to have one's basic needs met, this was accompanied significantly by postromantic aspirations: having personal freedom (78%), achieving one's potential (71%), having enough free time (67%), and being in harmony with nature (54%).[67] The Romantic method of forging a creative and fulfilled life became the standard mode of operation for finding meaning in an immanent frame.

Let me take a step back to press this point home. In contemporary times the aesthetic realm does not just include "high culture": going to art galleries, reading poetry, or attending the opera.[68] It also includes elements of "popular culture" where we increasingly assign aesthetic significance to our media consumption. It includes the fans rising in ritual action to celebrate their football team. It includes viewers of streaming television shows who feel that the characters of the sitcom are like family. It includes weekend warriors who find vital meaning and purpose in their participation in extreme sports.[69] The aesthetic realm is no longer the province of the elite, as it was during the Romantic era. We are all aesthetes now, and we have the Romantic movement to thank for it.[70] I can find meaning, beauty, and fullness in a flattened world by investing my everyday actions and associations with religious significance and depth. This was the final piece that completed construction of the immanent frame: the call to a quest! The aesthetic ideal—the search for the

facilitating condition of the new stance.... At other times and places [such as the developing world] such principled transgression seems insane, almost suicidal." Taylor, *Secular Age*, 493.

[67]The survey polled 1,821 U.S. citizens ages 18 and over. See https://newdream.org/resources/poll-2014. Accessed January 21, 2020.

[68]Taylor, *Secular Age*, 356.

[69]Indeed, these examples problematize the classical distinction between high and low culture. Classically, "high culture" refers to those elements that raise the human spirit to new levels, whereas "popular culture" (also called "folk culture" or "low culture") refers to those elements that simply reinforce the status quo. For example, *films* made by auteurs for a critical audience are high culture, while *movies*, made by studios for mass consumption are popular culture. The distinction has been attacked as arbitrary and Eurocentric. But it remains in the minds of many. For a discussion of this distinction see Herbert Gans, *Popular Culture and High Culture: An Analysis and Evaluation of Taste* (New York: Basic Books, 1999).

[70]As Taylor writes, "The post-Romantic space that the nineteenth century carved out is still being occupied. And it is good that it should be; many of us need it to live." Taylor, *Secular Age*, 411.

experience of depth and resonance—took on ethical force. It is the conviction that everyone *ought to* seek resonance and depth, composing an original life. This is called the ethic of authenticity, and it is important to discuss it at length.

THE AGE OF AUTHENTICITY

When I was in high school considering future possibilities, someone gave me this counsel: Don't ask yourself what the world needs. Ask yourself what makes you come alive. Go and do that, because what the world needs is people who have come alive.[71] This maxim, which I have since seen in books and greeting cards, illustrates the ethic of authenticity. Feeling alive is not just a means to fullness but a mandate, an aesthetic call to action: find something that makes you feel alive. Felt experience now becomes central; composing an original life that is deeply resonant with my embodied, emotive experience of the world is a moral imperative.[72]

Taylor defines authenticity as "the understanding of life which emerges with the Romantic expressivism of the late-eighteenth century, that each one of us has his/her own way of realizing our humanity, and that it is important to find and live out one's own, as against surrendering to conformity with a model imposed on us from the outside."[73] Taylor elaborates:

> There is a certain way of being human that is *my* way. I am called upon to live my life in this way, and not in imitation of anyone else's. But this gives a new importance to being true to myself. If I am not, I miss the point of

---

[71] I have seen the saying attributed to various authors but have not been able conclusively to identify the original source.

[72] Root's description of authenticity as resonant with our "embodied, emotive encounter with reality" is well put, and I will continue to use a version of this phrase throughout my argument. Root, *Faith Formation in a Secular Age*, 8.

[73] Taylor, *Secular Age*, 475. This conception of authenticity is related to but distinct from Martin Heidegger's use of the same term. Taylor clarifies this in an interview: "For Heidegger, the difference between authenticity and inauthenticity is whether you simply accept a routine version of your tradition or whether you go back to its very bases and roots and make a resolute decision for it. So what he's really talking about is resolute decisiveness, whereas I'm using authenticity as shorthand for the background idea that everyone has their own particular way of being human and that you can then be either true or untrue to that." Ronald A. Kuipers, "Religious Belonging in an 'Age of Authenticity': A Conversation with Charles Taylor (Part Two of Three)," *The Other Journal*, June 23, 2008, theotherjournal.com/2008/06/23/religious-belonging-in-an-age-of-authenticity-a-conversation-with-charles-taylor-part-two-of-three/.

my life, I miss what being human is for *me*. . . . Being true to myself means being true to my own originality, and that is something only I can articulate and discover. In articulating it, I am also defining myself. I am realizing a potentiality that is properly my own.[74]

In other words, we must forge our own way of being human, one that resonates with our sense of our place in the world.

The problem is that with the loss of widely shared orders of meaning there has been a dizzying proliferation of possibilities for being human.[75] This means a lingering identity crisis precisely because there are so many options, and each additional option weakens whatever identity we have forged. The realization that *my* orders of meaning are not shared by others makes my sense of the world seem much less stable. Imagine a student who has been educated in Christian schools all her life and who now finds herself at a public university in a secular setting. Perhaps she has always been aware that there are others who do not believe as she does. But now these others live in close proximity, and she finds that they are very different from her. If they seem to get on fine without faith, her faith will seem more fragile. Unbelief becomes imaginable, a visceral possibility.

But fragilization moves in both directions: neither belief nor unbelief is inevitable, and there is an ever-widening space in between. Taylor argues that it is because such an expansive neutral zone exists that the battles between belief and unbelief keep "running out of steam."[76] These skirmishes lose their gravity because they take place on the common ground of immanence. The nature of *reality* is never really felt to be at stake. Rather, what is actually at stake is sociological acceptance, institutional affiliation, and personal identification. Of course, these things do not necessarily exclude the recognition of divine action, but by themselves they fall short of faith in the transcendent.[77]

---

[74]Charles Taylor, *The Ethics of Authenticity* (Cambridge: Harvard University Press, 1992), 28-29.

[75]Taylor calls this the "nova effect," the "multiplication of a greater and greater variety of different spiritual options, from the most reductive atheist materialism to the most unreconstructed orthodoxy, through all possible variations and combinations in between." Taylor, "Afterword: Apologia pro Libro Suo," 306.

[76]Taylor, *Secular Age*, 351.

[77]See Root, *Faith Formation in a Secular Age*, 97-117.

Here is the key point: in the age of authenticity, acts of faith—whether defined immanently as the commitment to one identity over another or transcendently as the response to revelation—are not the result of an impartial weighing of the evidence. Rather, they are the result of a much more Romantic method, what the early Romantic philosopher J. G. Herder called *Einfühlung*: feeling the way in.[78] Whatever we make of the world must resonate deeply with our embodied, emotive experience. As Taylor writes, "Artistic creation becomes the paradigm mode in which people can come to self-definition. . . . Self-discovery requires *poiesis*, making."[79] In other words, achieving authenticity is less an analytic judgment and more an aesthetic project. Magic, in fact, has not disappeared: I may still be deeply affected by my life in this world. But the force of the magic is felt from within as I invest things with gravity and significance. Enchantment has been relocated from the realm of factual reality to the realm of subjective imagination.[80]

Thus we arrive at our hypermodern, expressivist moment in which we are so often commissioned to follow our hearts, where "individuals and groups are encouraged to define and express their own particular identities,"[81] and where the only abiding sin seems to be intolerance of someone else's unique way of being human. We live and move in an immanent space, consuming and creating culture that fits the narrative identity of who we want to become rather than living into an identity that has been bestowed. And it is in this space that the most decisive considerations of faith are made by paying greater attention to imaginative intimations ("What would it feel like to believe?") than epistemic obligations ("Here is why you ought to believe"). In a certain sense, *resonance*—a sense of existential "fit" with a particular vision of the world—becomes the most important criterion of believability.[82]

---

[78]See discussion in Jager, "This Detail, This History: Charles Taylor's Romanticism," 175.
[79]Taylor, *Ethics of Authenticity*, 62.
[80]See this argument in Paul Tyson, *Seven Brief Lessons on Magic*. (Eugene, OR: Cascade, 2019), 31.
[81]Taylor, "Afterword: Apologia pro Libro Suo," 306.
[82]Even a fierce materialist like Richard Dawkins is sensitive to this existential dimension, even though he seems perplexed by it, writing, "People, when given the right encouragement to think for themselves about all the information now available, very often turn out *not* to believe in God

After the ascendancy of authenticity, there is no longer any necessary embedding in a larger framework. We have been evicted from the Eden of embedded meaning, and the crisis is that it is now up to our imaginative sensibilities to forage for the depth of meaning that was once given. Taylor notes that religious practice itself is framed in terms of what it means to *me*: "The religious life or practice that I become part of must not only be my choice, but it must speak to me, it must make sense in terms of my spiritual development as I understand this . . . in the subtler languages that I find meaningful."[83] The question is whether the subtler languages of authenticity will ultimately be satisfying, whether they can reproduce in an immanent frame the depth that was a given in an enchanted world.

This raises another important question: Should apologists concede the game to authenticity? Should the expressivist imagination really be afforded such decisive power? Might it not be argued that the overemphasis on individual authenticity is among the faultiest features of modernity? There is certainly a dark side to individualism, and Taylor cites complaints that the focus on individual happiness has led to a culture of self-absorption and narcissism: "The dark side of individualism is a centering on the self, which both flattens and narrows our lives, makes them poorer in meaning, and less concerned with others or society."[84] The force of this critique is strong, and we can feel it, not least because of our own narrowness. Many discussions of authenticity major on this critique, demonstrating the ways that contemporary culture and Christian faith have been co-opted by the idol of expressive authenticity.[85]

Narcissism certainly merits a trenchant critique. And yet, narcissism is not the necessary destination of the ethic of authenticity. We should note that our age is not unique in its narcissistic trajectories: selfishness is as old as sin. What is unique to our age, however, is the "moral force" attached to personal fulfillment. Imagine a woman who

---

and to lead fulfilled and satisfied—indeed, *liberated*—lives." Richard Dawkins, *The God Delusion* (New York: Houghton Mifflin, 2008).

[83]Taylor, *Secular Age*, 486.

[84]Taylor, *Ethics of Authenticity*, 4.

[85]See footnote six in this chapter.

abandons her family because she "owes it to herself to be happy." Taylor highlights this: "It's not just that people sacrifice their love relationships, and the care of their children, to pursue their careers. Something like this has perhaps always existed. The point is that today many people feel *called* to do this, feel their lives would be somehow wasted or unfulfilled if they didn't do it."[86] This moral imperative can create versions of authenticity that are tremendously destructive, that seek fullness at any cost.

But the impulse of authenticity can also lead in the other direction. The thinness of individualistic narcissism produces a malaise that thicker versions of authenticity must seek to transcend. Insofar as authenticity involves ingenuity, it is not difficult to see how it could be set against convention and even morality itself, despite its original moral foundation.[87] The seeds of relativism are clear, but first we need to recognize the validity of the ideal apart from its flattened forms. What Taylor hopes to do, against those who advocate a return to some untroubled preromantic period, is to take authenticity seriously as a worthwhile moral ideal. This means showing that the ideal has both "flat" and "full" versions, the former being "debased and deviant forms."[88] If the ideal of authenticity is, as Taylor believes, "unrepudiable" to modern people, the missiological imperative is clear. We are already swimming in the water of authenticity, and so we must learn to paddle, aware that the undertow of narcissism is real.

So how might the ethic of authenticity be redirected toward thicker, even transcendent possibilities? At its best, Taylor argues, authenticity "points us towards a more self-responsible form of life. It allows us to live

---

[86]Taylor, *Ethics of Authenticity*, 17.

[87]Taylor traces the origins of authenticity to the eighteenth-century idea of an intuitive moral sense, over against Locke's idea that morality was rooted in the calculation of consequences. Earlier moral theories that identified this internal voice as with a transcendent source; we see in Augustine the inauguration of inwardness as the path to the divine. Yet with the buffering forces discussed above, by the eighteenth century this inwardness was increasingly discussed as self-contained. Rousseau argued that the "voice of nature" was all too often drowned by our dependence on others, and that moral integrity would be found in "recovering authentic moral contact with ourselves." Taylor, *Ethics of Authenticity*, 26.

[88]Taylor hopes to demonstrate that one can still make arguments about the conformity of practices to the ideal, and that such arguments matter. Taylor, *Ethics of Authenticity*, 21-23.

(potentially) a fuller and more differentiated life, because [it is] more fully appropriated as our own."[89] A thicker form of authenticity would lead to a life in which our embodied, emotive encounter with reality is deeply meaningful because it resonates with the life we have chosen to own. Notwithstanding the dangers of narcissism, this is an ideal worth defending. Indeed, this impulse to take responsibility for our lives and to make something of our situation derives from the call of creaturely agency, our answer to the question, "What will you do now?"[90] The question for believers is whether we are able to connect the impulse to look within and listen to the inner voice of authenticity with the possibility that Another voice is speaking, breaking through the immanent frame despite our best efforts to insulate ourselves.

Indeed, the fact that the project of authenticity—in its thick and thin forms—is pursued in the aesthetic realm presents us with an opening. Our projects of self-discovery are irrevocably shaped by our relationships, and the lives we curate are in a certain sense *addressed* to an audience. Resonance goes both directions. The making of identity—like the making of art and the making of meaning—requires a background of significance against which our projects can be set.[91] In other words, identity is not something that can be achieved in isolation; it must be forged against the background of relationship with significant others. As individual as my quest for authenticity might seem, I can never achieve it alone.

This means that the narcissistic modes of authenticity actually defeat themselves. They self-destruct because they exalt self-choice while denying any larger horizon against which those choices matter. If the pursuit of fullness can come at any cost, then I have no grounds for denying someone else's method of pursuit. As Taylor writes, "It may be important that my life be chosen . . . but unless some options are more

---

[89]Taylor, *Ethics of Authenticity*, 74.

[90]William A Dyrness, *The Earth Is God's: A Theology of American Culture* (Maryknoll, NY: Orbis, 1997), 20.

[91]Taylor argues that full versions of authenticity are necessarily rooted in the "fundamentally dialogical character" of human life: "We become full human agents, capable of understanding ourselves, and hence of defining an identity, through our acquisition of rich human languages of expression. . . . Including the 'languages' of art, of gesture, of love, and the like." Taylor, *Ethics of Authenticity*, 33.

significant than others, the very idea of self-choice falls into triviality and hence incoherence. . . . Which issues are significant, *I* do not determine. If I did, no issue would be significant. But then the very idea of self-choosing *as a moral ideal* would not be possible."[92] For our choices to be significant they must be set against a defined background of important questions, a horizon of what really matters, which requires taking things like tradition, culture, history, society, ethics, and religion into account.

Thus, for authenticity to be achieved, fullness must be found in terms of significant relationships. Our identities require *recognition*, which assumes a ground in some common humanity. Indeed, without attunement to created others—and I would add to wider the created order—the quest for authenticity produces a perpetual identity crisis, revealing the possibility of the failure of recognition.[93] We can see this expressed in one of the foremost spaces for negotiating authenticity, social media. Imagine posting a picture or opinion online that receives minimal recognition, few "likes" or emoji "reactions." Younger generations especially will feel the anxiety. Students tell me that they will delete posts that do not garner a minimum number of "likes." Why? Because it is not enough that the world resonates with me. My life must resonate with the larger world. The difference between flat and full versions of authenticity depends on the degree to which this recognition is achieved. Failure to find resonance leads to despair.

To make this more concrete, let me expand on the example I used in my introduction. We can see the ethic of authenticity embodied in the journeys of two pop culture heroines from the world of Disney: Princess Elsa of Arendelle and Moana of Mata Nui. Both are on journeys of self-discovery that take them away from convention and conformity. Elsa

---

[92]Taylor, *Ethics of Authenticity*, 39.

[93]Taylor writes, "The thing about inwardly derived, personal, original identity is that it doesn't enjoy recognition *a priori*. It has to win it through exchange. What has come about with the modern age is not the recognition but the conditions in which it can fail. And that is why the need is now acknowledged for the first time. In premodern times, people did not speak of "identity" and "recognition," not because people didn't have (what we call) identities or because these didn't depend on recognition, but rather because these were then too unproblematic to be thematized as such. Taylor, *Ethics of Authenticity*, 48.

leaves home, singing a ballad of authenticity if there ever was one: "It's time to see what I can do, to test the limits and break through; no right, no wrong, no rules for me. I'm free!"[94] Moana also leaves home, in response to a call that she first believes is from beyond the horizon, but she comes learn "isn't out there at all, it's inside me."[95] If each heroine's journey was no more than a song of the self, a celebration of self-determination, we might not find them that interesting. What makes their choices matter is the larger horizon of meaning, the matrix of relationships in which they find themselves. Elsa is, in fact, called back from her self-imposed exile by a sister who loves her and by a people that need her. She does discover who she is, but only in relationship to others in whom she finds recognition. Similarly, Moana's inner voice comes to be identified with the tradition of her ancestors, voyagers who have passed their pioneering spirit on to her. She discovers who she is, but only with reference to the larger story of those who have come before her. My aim here is not to valorize either princess or the larger narrative of their respective films. The point, rather, is that even in the most unabashed celebrations of authenticity we find a more subtle exploration, in conversation with culture, tradition, and external voices, as to what really makes a life resonant and fulfilled. The common message: we can only find ourselves in relationship to significant others, among whom we emerge and are embedded. This, then, leads to the question of which voices, which traditions, which significant others, are the most trustworthy.

Against those who lament the culture of authenticity, Taylor offers a shift in conversation: not merely to grant the ideal of authenticity but to negotiate the best way of realizing it. He writes, "The struggle ought not to be *over* authenticity, for or against, but about it, defining its proper meaning. We ought to be trying to lift the culture back up, closer to its motivating ideal."[96] We can meet people where they are, in the ethic of authenticity, and then seek to set it against a horizon that opens us up to thicker, even transcendent possibilities. Taylor makes it clear that he

---

[94]Shane Morris, Peter Del Vecho, and John Lasseter, *Frozen* (Disney, 2014).
[95]Jared Bush and Osnat Shurer, *Moana* (Disney, 2017).
[96]Taylor, *Ethics of Authenticity*, 73.

believes that Christianity is the best horizon—though not the only possible one—against which authenticity can be achieved. Which is to say, he
is reimagining an apologetic.[97]

TAYLOR'S METHOD: A REIMAGINED APOLOGETIC?

I am not the first to suggest that Taylor's work is an apology for Christianity. In response to multiple interlocutors, Taylor addresses this question
directly: "There's a certain amount of argument in the book, and the motivation partly comes from my faith position. Does this mean that the
book's an apology? Well, I suppose that I'm offering reasons for a certain
kind of Christian position. The first thing I'm trying to do is get this kind
of conversation going across as many differences as I can."[98]

In other words, Taylor is clearing a space, challenging the habits of
closed minds, trying to reopen a conversation that for years has been cut
short by subtraction stories. He seeks to achieve epistemic permission (to
show that it is reasonable and good to believe) rather than to argue for
epistemic obligation (to prove that you must believe).

But my interest is less on the epistemic aim of Taylor's work than on
its apologetic shape. That is, Taylor's narrative is precisely the kind of account that is appropriate to his understanding of secularity. It is an immersive story designed to give readers an aesthetic sense of what it means
to live in a secular age. Taylor practices what he preaches; he offers not
just an apologetic but an imaginative apologetic. As he writes early in
A Secular Age: "I want to talk about belief and unbelief, not as rival theories, that is, ways that people account for existence, or morality. Rather,
what I want to do is focus attention on the different kinds of lived experience involved in understanding your life in one way or the other, on
what it's like to live as a believer or an unbeliever."[99] Again, it is not that
premodern people believed one thing and we believe another; we have
very different lived experiences of reality. Taylor's intention is to make us

---

[97]Taylor's apologetic "fit" is explored in depth in Deane-Peter Baker, *Tayloring Reformed Epistemology: The Challenge to Christian Belief* (London: SCM, 2008).
[98]Taylor, "Afterword: Apologia pro Libro Suo," 320.
[99]Taylor, *Secular Age*, 4-5.

feel what it is like to undergo the shift to secularity, and then to ask, "What now?"[100] His goal is to lead us toward fuller versions of authenticity, grounded in the Christian story. This is an imaginative apologetic, and in the chapters that follow, I will be exploring what else this might look like and what other resources are available for the practice of apologetics in our postromantic situation.

CONCLUSION

Charles Taylor's account of secularity offers us an analysis of the soil of our social imaginary. The enchanted world has been lost, but the eclipse came about through unexpected sources: through trajectories of reform that shifted human consciousness toward inwardness and ordinary flourishing, through fascination with the created order for its own sake, through truncated theologies that shrunk the scope of apologetic defense, and finally through romantic expressivism that supplied the depth dimension that had been lost. The loss of extrinsic meaning has placed incredible pressure on the imagination to make sense of things, to forge a unique way of being human. This ethic of authenticity has become an inescapable feature of modern life. This situation is an imaginative crisis and an imaginative opportunity.

My argument is that the ethic of authenticity provides a profound space for engagement with the imagination: for what is deeply felt, for what sorts of possibilities are explored, and for what sorts of lives we make in response. With Taylor, I want to ask how apologetics might work within the parameters of this social imaginary, proposing thicker versions of

---

[100]Colin Jager argues convincingly that the shape of Taylor's method reflects Taylor's Romanticism, his Herderian conviction that the "alternative to the magisterial survey of Enlightenment historiography" is to "feel one's way in," empathetically experiencing, as far as possible, the difference in cultural and historical sensibilities. Jager writes that the closing sections of *A Secular Age* "are best read as a series of experiments in how one might best express, rather than resolve" the tension between the book's secularity and its Christianity, even if Taylor seems to argue for the "existential validity of Christianity as the best response to a secular age." Jager, "This Detail, This History: Charles Taylor's Romanticism," 177. To this assessment of his work, Taylor simply responds: "I plead guilty as charged: I'm a hopeless German romantic of the 1790s. I resonate with Herder's idea of humanity as the orchestra, in which all the differences between human beings could ultimately sound together in harmony." Taylor, "Afterword: Apologia pro Libro Suo," 320.

authenticity set against broader horizons. The goal is not to undo authenticity but to offer a better version. If our social imaginary is one in which we feel our way into faith, then how might we appraise apologetic methodology in light of this aesthetic ascendancy? This is the subject of the next chapter, in which I will survey and test apologetic methodologies in light of this diagnosis, to highlight the need for a more holistic approach, one that takes the imagination into fuller account.

two

Feeling the Way In

Schleiermacher and the Apologetics of Authenticity

Deeply felt personal insight now becomes our most precious spiritual resource.

CHARLES TAYLOR, *A SECULAR AGE*

KNOWING AND SHOWING:
AN APOLOGETIC QUANDARY?

When I was growing up, there was a hymn that my church used to sing on Easter Sunday. Written by Alfred Henry Ackley in the early twentieth century, the hymn celebrates the resurrected Christ. The hymn begins by expressing faith in the face of skepticism: "I serve a risen Savior; He's in the world today. I know that he is living, whatever men may say." The hymn notes the hand, voice, and presence of Jesus throughout the world, before building to its triumphant chorus: "He lives, he lives; Christ Jesus lives today. He walks with me and talks with me, along life's narrow way. He lives, he lives, salvation to impart. You ask me how I know he lives; he lives within my heart!"

I still enjoy the hymn, but now I see it as particularly expressive of the age of authenticity. For assurance of the resurrection, the hymn does not direct doubters to an external source, such as the testimony of eyewitnesses in Scripture or the authority of church tradition. Rather, the most significant reason for faith is profoundly existential and experiential: he walks with me and talks with me. Confidence that Christ is really risen is confirmed through my individual emotive, embodied experience as I turn to look within. You ask me how I know he lives? He lives within my heart.

Apologetic communication has always had experiential dimensions. But it is only with the rise of authenticity that the experiential dimension is given pride of place. The underlying theme is that the only way you can really know Christianity's substance is to experience it yourself. But this raises a significant challenge for the apologetic task. If Christian faith can only be adequately known from the inside, how can it be communicated to those on the outside? How can such deeply felt personal insight be commended, much less be convincing to those who contest the resurrection claim?

One option is to suspend the subjective, experiential dimension in an effort to establish the appeal on external evidences and rational proofs. Let us call this truth-oriented apologetics. To borrow a well-worn distinction from William Lane Craig, Christians may *know* the reality of the resurrection experientially (through the inner witness of the Holy Spirit), but that is not the way that we *show* that reality to others.[1] Such an approach seeks to demonstrate the truth of Christianity before appealing to its goodness or beauty. It builds on the facts rather than felt sense. "He lives within my heart" is fine as a word of personal testimony, directed toward the believing community. But as concerns Christian witness, "He lives within my heart" only has existential relevance after it has been demonstrated that the physical resurrection actually occurred. This approach has been so popular among evangelicals that for many "demonstrating Christianity's truth" is what the word apologetics means. But if our argument about authenticity in chapter one is persuasive, then we should expect such approaches to have uneven effectiveness. In the age of authenticity, truth must resonate with my emotional, embodied experience of

---

[1] William Lane Craig, *Reasonable Faith: Christian Truth and Apologetics* (Wheaton, IL: Crossway, 2008), 43-58.

the world. It must "speak to me" in languages of feeling that I can understand. That is to say, it must engage the imagination, not just the intellect. But how does one communicate internal resonance while also staying tethered to external reality?

A second approach, responsive to the perceived impotence of the first method, is to suspend evidential argumentation altogether and to insist that the church's communal witness and proclamation of the gospel is the best apologetic. Let us call this church-oriented apologetics. Here the modest claims of testimony replace the empirical claims of proof and the reality of the resurrection becomes intelligible in the concrete, lived out reality of the church's corporate life. So, we might adjust the words of the hymn to something like, "He lives in the embodied practices of our community." This may not pack a punch like the original version, but that is not a major concern. For although outsiders are invited to "taste and see" the coherence of Christianity, there is less of a concern to establish common ground between rival visions of the world. This approach seeks to commend the Christian faith as an imaginative whole. Apologetics is embodied in a revitalized and robust church whose distinctiveness is its most attractive element. Insofar as it takes the imagination more seriously, this approach to apologetics has wider purchase in the age of authenticity. But at its best it requires a high level of imaginative empathy from outsiders. At worst it ignores them.

This leads us to a third route, one that seeks to alert outsiders to the way that their embodied, emotional experience of the world may already bear the marks of divine presence and address. I will call this the apologetics of authenticity: an apologetic that begins by exploring our intuitive and imaginative sense of our place in the world, locating the appeal of faith in the aesthetic dimension. Adopting the apologetics of authenticity does not necessarily mean we must leave the first two approaches behind. I want to encourage all sorts of ways of working together to bear witness to the good news of Jesus. And so, I will seek to honor the best impulses and sharpest criticisms of both the truth-oriented and church-oriented approaches in order to create a robust, reimagined apologetic.

Indeed, this chapter puts these three approaches in conversation, sketching the contours of an apologetic that takes the aesthetic dimension seriously. In order to orient the discussion, I will begin with the apologetic project of German theologian Friedrich Schleiermacher (1768–1834).[2] Schleiermacher's project was the first real attempt at an apologetic resonant with Romantic sensibilities, an apologetic of feeling. In orienting the discussion around Schleiermacher, I am not so much commending his body of work so much as his basic impulse to make sense of new conditions of belief. Schleiermacher's program functions as a sort of test case: if secularity is indeed a crisis in which we feel our way into faith imaginatively and aesthetically, then that crisis ought to shape Christian witness. Like authenticity itself, we should expect the apologetics of authenticity to have both thicker and thinner varieties. The deficiencies of a particular approach may invite us to consider how the impulse might be salvaged, and what a thicker version might require. This will require Schleiermacher's voice along with other conversation partners in resonance and reaction, including other apologetic schools and thinkers: William Lane Craig, Alvin Plantinga, and George Lindbeck. My goal in highlighting the place of the imagination in various apologetic methodologies is to discover some promising points of entry for a reinvigorated approach. I hope to show that a thicker apologetics of authenticity is possible, though it will require broader theological horizons—indeed, a theology of imagination, the subject of chapter three.

SCHLEIERMACHER AND THE APOLOGETICS OF AUTHENTICITY

Schleiermacher's apologetic project. Friedrich Schleiermacher seems the ideal place to start an inquiry about the apologetics of authenticity, not least because of his personal history. He was raised by the Moravians,

---

[2]Schleiermacher is already a noteworthy figure in the history of apologetics, the first Protestant thinker to carve out space for apologetics as a separate discipline. Friedrich Schleiermacher, *Brief Outline of Theology as a Field of Study: Revised Translation of the 1811 and 1830 Editions*, trans. Terrence N. Tice (Louisville: Westminster John Knox, 2011), 17-24.

ordained in the Reformed church, and deeply influenced by the German Romantic movement. Accordingly, he sought to draw together all of these streams, in the words of Avery Dulles, "to mediate between the Pietistic Christianity of his forebears and the enlightened romanticism of his intellectual companions."[3] Schleiermacher hoped to show his contemporaries how to hear the divine in the Romantic inner voice.

Addressed to his Romantic associates, Schleiermacher's book *On Religion: Speeches to Its Cultured Despisers* was a revolutionary work of apologetics. In it, he endeavored to free religion from finding its center in either metaphysics or morality. Instead, he argued that the essence of religion was a feeling of absolute dependence (*Gefühl*). Religious piety was not a rationalistic deduction from evidences found in the natural world. Rather, it was an immediate "consciousness of the universal existence of all finite things, in and through the Infinite, and of all temporal things in and through the Eternal."[4] If this framing of things seems opaque, let us consider his particular audience: Romantic writers, poets, and aesthetes, whom he called "cultured despisers of religion." These contemporaries had rejected religion as irrational and irrelevant, but Schleiermacher wanted to show them that their love of natural beauty and artistic creation were fundamentally religious. In their aesthetic appropriation of these things, they were tapping into an irrefutable sense or hunger for the infinite.[5] What if, he asked his friends, you are still deeply religious, and your aesthetic pursuits are deeply responsive to a religious sense that is impossible to eradicate?[6]

---

[3] Avery Cardinal Dulles, *A History of Apologetics* (San Francisco: Ignatius, 2005), 210. Despite being expelled from a Moravian seminary, Schleiermacher nevertheless retained their characteristic interest in personal experiences of faith.

[4] Friedrich Schleiermacher, *On Religion: Speeches to Its Cultured Despisers*, trans. John Oman (New York: Harper and Row, 1958), 36.

[5] Schleiermacher rarely speaks of "divinity" or of "God," opting instead to speak of "the Universe," "the Infinite," "the World-Spirit," and the like. Robert Johnston argues that this is integral to his apologetic strategy, writing for his contemporaries who no longer took God's existence for granted. Robert K. Johnston, *God's Wider Presence: Reconsidering General Revelation* (Grand Rapids: Baker Academic, 2014), 145. I am indebted to Dr. Johnston's reading of Schleiermacher, drawn primarily from a doctoral seminar in the fall of 2014.

[6] Schleiermacher was convinced that although "the rage for calculating and explaining" attendant to his time tended to suppress this sense of dependence, it could not be altogether extinguished. Schleiermacher, *On Religion*, 124.

Schleiermacher wanted to take the aesthetic experience of his colleagues seriously. As Dulles writes, Schleiermacher's is the first construction of "a thoroughgoing 'inner apologetic' that proceeds through the progressive unfolding of the innate longing for communion with God."[7] This new apologetic represented a new way forward for religion after the Kantian revolution. Kant insisted that we have no access to things as they are, but only as they appear to us. This seemed to block the way to primary reality, enclosing the human subject in the echo chamber of immanence. Schleiermacher's solution was to look inward with vigor. Humanity's intuitive, imaginative sense of dependence became the cornerstone of his theology. Feeling displaced reason as the criterion for legitimizing faith.

The abiding relevance of Schleiermacher's apologetic is connected to the rise of authenticity. Since he agreed with Kant's critique of speculative reason, Schleiermacher had no desire to prove God's existence through traditional proofs.[8] His master stroke was to start and stay in the inner realm of feeling. This diluted the power of rational critique, which missed the core of the Christian faith in any case. The truth of Christianity could only be validated through an *experience* of redemption.[9] Taylor explicitly designates Schleiermacher's attempt as an example of the sort of "subtler language" that characterized the Romantic movement. He writes:

> Now it appears to many that desiccated reason cannot reach the ultimate truths in any form. What is needed is a subtler language which can make manifest the higher or the divine. But this language requires for its force that it resonate with the writer or reader. Getting assent to some external formula is not the main thing, but being able to generate the moving insight into higher reality is what is important. *Deeply felt personal insight now becomes our most precious spiritual resource.* For Schleiermacher, the crucial thing to explore is the powerful feeling of dependence

---

[7]Dulles, *History of Apologetics,* 213.

[8]Schleiermacher also discounted apologetic arguments based on miracles or prophecy, though he did allow them corroborative value for the already convinced. Friedrich Schleiermacher, *The Christian Faith,* ed. H. R. Mackintosh and James S Stewart (Edinburgh: T&T Clark, 1999), 70-76.

[9]Schleiermacher, *Christian Faith,* 68-69.

on something greater. To give this reign and voice in oneself is more crucial than getting the right formula.[10]

Bernard Reardon writes that Schleiermacher's theology was successful because it targeted the area where Kant was the weakest, namely his "inadequate appreciation of the part of the emotions and the imagination in the religious consciousness."[11] In his sensitivity to the imagination, Schleiermacher is not just valorizing feeling for its own sake. He is attempting to identify God's presence within the parameters of authenticity, looking for a divine source for the internal voice. Indeed, he is characteristically Romantic in his method: his speeches do not merely try to articulate the concept of *Gefühl*; they aim to provoke it. Genuine prophets and priests, he argues, are those who are able to make others feel this intuition of the universe. This means that we ought to expect prophetic ministry not just from pulpits but also from the pens and brushes of writers and artists, who excel at giving us images and stories that resonate with our intuitive sense of our place in the world. As Taylor puts it, this deeply felt personal insight "is more crucial than getting the right formula."[12]

In Schleiermacher the Reformed sense of the divine (*sensus divinitatis*) meets the Romantic inner voice. But is there any way to tell the difference? Has Schleiermacher gone too far in his accommodation to Romanticism, betraying the theocentric legacy of the Reformed Church in which he was ordained? Karl Barth, despite being deeply impressed by Schleiermacher, vigorously resisted and criticized the latter's theological method for starting with humanity rather than God.[13] Earlier thinkers like Locke had made the misstep of attempting to ground Christian faith in universal human reason. Schleiermacher had made the opposite error, attempting to ground Christian faith in universal human experience. In either case the ground of the Christian faith lay outside of itself, outside of God's self-revelation in Christ. Schleiermacher

---

[10]Charles Taylor, *A Secular Age* (Cambridge: Harvard University Press, 2007), 489. Emphasis added.
[11]Bernard M. G. Reardon, *Religious Thought in the Victorian Age: A Survey from Coleridge to Gore* (London: Longman, 1971), 12.
[12]Taylor, *Secular Age*, 489.
[13]Karl Barth, *The Theology of Schleiermacher: Lectures at Gottingen, Winter Semester of 1923-24* (Grand Rapids: Eerdmans, 1982).

interpreted the Christian faith as a particular instance of the general phenomenon of human religiosity. But Barth set a sharp antithesis between the Christian faith and human religion. The latter was more an expression of human sinfulness than a point of contact for clarifying revelation. We are always in danger, Barth believed, of mistaking our best imaginings about God for the real thing.

By contrast, Dutch theologian Herman Bavinck had a more positive appraisal of Schleiermacher's central insight, even though he was critical of his larger project. He writes, "The core of our self-consciousness is, as Schleiermacher perceived much more clearly than Kant, not autonomy, but a sense of dependence. In the act of becoming conscious of ourselves we become conscious of ourselves as creatures."[14] Although Bavinck affirms Schleiermacher's contention that creaturely self-consciousness means both dependence and freedom, Bavinck is careful to emphasize that Schleiermacher understates the effects of sin. Sin twists our dependence toward idolatry and our sense of freedom toward autonomy.

In either case, the assessment that Schleiermacher has overcompensated for the nineteenth century's turn to the subject and thus betrayed Calvin's theocentric legacy continues to be shared by many Reformed scholars.[15] The concern expressed by Barth and many after him is that Schleiermacher has only charted a new path toward making much of oneself. Rather than discerning the voice of God within the Romantic inner call, he has confused them. Indeed, this was the route taken by Schleiermacher's student, Ludwig Feuerbach. Feuerbach argued that anthropology was the secret of theology and that divinity is the imaginative projection of the best impulses in humanity.[16] We imagine the biggest and best human and call it divine, as if we could whisper "God" by shouting "man."

---

[14]Herman Bavinck, *The Philosophy of Revelation* (Grand Rapids: Baker, 1979), 42.

[15]Charles Partee sketches a parting of ways, writing that the Protestant scholastics tended to "ignore Hume's critique of reason and Kant's resolution while their liberal opponents accept Kant's critique and embrace Schleiermacher's resolution." Charles Partee, *The Theology of John Calvin* (Louisville: Westminster John Knox, 2010), 318.

[16]Ludwig Feuerbach, *The Essence of Christianity*, trans. George Eliot (Buffalo: Prometheus, 1989). This recalls the witch's argument to the children in the *Silver Chair* (discussed in the last chapter).

The limits of imaginative apprehension. I should make it clear that my goal is not to critique Schleiermacher's larger theological project. Barth called Schleiermacher "the great Niagara Falls" of modern theology. Such a prospect calls to mind the joke about the young plumber who upon visiting Niagara Falls said, "I think I can fix this." I will leave Schleiermacher's body of work to others above my station. My intention is to consider Schleiermacher's *starting point* ("deeply felt personal insight") rather than his decision to take such insight as theology's primary *source*. There is a difference between taking authenticity as a fact on the ground of our current situation and taking it as the ground of Christian faith.

This more modest proposal, of course, does not exempt me from Barth's larger critique.[17] But it is not the case that Schleiermacher's starting point must proceed inevitably toward Feuerbach. A charitable reading of Schleiermacher considers his apologetic sensitivities. Writing for peers who no longer took God's existence for granted, he endeavored to meet them where they were and to lead them along toward Christian faith. Recognizing the eternal is the first step to recognizing the Eternal One.[18] The question is this: Does our sense of deeply felt personal insight mean we are experiencing something wholly immanent or wholly Other. There are certainly places in the speeches where the latter reading can be sustained, as when Schleiermacher says, "Every intuition and every original feeling proceeds from revelation."[19] Barth was so intrigued by this dynamic in Schleiermacher that in his later career he wondered if he had misinterpreted him:

---

[17]As Robert Jenson warns with specific reference to Schleiermacher: "If theological prolegomena lay down conceptual conditions of Christian teaching that are not themselves Christian teaching . . . the prolegomena [will] soon turn against the *legomena*." Robert W. Jenson, *Systematic Theology: The Triune God* (Oxford: Oxford University Press, 2001), 9.

[18]Johnston argues convincingly that there is a critical difference in Schleiermacher's vocabulary between intuition (*Anschauung*) and feeling (*Gefühl*). Whereas the latter is indeed an inner awareness of our dependence, the former is immediate perception of otherness—the presence of the Spirit. Johnston, *God's Wider Presence*, 146.

[19]Schleiermacher, *On Religion*, 89. Gerrish argues that Schleiermacher drew his understanding of religion as an unavoidable dimension of human experience directly from Calvin, and that for Schleiermacher as for Calvin, God's revelation comes generally through religious experience, though only decisively through an experience of Christ, by the power of the Spirit. B. A. Gerrish, *A Prince of the Church: Schleiermacher and the Beginnings of Modern Theology* (Eugene, OR: Wipf and Stock Publishers, 2001), 43.

In Schleiermacher's theology or philosophy, do persons feel, think, and speak . . . in relationship to an indispensable Other, in accordance with an *object* which is superior to their own being, feeling, perceiving, willing, and acting, an object toward which adoration, gratitude, repentance, and supplication are concretely possible and even imperative? Were that the case, then I would prick up my ears and be joyfully prepared to hear further things about this Other, in the hopes of finding myself fundamentally at one with Schleiermacher.[20]

In other words, although there is unquestionably an expressivist impulse in Schleiermacher's project, it does not preclude an external "indispensable Other" that calls forth the expressivist response.

This is an important distinction. But the fact remains that Schleiermacher does not offer any significant criteria for distinguishing between an awakening to the eternal and to the Eternal One. How can we know if we have mistaken highest imagination for revelatory presence? More pointedly, will a general sense of imaginative apprehension felt in aesthetic encounter ever get us to the particularity of the God revealed in Jesus Christ? Profound tensions remain in Schleiermacher's Romantic theology and its attendant apologetic methodology. If we are to proceed with the apologetics of authenticity, we need to listen to Schleiermacher's critics.

I have two primary criticisms in mind in this chapter. One stream of critics sees Schleiermacher's project as a dangerous overreaction that placed an unwarranted emphasis on the human person. They seek to suspend the aesthetic dimension, insisting that human faculties be first aimed at the truth. Only once we are convinced of Christianity's truth may we consider its resonance. In keeping with the categories from this chapter's introduction, let us call this the *truth* corrective. A second stream of critics questions the assumption that any *universal* feeling underlies human culture and religion. Different religious systems yield different sorts of feelings, and only uniquely Christian practices will engender uniquely Christian imaginings. These critics seek to speak with a uniquely Christian voice, using a grammar that can only be understood by those

---

[20]Barth, *Theology of Schleiermacher*, 275.

who are willing to immerse themselves in Christianity as a unique form of life. We will call this the *church* corrective. When both correctives are taken into account, we find that a thicker apologetics of authenticity, requiring sharper theological horizons.

THE STATUS OF THE IMAGINATION
IN APOLOGETIC METHOD

The truth corrective: Suspending the imagination. If authenticity means that people *feel* their way into faith, then what becomes of truth? Here we find the primary concern of conservative apologetic approaches. *Conservative* is a slippery word, but I use it throughout this chapter to refer to those apologetic approaches that take defending the truth claims of Christianity as the primary task of apologetics. Keeping the focus on the truth guards against subjectivism, which leaves us without any objective criteria for adjudicating between differing religious senses. William Lane Craig articulates this concern with direct reference to Schleiermacher:

> The warm Pietism of eighteenth-century Germany found its issue in F. D. E. Schleiermacher and the liberal theology of the next generation. In the same way, if out of deference to the "postmodern mentality" we abandon natural theology and Christian evidences and tell people to attend to the inner divine sense as they watch the sun set over the mountains or on the ocean, then I fear that what we shall reap in the next generation is a whirlwind of religious relativism and pluralism.[21]

This desire to avoid relativism leads many conservative apologetic texts to define apologetics *solely* in terms of defending the truth of Christian claims. Stephen Cowan's introduction to "five views of apologetics" is emblematic, defining the discipline as "concerned with the defense of the Christian faith against the charges of falsehood, inconsistency, or credulity," and with "making a case for the truth of the Christian faith."[22] Although the conservative evangelicals in Cowan's

---

[21]William Lane Craig, "Response to Kelly James Clark," in *Five Views on Apologetics*, ed. Stephen Cowan (Grand Rapids: Zondervan, 2010), 290.
[22]Stephen Cowan, ed., *Five Views on Apologetics* (Grand Rapids: Zondervan, 2010), 8.

book disagree on whether the truth of Christianity should be presupposed, or whether to start with proofs for theism or proofs for the resurrection, they are united by their focus on the *truth* of Christianity. A sampling of definitions from across the evangelical spectrum further bears this out. John Warwick Montgomery, who relies heavily on evidentiary arguments, writes that apologetics is about "the compelling facticity of Christian arguments."[23] K. Scott Oliphint, who presupposes Christian faith, writes that apologetics is "the application of biblical truth to unbelief."[24] Douglas Groothuis, who makes a "cumulative case" argument for Christianity, writes that apologetics is "the rational defense of the Christian worldview as objectively true, rationally compelling and existentially or subjectively engaging."[25] As we see with this last definition, it is not that evangelical apologists necessarily neglect the affections or the will. It is rather a matter of what comes first in their apologetic method. Rationality and truth are primary; apologetics must first defend the rational grounds of Christianity.

Similarly, apologetic practitioners in the conservative camp are quite happy to demonstrate imaginative impulses for belief. Craig himself often notes the secondary value of aesthetic experience. Responding to a letter from a skeptic who, convinced by Craig's arguments, still cannot bring himself to believe, Craig gives this counsel:

> Seek experiences that put you in touch with the transcendent. You need to escape the cloying bonds of naturalism by catching glimpses of a transcendent reality beyond the material world. This will help to prepare your heart for belief in God. So open yourself to experiences of sublime beauty. . . . Watch a sunrise or sunset over a beautiful landscape or take in the beauty of pristine nature. Such beauty can sometimes produce an almost painful ache in us because of our inability to take it all in.[26]

---

[23]John Warwick Montgomery, *Faith Founded on Fact: Essays in Evidential Apologetics* (Nashville: Thomas Nelson, 1978), xvii.

[24]K. Scott Oliphint and William Edgar, *Covenantal Apologetics: Principles and Practice in Defense of Our Faith* (Wheaton, IL: Crossway, 2013), 29.

[25]Douglas R. Groothuis, *Christian Apologetics: A Comprehensive Case for Biblical Faith* (Downers Grove, IL: IVP Academic, 2011), 24.

[26]William Lane Craig, "You've Ruined My Life, Professor Craig!" ReasonableFaith.org, accessed February 28, 2017, www.reasonablefaith.org/you-have-ruined-my-life-professor-craig.

Compare this with Craig's earlier stated suspicion of "sunset spirituality." By contrast, this celebration of the sublime might have come from Schleiermacher himself! But the key difference between Craig's suspicion in one case and celebration in the other is the timing of the imaginative provocations. It is only after being persuaded of the truth of Christianity that the aesthetic dimension is explored in order to give the extra "push" into belief. Otherwise faith would be grounded on feeling instead of fact.

Craig is quite willing to accept any number of subjective, imaginative, and inwardly oriented foundations for faith, but only when it comes to *knowing* the truth of Christianity for oneself. *Showing* the truth of Christianity, however, is a different matter entirely, since a non-Christian will not accept the sense of the divine or the inner testimony of the Spirit.[27] Thus, some common ground is sought for shared rationality. In seeking this common ground, conservative apologetic approaches often are inclined to defend the correspondence theory of truth. This defense is also often accompanied by epistemic foundationalism, the view that all truth claims must ultimately rest on indubitable foundations.[28] For these apologists, the apologetic project includes defending truth itself: to show that Christianity is true, you must show that there is such a thing as truth.[29]

---

[27]Myron Penner challenges this distinction (between *knowing* and *showing* Christianity's truth), arguing that witness is always embodied in a person's life, composed of the dialogical relationship between what is claimed and how those truths are embodied: "What is needed in our witness, if those we engage are to be edified, is a poetics that performs the essentially Christian, in which there is no gap between the form of witness and its content." Penner, *End of Apologetics*, 90.

[28]This is not always the case. Presuppositional apologists usually reject epistemic foundationalism and assert that the basis of Christian faith is special revelation. Nevertheless, many Reformed apologists join other conservative models in preoccupation with the methodological primacy of truth, substituting Scriptural revelation for reason as the foundation, and proceeding in the usual way. See Cornelius Van Til, *Christian Apologetics*, ed. William Edgar (Phillipsburg, NJ: P&R, 2003).

[29]Normal Geisler makes an effort to defend the modern paradigm of knowledge, arguing that the Christian faith requires both ontological realism and epistemic foundationalism. Norman L. Geisler, *Christian Apologetics* (Grand Rapids: Baker Academic, 1988), 8-9. There can certainly be value to such an approach: it aims to avoid circular reasoning and seems to offer an accessible foundation for belief for all people. But as the Reformed epistemologists argue, classic foundationalism does not offer a reliable account of how belief actually works. Large numbers of people have neither access nor ability to assess theistic arguments yet find themselves believing. Moreover, such an epistemological paradigm owes much to Cartesian universal methodic doubt, aiming not just for trustworthiness but for Enlightenment certainty. The problem, as we have seen in Taylor's narrative, is that in search of sure foundations, eighteenth

The problem is that fixation on truth tends to suspend the aesthetic and experiential dimensions of faith, which are more decisive in the age of authenticity. Let us take as an illustration the truth-oriented approach of Benno Van den Toren. Van den Toren defines the scope of apologetics as related to "the intellectual justification of the truth and relevance of the Christian faith."[30] He operates with a robust conception of the intellect, which "can only flourish together with the will and the affections," and a more personalistic concept of truth.[31] In other words, what we encounter is not just abstract truths of Christianity but the reality of a present God, who makes universal claims on humanity in the gospel and addresses answerable human beings.[32] Van den Toren tends to avoid speaking about the imagination, but there is an implicit imaginative theory at work in his project, concerned with the Christian faith as an orienting vision of reality.[33] He is interested in the presentation of the Christian faith as a way of seeing and being in the world which "can only be adequately acclaimed as a whole."[34] Moreover, Van den Toren makes it clear that human inquiry after truth always exists in a field of social, cultural, psychological, and religious forces, of which we are a product but not passive victims. This nuanced view of the intellect is a significant advance over most other conservative approaches. Yet insofar as Van den Toren remains centered on demonstrating the truth of Christianity, relying on the unity and coherency of the

---

century apologists narrowed apologetic defense to the demands of generic theism, unwittingly aiding the rise of exclusive humanism. Insofar as apologetics capitulates to the Enlightenment fixations with objectivity, neutrality, and universality, it takes up a posture of apprehending truth that is inconsistent with Christian theology, which has long maintained that there are moral and affective dimensions to knowledge. See Sarah Coakley, ed., *Faith, Rationality and the Passions* (Malden, MA: Wiley-Blackwell, 2012).

[30]Bernard Van den Toren, *Christian Apologetics: Religious Witness as Cross-Cultural Dialogue* (London: T&T Clark, 2011), 27.

[31]Van den Toren, *Christian Apologetics*, 212.

[32]Van den Toren distinguishes between universal validity from the start (a universal starting point, such as the law of noncontradiction) and universal validity in principle (but without a universal starting point) Van den Toren, *Christian Apologetics*, 60-62.

[33]Van den Toren's descriptions of the imagination tend toward the Romantic caricature so that he distinguishes "products of human imagination" from reality. Van den Toren, *Christian Apologetics*, 28.

[34]Van den Toren, *Christian Apologetics*, 63. Apologetic witness invites outsiders to consider Christianity an imaginative whole, and Van den Toren makes special note of the apologetic uses of narratives, which can "plunge us right into the middle" of the Christian imaginative vision. Van den Toren, *Christian Apologetics*, 182-86.

Christian vision, he struggles to make sense of apologetic situations when no intellectual integration is sought. He writes of the challenge: "A person may, all at the same time, think as a materialist in relation to science, as a romanticist in relation to art, as an idealist in relation to politics, and as a Christian or Hindu in relation to death."[35] But if our diagnosis is correct, what is more significant is not the fact that a person may "think as" different identities but that they "feel their way in" to their place in the world and that they are actively engaged in making something of their situation. Both of these aspects of human inquiry are more responsive to the imagination than the intellect, and here Van den Toren's project would benefit from including a broader imaginative theory.

Notwithstanding this criticism, the basic impulse of the truth corrective is to anchor the imagination to reality. This should be taken seriously. Groothuis is correct: we should do our best to "get reality right" lest we "forfeit the humility of being beholden to a reality outside of [ourselves]—a reality that may prove right or wrong, but which [we] do not command."[36] The challenge is how the apologetics of authenticity can take truth seriously without leaving the imagination on the shelf until the end of the inquiry. Here Reformed epistemology provides a resource.

Reformed epistemology: Aiming the imagination at truth. At first glance, the school of thought known as Reformed epistemology (represented here by Alvin Plantinga) seems to share much in common with Schleiermacher's Romantic convictions. Both propose an alternative to classic foundationalism. Both are children of the Reformation working with Calvin's sense of the divine (*sensus divinitatis*). Both are sensitive to a noninferential awareness of God, especially as occasioned through aesthetic experience. But there is a key divergence in their philosophical lineage: whereas Schleiermacher attempts to transcend the problem laid out by Hume and Kant, Plantinga combines Scottish realism with the Calvinist insistence on the necessity of special revelation.[37] With the

---

[35]Van den Toren, *Christian Apologetics*, 7.
[36]Groothuis, *Christian Apologetics*, 137.
[37]Plantinga's more positive posture toward apologetics (relative to his Kuyperian tradition) derives from his dependence on *both* Kuyper and Reid. See Keith A. Mascord, *Alvin Plantinga and Christian Apologetics* (Eugene, OR: Wipf and Stock, 2007), 12-18.

Calvinists he rejects neutrality as a fiction, and with the realists he rejects Hume's epistemological strictures and Kant's cautions about knowledge. Plantinga writes, "Why think that we can't have *a priori* knowledge of what is real? Couldn't God create persons who were capable of that? . . . And might we not be creatures of just that sort?"[38]

This leads to Plantinga's well-known proposal that Christian belief is properly basic, that is, it is not accepted on the basis of other beliefs. Belief in God, he argues, sits in the same intuitive category as belief in other minds, or the belief that the world was not created ten minutes ago. These are rationally held beliefs rooted in the general reliability of human perception. As basic beliefs, we reason *from* them rather than reasoning *to* them. Basic beliefs are still subject to criticism, but we hold them intuitively, not inferentially. As Plantinga writes, "I am a theist; I believe that there is such a person as God; but I have never decided to hold this belief. It has always just seemed to me to be true. And it isn't as if I could rid myself of this belief just by an act of will."[39] In the normal course of events, a person does not believe because she has examined all possible arguments. She simply finds herself believing; even after encountering objections she continues to find the object of her faith to be trustworthy.

Plantinga explicitly connects the phenomenon of faith to the sense of the divine, which he understands as a natural—though confused—awareness of God implanted in humanity, "a disposition to form beliefs about God under a variety of conditions and in a variety of situations."[40] This awareness of divinity is an imaginative sense that has to do more with *capacity* than *content*. As a noninferential awareness of God's presence, it is simply there. Plantinga writes,

> It isn't that one beholds the night sky, notes that it is grand, and concludes that there must be such a person as God: an argument like that would be ridiculously weak. . . . It is rather that, upon perception of the night sky . . . these beliefs just arise within us. They are *occasioned* by the circumstances;

[38]Alvin Plantinga, *Knowledge and Christian Belief* (Grand Rapids: Eerdmans, 2015), 6.
[39]Plantinga, *Knowledge and Christian Belief*, 17.
[40]Plantinga, *Knowledge and Christian Belief*, 32.

they are not conclusions from them. . . . In this regard, the *sensus divinitatis* resembles perception, memory, and *a priori* belief.[41]

The *sensus* is a cognitive mechanism, a faculty of perception that is occasioned by a variety of circumstances: gratitude, guilt, and grave danger.[42] Nevertheless, he writes, "it isn't only grandeur and majesty that counts . . . [but also] the subtle play of sunlight on a field in spring, or the dainty, articulate breeze of a tiny flower, or aspen leaves shimmering and dancing in the breeze."[43] This perception of glory in the ordinary, as we will see in the chapters that follow, is a hallmark of the Protestant imagination.

What Plantinga wants to demonstrate is that Christians are rationally justified in believing in God even if there are no arguments to support that belief. To use the technical distinctions, Plantinga is arguing for the rationality of faith (a de jure argument) rather than for its veracity (a de facto argument). This is because we cannot consider the rationality of belief apart from a decision on its truth. Imagine an elderly woman who has never read a book of apologetics and yet finds herself believing in God. The only way we can decide about the rationality of her belief is if we know whether that belief is true: "What you properly take to be rational or warranted depends upon what sort of metaphysical and religious stance you adopt."[44] Marx and Freud look for alternative explanations for religious belief because they are convinced that religious belief is false. But religious belief, Plantinga argues, is warranted if it is true: "A belief is rational if it is produced by cognitive faculties that are functioning properly and successfully aimed at truth . . . as opposed, for example, to being the product of wishful thinking [Freud] or cognitive malfunction [Marx]."[45] The rationality of a belief is ultimately connected to it being successfully aimed at the truth. Thus, if it is true that God created humanity with a built-in

---

[41]Alvin Plantinga, *Warranted Christian Belief* (Malden, MA: Oxford University Press, 1999), 175.

[42]David Tracy calls these occasions "limit-experiences," which disclose a religious dimension to life: "sickness, guilt, anxiety, and the recognition of death as one's own destiny," as well as ecstatic experiences of "love, joy, the creative act . . . authentically self-transcending moments in our lives." David Tracy, *Blessed Rage for Order: The New Pluralism in Theology* (Chicago: University of Chicago Press, 1996), 105.

[43]Plantinga, *Warranted Christian Belief*, 174.

[44]Plantinga, *Knowledge and Christian Belief*, 40-41.

[45]Plantinga, *Knowledge and Christian Belief*, 46.

cognitive mechanism (a sense of the divine), then we should expect belief
in God to be occasioned in various situations.[46]

Here is the point of this somewhat technical foray into the philosophy
of knowledge: Plantinga offers an epistemology in which Schleiermacher's
basic aesthetic impulse can be grounded. Plantinga shares Schleiermacher's recognition of occasions that elicit the sense of the divine, but
he also gives us theological reasons to trust our imagination, so that
reason and imagination need not be set against one another. As we intuit
God's presence and address, the imagination is not just sensing but also
seeing: it is not simply gripped by a desire for God's existence but is also
aimed at the truth. That is what the imagination is for: it feels its way into
the possibility of God in search of truth. And if there really is a God, that
is, if the reaching out of the human imagination is responsive to the self-
giving revelation of God, then we can say that the imagination is not only
an organ of meaning but also an organ of truth. This epistemological
framework helps keep the apologetics of authenticity from sliding into
mere self-expression. It operates on the conviction that the imagination
must be responsive to a reality not of its own making, and that the criteria
for discerning this reality may be gleaned apart from our aesthetic sense.[47]

In arguing that Reformed epistemology supplies necessary guardrails
for Schleiermacher's basic impulse, I am seeking a thicker authenticity that
remains connected to the search for truth without allowing facticity to be
the primary criterion of believability. Apologetics is certainly not less than
a defense of the truth of Christianity. But for Christians throughout
history it has always meant more than this; apologists have endeavored

---

[46]If Christian faith is true, Plantinga argues, it is the unbeliever "who displays epistemic malfunction; failing to believe in God is a result of some kind of dysfunction with the sensus divinitatis."
Plantinga, *Knowledge and Christian Belief*, 37.

[47]Nevertheless, Craig maintains that Reformed epistemology still needs natural theology to keep
it from subjectivism. Indeed, the context for Craig's critique of Schleiermacher (quoted above)
is a larger caution about Reformed epistemology. For Craig, the latter bears a troubling resemblance to Schleiermacher's Romanticism, which to Craig is the seedbed for rampant subjectivism. Without the additives of Christian evidences, the seed of religion operative in Reformed
epistemology will break forth in unrecognizable growths. He writes, "It is terrifyingly easy to
see how, in the absence of a vigorous emphasis on natural theology and Christian evidences,
Reformed epistemology can give birth to such deformed progeny." Craig, "Response to Kelly
James Clark," 290.

not merely to show that Christianity is true but also that it is beautiful and good. One of the first such attempts, Aristides's *Apology* (ca. AD 125) made the argument for the moral value of Christianity as an indication of its resonance with reality. Christians tell the truth, show mutual love, and even have compassion on their enemies. For Aristides, the ultimate proof is to say, look at the lives and unity of the Christians. Similarly, Justin Martyr's *First Apology* (AD 150) sets out to demonstrate Christianity's civic value. Writing to the emperor, Justin argues that civil magistrates should investigate whether Christians have actually done anything destructive to civil society. Even if Christians are found to be foolish or misguided, they do not deserve to die. This is much more than justification for the truth and relevance of Christianity. Finally, Augustine's *City of God*, the high-water mark of Christian apologetics in the classical world, defends Christianity not only as true but also as the best hope of establishing peace and cultivating love in the late Roman Empire. Augustine's apologetic strategy was, in John Milbank's apt description, not to "outreason" his detractors but to "outnarrate" them, offering a larger story of the world rooted in an ontology of peace rather than violence.[48] All three of these examples are more than intellectual justifications of Christian truth; they are imaginative provocations of the goodness and beauty of the Christian way of life.

Truth-oriented apologists will likely respond that Christianity is morally generative, worthy of toleration, and capacious for peace and justice precisely because it is *true*. Or to put it more precisely, Christianity is beautiful because it is good, and good because it is true. Just so. But if the transcendentals are thus vitally connected, it means that we can also reverse the order: we are drawn to Christianity's truth by its goodness, and to its goodness by its beauty. Indeed, it is not enough to assent to Christianity's truth; we must love the truth (2 Thess 2:10) who comes to us in grace and glory as a person (Jn 1:14).

Consider the example of Catholic theologian Hans Urs von Balthasar, who opened his theological oeuvre with seven volumes on aesthetics.[49]

---

[48]John Milbank, *Theology and Social Theory: Beyond Secular Reason* (Oxford: Blackwell, 2006), 4.
[49]Hans Urs von Balthasar, *The Glory of the Lord, Vol. 1*, ed. John Riches (San Francisco: Ignatius, 2009).

Why did he do this? He described his choice to start with aesthetics as "comparable to what was once called apologetics."[50] He writes, "In a world without beauty . . . the good loses its attractiveness, the self-evidence of why it must be carried out. Man stands before the good and asks himself why it must be done and not rather its alternative, evil. . . . The logic of these answers is itself a mechanism that no longer captivates anyone. The very conclusions are no longer conclusive."[51] Truth, divorced from goodness and beauty, lacks the power to enthrall. By all means, let Christians seek and contend for the truth. But why should we think that the imagination is any less aimed at truth than the intellect? As I will argue in the next chapter, in imagining we may disconnect from the actual, but only so that we may grasp reality more firmly. Perhaps truth-oriented apologists have it backwards. Perhaps it is truth that provides the final "push" into belief once the imagination is already captivated by the goodness and beauty of the Christ.

But this raises a second question. How exactly does the apologetics of authenticity move outsiders from an apprehension of the beauty of a sunset (to use Craig's example) to the beauty of Jesus? Let us not insult the sun, which sings the glory of Christ (Ps 19:1). The problem is with fallen powers of perception. To outsiders, the sun speaks in glossolalia, a heavenly tongue that cannot be understood without Spirited interpretation.[52] Apart from the Spirit, the sunset may lead just as surely to a sense of self-satisfaction as to surrender. It may evoke a kind of spiritual feeling, but that intuition may not necessarily be followed to Christian faith. C. S. Lewis put it memorably:

> When you are feeling fit and the sun is shining and you do not want to believe that the whole universe is a mere mechanical dance of atoms, it is nice to be able to think of this great mysterious Force rolling on through the centuries and carrying you on its crest. If, on the other hand, you want to do something rather shabby, the Life-Force, being only a blind force,

---

[50]Hans Urs von Balthasar, *Theo-Logic: Theological Logical Theory: The Truth of the World, Vol. 1* (San Francisco: Ignatius, 2001), 20.

[51]Von Balthasar, *Theo-Logic, Vol. 1*, 19.

[52]I owe this analogy to Calvin Seerveld, *Rainbows for the Fallen World: Aesthetic Life and Artistic Task* (Toronto: Tuppence, 1980), 13.

with no morals and no mind, will never interfere with you like that troublesome God we learned about when we were children.[53]

To put it another way: feeling a sense of the divine may not even get you to theism, much less to the God of Abraham, Isaac, and Jacob, the God of Jesus Christ.

The church corrective: Situating the imagination. This brings us to the second critical issue with Schleiermacher's apologetic of feeling: whether it has any concrete content. If the first concern is subjectivism, the second concern is specificity. The complaint is put incisively by "postliberal" theologians, of whom will I take George Lindbeck as representative. The "post-" refers to these theologians' rejection of all varieties of foundationalism, and any approach that seeks to justify Christian faith by any criteria external to the faith itself.[54] To place either foundational truths (as conservative thinkers tend to do) or a foundational religious experience (as liberal thinkers following Schleiermacher have done) underneath religious dogma is to neuter the particularity of religious faith. This is because it is precisely the particularities of belief that enable the sorts of experiences we have. Lindbeck writes, "Different religions seem in many cases to produce fundamentally divergent depth experiences of what it is to be human. . . . The significant things are the distinctive patterns of story, belief, ritual, and behavior that give 'love' and 'God' their specific and sometimes contradictory meanings."[55] In other words, as I stand before a sunset, I don't just intuit a general sense of the divine. The sort of religious sense I have (if any) is always already colored by my imaginative universe, shaped by particular stories, songs, prayers, liturgies, dispositions, and doctrines.[56] To remove the particularities that have trained my imagination over time is to empty religious experience of any real meaning.

---

[53]C. S. Lewis, *Mere Christianity* (Harper Collins, 2009), 26-27.

[54]In this way postliberal thinkers bear a family resemblance to presuppositionalism. Yet the latter often remains foundationalist, but with the key difference that revelation stands in for reason in providing the foundation. By contrast, postliberals reject the foundationalist epistemic picture in toto.

[55]George A. Lindbeck, *The Nature of Doctrine: Religion and Theology in a Postliberal Age* (Philadelphia: Westminster, 1984), 41-42.

[56]Lindbeck argues that doctrine is not primarily "an array of beliefs about the true and the good (though it may involve these), or a symbolism expressive of basic attitudes, feelings, and

This brings the church right into the forefront of the conversation. Indeed, thinkers following Lindbeck's approach prefer to speak of mission and catechesis rather than apologetics.[57] The problem with apologetics is that it seeks to translate, and too much is lost in translation. The corollary to this is that Christianity and other religious systems are "incommensurable." This does not mean that there is no common ground for some shared understanding (or else we would not even recognize the discontinuity). It means that as soon as translation begins to occur, a particular interpretive frame is imposed on the translation. Common ground is still possible, but finding it will always be a nonsystematic process, a matter of making whatever connections exist between two interlocutors. This is why the only acceptable apologetics will be "ad hoc apologetics," because there is no neutral, middle language into which incommensurable systems can be translated.[58] For postliberals like Lindbeck, the only way to truly understand faith and to find it believable is to experience it as a unique form of life in all its particularities. Like a language, Christianity is a thick form of life with an internally consistent grammar that will not make sense to those who do not speak it.[59] Thus, we must learn by immersion, plunging into the formative doctrines and practices of Christian community, for it is only within this matrix that the Christian faith becomes intelligible.

---

sentiments (though these will be generated). Rather it is similar to an idiom that makes possible the description of realities, the formulation of beliefs, and the experiencing of inner attitudes, feelings, and sentiments." Lindbeck, *Nature of Doctrine*, 33.

[57]Lindbeck writes: "Postliberals are bound to be skeptical, not about missions, but about apologetics and foundations." Lindbeck, *Nature of Doctrine*, 129. To be clear, Lindbeck and other postliberal thinkers are not really against apologetics in principle so much as apologetic systems grounded in foundationalism.

[58]So Lindbeck: "In regard to some Muslims you might say, Look, this is why I recommend Christ rather than Muhammad to you. To other Muslims you might present a different set of reasons. . . . There is no single logic of coming [to faith]. There is a logic of belief. There is a structure of Christian faith. But the ways in which God calls us through the Holy Spirit to come to believe are so varied that you cannot possibly make generalizations." Timothy R. Phillips and Dennis L. Okholm, eds., *The Nature of Confession: Evangelicals and Postliberals in Conversation* (Downers Grove, IL: InterVarsity Press, 1996), 252. Jeremiah Gibbs gives a wry reply: "Apologetics has always been *ad hoc* in the way that Lindbeck describes." Jeremiah Gibbs, *Apologetics After Lindbeck*, 30.

[59]Lindbeck and other postliberal theologians are drawing from Ludwig Wittgenstein's proposal that meaning is intelligible in light of the rules of particular "games" that govern the use of language. Ludwig Wittgenstein, *Philosophical Investigations*, trans. G. E. M. Anscombe (Englewood Cliffs, NJ: Pearson, 1973).

The point is that it is not enough to unleash the imagination in the realm of aesthetic possibility, in search of the divine. To explore Christian possibilities, there must be some approximation of Christian practices, which will lead to particularly Christian imaginings.[60] In the volume *Imaginative Apologetics*, Andrew Davison continues this line of argument, connecting apologetic witness to Christian worship. Rather than seeking to persuade on "neutral" grounds, Davison argues that the only truly persuasive logic is situated, embodied in vibrant Christian community. He writes,

> Whatever the apologist might say about the Christian faith, it can only be incomplete without an introduction to a community where the faith is practiced. Christian rationality is inseparable from Christian disciplines. They are woven into the life of the Church. . . . The Christian does not therefore simply talk about creation (and its goodness) and the human heart (and its selfishness); he or she joins with others to live out these ideas in practices and a form of life.[61]

Thus, to invite a person to consider Christian belief also involves an invitation to Christian community. The community itself becomes the most powerful apologetic, a community that affects the structures of plausibility, making belief believable.

These church-oriented thinkers provide another important corrective to the apologetics of authenticity. Christian faith is more than assent to foundational truths, and it is more than a response to a foundational feeling. It is a particular way of seeing and being in the world, cultivated as we live into and out of the Christian story. We must immerse the imagination in Christian meaning, to feel its internal coherence, the "illuminating power of the whole."[62] This is a more holistic account of faith, sensitive to the way that properly *Christian* intuitions are formed. If the truth-oriented model seeks the connection of the imagination to reality,

---

[60]William Wepernowski argues that short of conversion, outsiders can only arrive at most at an "approximation of Christian belief." William Werpehowski, "Ad Hoc Apologetics," *The Journal of Religion* 66, no. 3 (1986): 192.

[61]Davison, "Christian Reason and Christian Community," 28.

[62]Lindbeck, *The Nature of Doctrine*, 11.

the church corrective seeks the cultivation of the imagination through vital participation.

Here is an approach that takes the imagination seriously. Let us recall that if the quest for authenticity is to avoid narcissism, there must be resonance with some larger story than my own, a storied tradition, a formative community against which my choices are measured. In the same way that the truth corrective compels us to remain tethered to "a reality not of our making," the church corrective compels us to situate our imaginings within the practices of Christian faith: the Christian way of seeing, speaking, listening, and loving. Indeed, if outsiders are truly to understand the Christian faith, there is simply no substitute for participation in Christian community.

Nevertheless, there are two areas where I believe that the postliberal approach runs into difficulties and would benefit from an expanded conception of imagination. First, conceiving of Christian faith as a language has limitations. When we compare languages, we are not in search of normativity, "one tongue to rule them all." But when we compare religious systems, we are often required to make normative judgments between them. They describe reality very differently, engendering different imaginative experiences and leaving us with a different kind of subjectivity.[63] If Christianity (or any other religious system) must be experienced from within to be found intelligible much less believed, what claim could this make on other religious traditions?[64] A second difficulty is related to

---

[63]Some critics may also wish to apply the truth corrective to the postliberal project. But Gibbs proposes that postliberal "ad hoc apologetics" is actually a version of the cumulative case method, insofar as both present Christianity as a comprehensive "take" on reality that commends itself on the grounds of consistency, comprehensiveness, livability, and simplicity, and not just correspondence. Gibbs, *Apologetics After Lindbeck*, 122.

[64]Lindbeck himself acknowledges two dimensions to this problem: "first, [it] seems wholly relativistic: it turns religions, so one can argue, into self-disclosed and incommensurable intellectual ghettos. Associated with this, in the second place is the fideistic dilemma: it appears that choice between religions is purely arbitrary, a matter of blind faith." Lindbeck, *Nature of Doctrine*, 128. I find that the postliberal picture here of religious imaginaries as sharply-defined, self-contained systems is not really accurate. The reality is that imaginaries overlap, interpenetrate, and integrate with each other. As Kathryn Tanner points out, there is no engagement as a "face-off between distinct wholes"; rather, the Christian way of life must be situated "within a whole field of alternatives," resulting in a "step-by-step process of engagement with particulars." Kathryn Tanner, *Theories of Culture: A New Agenda for Theology* (Minneapolis: Fortress, 1997), 111-17. There are boundaries, but the boundaries are porous. There are real differences, but the

this. The church-oriented approach assumes the intrinsic appeal of the Christian faith as well as a high degree of imaginative empathy from outsiders. It assumes that non-Christians will be able to see the greater fecundity of the Christian vision. Yet there is no clear motive for an outsider coming to Christianity to do the arduous work of learning a "second first language" in order to experience the Christian faith from the inside.[65]

What is needed is a more expansive metaphor than linguistic competence, or at least a metaphor that takes into account the generativity of cross-cultural communication. Perhaps in the beginning understanding Christian faith from the outside is less like *learning* to speak a language and more like watching fluent speakers in spirited conversation. Even if the language is not understood, the conversation is beautiful. Or to shift to the other analogy, understanding begins as a matter of artistic appreciation, which provokes a desire to listen and look further. An aesthetic appeal engages the desire. And insofar as works of imagination enable vision and cultivate empathy, they can also initiate outsiders into a new grammar of meaning making.

Here we may take a page from Catholic theologian David Tracy. Tracy notes the emergence of "classic" works in every human culture. Classics are imaginative expressions "of the human spirit [which] so disclose a compelling truth about our lives that we cannot deny them some kind of normative status." A classic work has something to say to every generation; it continually rewards re-examination. This concept offers a way to move beyond the subjectivity of personal feeling toward normative claims. This normativity, however, is not discerned by empirical investigation, but

---

differences do not preclude the possibility of deep understanding, for what may be shared are not necessarily common concepts but common concerns. Within these common concerns, which may be epistemic, ethical, or aesthetic, there is the potential for intelligibility and translation, just as deep communication can still occur across significant linguistic boundaries.

[65]"Second first language" is Alasdair MacIntyre's phrase. As a person learns a language, MacIntyre notes, she inevitably begins by continually translating the language in her mind; but over time she is immersed enough in the language to begin *thinking* in that language without translation. Moreover, MacIntyre argues that the best model for understanding is the way that a child learns a language: by immersion. True fluency means not just understanding the rules of the language but absorbing the logic of the culture, so that one experiences the world "so far as it is possible," as a native inhabitant would experience the world. Alasdair MacIntyre, *Whose Justice? Which Rationality?* (Notre Dame: University of Notre Dame Press, 1989), 374.

by a spirit of recognition. Tracy writes, "What we mean in naming certain texts, events, images, rituals, symbols and persons 'classics' is that here we recognize nothing less than the disclosure of a reality we cannot but name truth."[66] While classics in other disciplines speak to particular areas of the human experience, *religious* classics involve a "claim to truth as the event of a disclosure—concealment of the whole of reality by the power of the whole—as, in some sense, a radical and finally gracious mystery."[67] Tracy argues that religious classics reach across boundaries. They even provide public criteria for testing the truth to which the classic testifies: meaningfulness, internal coherence, and adequacy to experience. We can note that these criteria bear a family resemblance to the value that we have been chasing: authenticity.

The postliberals are right that there is no substitute for life inside the Christian story. But what Christian communicators can provide is a glimpse of the world through Christian eyes, vicarious participation as if from the inside. Here even an approximation of belief is sufficient to compel further interest and engagement in the Christian imaginary. Understanding the imaginative dimension to include not just sensing but also seeing and shaping offers us a threefold cord binding the imagination to the greater reality to which it responds. Such a conception of the imagi- nation connects the concern for specificity together with the concern for truth but also leaves room for surprise, for the gospel to flower forth in ways hitherto unseen.

This is why taking the imagination seriously is so important for apolo- getic communication. Although our social locations *privilege* our religious imagining in particular directions, they do not *determine* what we are able to imagine. We can and regularly do use our imaginations to transcend the horizon of our context in empathetic identification, creative invention, or hopeful anticipation. Indeed, we often speak of "visionaries" as those who possess the power to visualize possibilities that ordinary people fail to see. Conversely, when we say that a person "lacks imagination," we

---

[66]David Tracy, *The Analogical Imagination: Christian Theology and the Culture of Pluralism* (New York: Crossroad, 1998), 108.
[67]Tracy, *Analogical Imagination*, 163.

mean that they are unable to break out of the prison of their own narrow perspective. In the same way our context limits but does not determine what we are able to imagine. Similarly, it is the imagination that makes translation possible, our ability to put ourselves in the shoes of another and to "see as" others see. In such cases, we make sense of unfamiliar experiences in terms we can understand, but those experiences also reciprocally shape our horizon of what is possible.

CONCLUSION

We began by asking how the reality of Christianity, which can only be fully appreciated from the inside ("He lives within my heart!"), could be communicated to those on the outside, particularly within the parameters of authenticity. What would the apologetics of authenticity look like? I oriented the discussion around Schleiermacher's apologetic project, which I took as an early prototype of an apologetic approach engaged with the value of authenticity. Schleiermacher begins with emotional and aesthetic experience and is the founder of a uniquely postromantic apologetic method. Schleiermacher's key source is "deeply felt personal insight," resonant with the desire for authenticity. But Schleiermacher's critics worry that Schleiermacher has simply traded one kind of foundationalism for another. Conservative critics wish to inquire of the relationship of religious feeling to external reality. Postliberal critics wish to demonstrate the relationship of religious feeling to the concrete ecclesial frameworks that makes that sense intelligible. My goal was to carry forward Schleiermacher's basic impulse to work within the parameters of authenticity while also thickening it in response to the critics.

In response to the truth corrective, I noted the resources of Reformed epistemology for grounding Schleiermacher's impulse, especially given the former's orientation toward truth as well as meaning. Nevertheless, I argued that fixation on truth can flatten the multidimensional nature of divine address, and so truth must be held tightly together with beauty and goodness. In response to the church corrective, I argued that although Christian faith requires Christian practices to form Christian intuitions, works of imagination have the power to grant vicarious vision. Rather than asking a seeker to learn the language of Christian faith, aesthetic artifacts can plunge the seeker into the Christian world of meaning. They can expand the field of vision, provoke desire, and even provide the feel of faith from the inside. The promise of such an apologetic is its potential to use the power of the imagination to create a visceral space for imaginative empathy, which creates the possibility of understanding.

Following Schleiermacher's impulse, the apologetics of authenticity seeks to discern God's presence in the questions, joys, and anxieties of those outside the walls of the church, as they feel their way into and out of faith. Yet this imaginative exploration cannot merely be a matter of sensing the divine. It must also include seeing (which requires wrestling with Christian vision of the world) and shaping (which requires vicarious participation in the Christian story). To put it another way, what is needed is an account of the imagination that makes clear how the imagination is aimed at reality and responsive to revelation. It must also offer an account of how the fluency of faith might be cultivated imaginatively in the absence of an explicit commitment. Our exploration in this chapter has laid out the project for the next chapter. It is now time to take a careful look at the imagination itself.

three

Reaching Out

Getting a Grip on the Imagination

*The reaching of the imagination towards a new world
is the result of God's reaching towards us.*

PAUL FIDDES, *FREEDOM AND LIMIT*

DEFINING THE IMAGINATION: SEEKING POSSIBILITY

What exactly *is* the imagination? That depends on whom you ask. Scholars
have noted "a groundswell of philosophical interest in imagination" in the
twenty-first century.[1] Yet the imagination is so multidimensional (one
scholar lists twelve irreducible conceptions!) that it is notoriously difficult
to define. Perhaps imagining is better recognized than defined: we know
it intuitively when we see it (or do it!).[2] Yet the danger is that without a

---

[1]Amy Kind, "Exploring Imagination," in *The Routledge Handbook of Philosophy of Imagination*, ed.
Amy Kind (London: Routledge, 2016), 1.

[2]Leslie Stevenson writes that the topic now "sprawls promiscuously over philosophy of mind,
aesthetics, ethics, poetry, and even religion." Leslie Stevenson, "Twelve Conceptions of Imagination," *British Journal of Aesthetics* 43, no. 3 (July 2003): 238. There is greater consensus on what
the imagination is *not* than what imagination is, and this leads Walton to argue that an intuitive
understanding of the imagination is sufficient, even if we cannot unite all of its dimensions under

clear definition, the imagination might become a conceptual junk drawer gathering many miscellaneous things.[3]

In order to make my argument that taking the imagination seriously is central to the task of making belief believable in an age of authenticity, I need to clarify what I mean by imagination. That is the aim of this chapter: to create a philosophical and theological framework for a reimagined apologetic. This chapter will proceed in three movements. First, I wish to define the imagination as a faculty concerned with *possibility*. Second, I will defend the imagination as responsive to real *presence*. Third, I want to direct the imagination for *participation* in the theodrama of Scripture. My goal is to sketch an account of the imagination in which the human person responds to divine presence by seeing, sensing, and shaping possibility in the created world.

Let me begin with a clarifying claim. *Imagining is a strategic, intentional, and embodied activity that suspends actuality for the sake of reality.* If that sounds dense, let me break it into four parts, which I will examine and illustrate in turn. First, imagining is a strategic activity. In imagining we aim to accomplish something we could not accomplish any other way. Second, imaginings have intentional content: we always aim the imagination *at* something. Third, there is a bodily basis for all human imagining: our embodied experience of the world provides structure for what we can imagine. Fourth, the imagination suspends actuality for the sake of reality: we can imagine things that do not exist, but our ultimate goal is to grasp the world more securely.

Let us consider these claims using a line from John Lennon's classic song: "Imagine all the people living life in peace."[4] My purpose here is not to deliberate over the content of Lennon's proposal but to examine his use of the word *imagine* as illustrative of my claims.

First, imagining is a strategic state. Notice that Lennon is using the word *imagine* in a way that exceeds some ordinary uses of the word. For

a common definition. Kendall L. Walton, *Mimesis as Make-Believe: On the Foundations of the Representational Arts* (Cambridge: Harvard University Press, 1990), 19.

[3]Kind quotes Noël Carrol's expression, "the junkyard of the mind." Kind, "Exploring Imagination," 1.

[4]John Lennon. "Imagine." Genius. Accessed October 4, 2018. genius.com/John-lennon-imagine
-lyrics.

example, I might say, "I *imagined* that traffic would be light today, but my commute took an hour." In this case, the word *imagine* is used to refer to a mistaken assumption, an ill-considered projection. Alternatively, in response to complaints that there is "nothing to do," I might say to my son, "Use your imagination!" In this case, I mean something like "make-believe," proposed as a way to cope with childhood boredom.[5] In neither example is the imagination granted "real world" significance. Imagining consists either of idle speculation or immature escape. The real world, it would seem, requires evidence-based investigation and concrete thinking.[6] But it is clear that Lennon is using "imagine" in a way that exceeds both conjecture and escape. He is counseling a consideration of possibilities—a suspension of disbelief—which he believes can erupt into reality.[7]

If the imagination is nothing more than an idle faculty for amateur thinkers and immature dreamers, no serious theory of imagination would be necessary. What requires a theory of imagination is the recognition that we use the imagination strategically to get a better grasp of the world. Lennon clearly believes that responding to his imaginative invitation will result in a more peaceful, united world. Imagining is strategic: there is something that can be accomplished by imagining that cannot be accomplished by any other mental state. And therefore, as philosopher Amy Kind puts it, "imagination deserves its own box."[8]

---

[5]My point here is not to discount the creative imagination (employed in make-believe), of which I will have more to say below. My point is that some of our ordinary uses of the word imagine fall short of granting the imagination any real power beyond mere amusement. If we regard the imagination as idle and infantile, we miss its potency. But if the childlike imagination can become a model for a constructive creative imagining for all ages, we are now talking about a faculty worth taking seriously. See Walton, *Mimesis as Make-Believe.*

[6]This tendency to discount the imagination dates back at least to Plato, who in the *Republic* labeled imagination (*eikasia*) as the weakest mode of knowledge and expelled the image-making poets from the ideal city. Imagination is imitation, he reasoned, and well-ordered souls need to be in touch with the substance of reality rather than shadows. Plato, *The Republic*, trans. Allan Bloom (New York: Basic Books, 2016).

[7]"Suspension of disbelief" is Coleridge's phrase for describing "poetic faith." Samuel Taylor Coleridge, *Biographia Literaria, or, Biographical Sketches of My Literary Life and Opinions*, ed. James Engell and Walter Jackson Bate (London: Routledge, 1983), 174.

[8]Three of my claims follow the discussion of Amy Kind, who makes four similar claims. I have collapsed her first two claims into one, emphasizing the strategic nature of the imagination, as well as added an additional claim about the bodily basis of imagining. Kind's first claim is that not all

Second, imaginings have intentional content. This is a technical way of saying that we don't just "imagine" in general; our imaginings are always *about* something. This is even the case in the cases I gave above. I may tell my son "use your imagination," but without additional context, he will be unable to comply with my command. The imagination only works by latching onto concrete content, aiming at some possible object or situation. For my son, the implied context is a room full of Legos. What I mean is something like, "Point your imagination at your Legos, and see what you come up with." But this intentionality can go either direction: either we point the imagination toward the world, or we find the world pointing into us, impressing something on our imaginations. So, I could just as easily mean, "Let the Legos stimulate your imagination and see what you come up with." Both the projection of his imagination toward the Legos and the Legos' impression of particular images on his imagination are acts of imagining, as is the negotiation of the two, the "seeing what you come up with."

Similarly, when we consider the more sophisticated imaginative activity recommended by Lennon, we find that he is not prescribing imagination in the abstract but the exploration of a very particular set of possibilities. We are directed to consider the possibility of a world without national or religious boundaries. How do we imagine this? What images impress themselves on us? How do these images resonate with our sense of the way that things are and the way that they could be? Another way of saying this is that imagining is not mere daydreaming, empty-minded musing on nothing in particular. Imagining seeks to bring real content before our field of perception.

Third, there is a bodily basis for all human imagining. Imagining doesn't just take place in brains on sticks but in bodies.[9] This means that our

---

ordinary uses of the word imagination describe the imagination's proper exercise. Her second claim is that imagining is a unique mental state. It is related to but not identical with other mental states like memory. It is related to other modes of perception like theorizing, speculating or conceiving, but it exceeds those modes in degree if not in kind. Kind, "Exploring Imagination," 2-4.

[9]Or more accurately, in the mind with a body, embedded in the world. So Merleau-Ponty: "Rather than a mind and a body, man is a mind with a body, a being who can only get at the truth of things because its body is, as it were, embedded in those things." Maurice Merleau-Ponty, *The World of Perception* (London: Routledge, 2004), 43.

embodied experience of the world provides the structure for what we imagine. We can imagine all sorts of possibilities but not anything we wish. As philosopher Julia Jansen explains, "An imagined object or scene is imagined as being seen, heard, smelled, tasted and/or touched. An object that . . . cannot be experienced in at least one of these modes is 'unimaginable' in the relevant sense."[10] Furthermore, the world around us is already organized (as we perceive it) according to our bodily position in it. Think of our most common prepositions: up, down, in, out, around, and through. All of these have an unavoidable connection to our bodily existence in the world.[11] Our embodied embeddedness in the world is the ground of us being able to make meaning of the world, as well as the impetus for the search. We are inescapably invested; "because we are in the world," Merleau-Ponty reminds us, "we are *condemned to meaning*."[12] We cannot separate imaginative cognition from embodied coping. As the imagination does its work, it works within the limiting structure of the body.

When Lennon asks us to "imagine all the people living life in peace," imaginative clarity requires the simulation of sensory details. Perhaps we imagine the sight of people smiling and simply going about everyday activities undisturbed by violence. Perhaps we imagine the sound of laughter and celebration. Perhaps we imagine the smell of food as people eat together. Without sensory details, imaginings fail to captivate and connect. We are aware that the objects evoked are not present, and yet we make them present to our consciousness through the act of imagining.[13] Though the imagination is capable of tremendous flights of fancy, it remains anchored to reality by the body, which always remains part of the real world.[14]

---

[10]Julia Jansen, "Husserl," in *The Routledge Handbook of Philosophy of Imagination*, ed. Amy Kind (London: Routledge, 2016), 71.

[11]As Taylor writes, "The most primordial and unavoidable significances of things are, or are connected to, those involved in our bodily existence in the world: our field is shaped in terms of up and down, near and far, easily accessible and out of reach, graspable, avoidable and so on." Charles Taylor, "Merleau-Ponty and the Epistemological Picture," in *The Cambridge Companion to Merleau-Ponty* (New York: Cambridge University Press, 2005), 46.

[12]Maurice Merleau-Ponty, *Phenomenology of Perception*, trans. Donald A Landes (London: Routledge, 2012), xviii.

[13]Indeed, to imagine something is to simulate the experience of it. Jansen, "Husserl," 73.

[14]Merleau-Ponty emphasizes how embodiment grounds all human perception, including imagination. He writes: "My body is geared into the world when my perception provides me with the most varied and the most clearly articulated spectacle possible, and when my motor intentions,

This leads to our final claim, that the imagination suspends actuality for the sake of reality. Here we see the goal of the strategic intentionality described in the first two claims. What sets the imagination apart from other sorts of perception like memory, belief, or speculation is that the imagination need not be directed toward something that actually exists. The possibilities we ponder often side-step the real world: reimagining history, violating social and cultural convention, even ignoring physical laws, such as, "It's a bird, it's a plane, it's Superman!" When I imagine Superman leaping tall buildings with a single bound, the fact that Superman does not actually exist cannot keep me from imagining him. To put it technically: Superman's existence (his ontological status) is not a necessary condition for the imagination. We may have mistaken memories, beliefs, or perceptions, but these faculties are at least aimed at actuality. We expect our memories, beliefs, or perceptions generally to be accurate as they can guide us to grip the world. But the imagination can also consciously aim itself toward non-actuality, toward what we know to be fictional.

With respect to Lennon's song, even if I know that the world actually has national borders and religious affiliations, I am nevertheless able to ponder a fictional world without these features. But here is a critical distinction: to say that the imagination need not be aimed at the real world (of what is actual) *is not the same as saying that the imagination is not aimed at reality itself.*[15] As I will argue later in this chapter, it is precisely this capacity to disconnect from actuality that enables it, by simulation, to grasp reality more fully.

With this foundation in place, let me restate my claim in a less technical way: the imagination is the embodied human faculty concerned with

---

as they unfold, receive the responses they anticipate from the world. This maximum clarity in perception and action specifies a perceptual ground, a background for my life, a general milieu for the coexistence of my body and the world." Merleau-Ponty, *Phenomenology of Perception*, 261. For Merleau-Ponty, we make sense of the world as we alternate between our actual position in the world and imagined possibilities, between what he calls the "body schema" and the "virtual body." See my longer discussion of this point in Justin Bailey, "The Body in Cyberspace: Lanier, Merleau-Ponty, and the Norms of Embodiment," *Christian Scholar's Review* 45, no. 3 (2016): 217-18.

[15]For Husserl, imagining that takes place in a mode he called "irreality" rather than "unreality." See Jansen, "Husserl," 70-71.

possibility. The imagination perceives possible ways of being in the world, is captivated by other possibilities, and seeks to negotiate a space for life amid possibility. We may use our imagination to relive memories, make metaphors, or to escape from boredom, but what I am most interested in is *why* we do all these things. In exercising out imaginations, we are looking for connection amid chaos, using our imagination as an "organ of meaning."[16] We *must* make sense of the world. But paradoxically, we seek concrete meaning by moving in a subjunctive mood, exploring possibilities, in search of a firmer grip on reality, using the imagination as an organ of truth.

Thus far I have been content simply to describe the activity of the imagination in terms of how it helps humans "feel their way into" making sense of the world.[17] In doing so I have sidestepped several significant philosophical conversations about the relationship of imagination and objective (noumenal) reality. But now it is time to step back briefly into those conversations. Insofar as my argument concerns an exploration of specifically Christian possibilities, it is necessary to move from descriptive to normative claims. Thus far I have argued that we cannot separate our imagining from the everyday search for meaning. Our imaginings help us cope with the world in which we are inescapably invested.

But while our imaginings are not less than coping mechanisms for existential crises, they can also be more. We use our imaginations not just to cope with crisis but also to connect with community, responding to embodied others and perhaps to an Absolute Other as well. So how might we defend the imagination as a means of not just practical knowledge (how to navigate the world) but also contemplative knowledge (how to

---

[16]C. S. Lewis, "Bluspels and Flalansferes: A Semantic Nightmare," in *Selected Literary Essays*, ed. Walter Hooper (Cambridge: Cambridge University Press, 2013), 265.

[17]I am working within the tradition of phenomenology, a philosophical method that suspends questions of ontology in order to describe our conscious experience of the world. Rather than hypothesizing about how we can know the world outside our consciousness, phenomenologists attend to the objects of consciousness and acts of consciousness, seeking to describe the relationship between the two. Edmund Husserl, the father of phenomenology, rejected Kant's category of *noumena*, insisting that objects as perceived are indeed "the things themselves." Edmund Husserl, *Logical Investigations*, ed. Dermot Moran (London: Routledge, 2001), 168. This meant an "epistemological reduction" in which "we parenthesize everything . . . with respect to being." Edmund Husserl, *Ideas Pertaining to a Pure Phenomenology and to a Phenomenological Philosophy*, trans. F. Kersten (The Hague: Nikhoff, 2001), sec. 32.

connect with ultimate reality)? Can we ground our imaginings in reality? And is it possible that some of the possibilities we ponder might actually be "authored," bearing the signature of the divine? This section requires a more technical level of discussion, and those who are not as philosophically inclined may wish to proceed to the third section of this chapter, titled "Directing the Imagination."

DEFENDING THE IMAGINATION:
SIGNIFYING PRESENCE

There is a long tradition in philosophy of being skeptical about the connection between perception and reality.[18] David Hume is representative: he held that since all knowledge is mediated through the senses, we only have access to our image-ideas of the world. Do I really know my wife, or do I merely know my idea of my wife? Hume exposed the imaginative leaps inherent in staples of human thought: abstract ideas, causality, personal identity, historical knowledge, and moral sentiment. Under the scrutiny of Hume's empiricism, all of the above were reduced to subjective invention without an empirical ground. The situation was unenviable and intractable: "the worlds of reason and of reality . . . are both fictions of imagination. . . . We have therefore, no choice but betwixt a false reason and none at all."[19]

Plenty of thinkers rose to answer Hume's challenge. Some, like Thomas Reid, argued for a common-sense realism, arguing that a person who is not sure that the world external to his senses actually exists is akin to a person who believes himself to be made of glass.[20] But more followed Immanuel Kant, who doubled down on the imagination's synthetic power. Hume was right, Kant argued, that categories like time and space had to be imagined. But far from being arbitrary, these imaginative projections

---

[18]For a treatment of the imagination in the history of philosophy up until the twenty-first century, see Mary Warnock, *Imagination* (Berkeley: University of California Press, 1976); Richard Kearney, *The Wake of Imagination: Toward a Postmodern Culture* (Minneapolis: University of Minnesota Press, 1988).

[19]David Hume, *A Treatise of Human Nature*, ed. David Fate Norton and Mary J. Norton (Oxford: Oxford University Press, 2000), 174.

[20]Thomas Reid, *Thomas Reid's Inquiry and Essays*, ed. Ronald E. Beanblossom and Keith Lehrer (Indianapolis: Hackett, 1983), 53.

were feats of consciousness, reflexively provided to facilitate an intelligible experience of the world.[21] This radical affirmation of human consciousness ushered the imagination from the philosophical margins to the center of discussions of ontology, epistemology, and aesthetics.[22] With the Romantic movement a visionary paradigm of imagination rose to ascendancy. Aristotle's mirror, which reproduced reality, was replaced by a lamp, which could provide the world a light of its own.[23] Shelley famously announced that poets were society's new priests, "hierophants of unapprehended in-spiration . . . the unacknowledged legislators of the world."[24]

This visionary paradigm was not unprecedented, having roots in Neo-platonic philosophy and medieval mysticism.[25] But what was new was the way that the mystical vision was increasingly domesticated. In other words, rather than receiving meaning from the depths of some external reality (God or being), the imagination was seen as its own source. William Desmond sees in the Romantic movement an "aesthetic will to power,"[26] and it is not surprising that the imagination would be subjected

---

[21]Immanuel Kant, *Critique of Pure Reason*, ed. Paul Guyer and Allen W. Wood (Cambridge: Cambridge University Press, 1999), A50/B74, p. 193.

[22]Thinkers like Descartes and Locke had reinvigorated mistrust of the imagination, as they applied methodic doubt to human fancy in search of the facts of existence. Locke even encouraged parents "to stifle and suppress" imagination in their children as much as possible. Not for noth-ing did the Romantic poets rail against the reduction of the mind to a fact-finding machine! Kant's revolution paved the way for the idealism of Schiller, Fichte, and Hegel and for the Ro-mantic movement that flourished early in the nineteenth century. Kearney, *Wake of Imagina-tion*, 164.

[23]This is the central argument of Meyer H. Abrams, *The Mirror and the Lamp: Romantic Theory and the Critical Tradition* (New York: Oxford University Press, 1971).

[24]Percy Bysshe Shelley, *A Defence of Poetry* (Indianapolis: Bobbs-Merrill, 1904), 90.

[25]Plato himself added a mystical dimension to the mimetic imagination, whereby the gods direct humanity. In *Philebus*, he explored how thought-images—either of fear or flourishing—orient ethical action. He writes that the good tend to have good images presented to them "because they are friends of the gods," and thus live virtuously. In *Timaeus*, he develops the connection between divine agency and the imagination with a conception of the dream vision, whereby the gods direct humanity. Plotinus took up the visionary paradigm, arguing that the imagination, rather than merely imitating nature, "flowed in parallel from the same source" as nature, afford-ing it the power of special vision. Medieval thinkers like Bonaventure, Richard St. Victor, and Dante drew on this Neoplatonic tradition, casting the imagination as a revelatory vehicle for the divine, the site of orienting dreams and visions. See Murray Wright Bundy, *The Theory of Imagi-nation in Classical and Mediaeval Thought* (Urbana, IL: University of Illinois Press, 1927), 52-53; Raymond Barfield, *The Ancient Quarrel Between Philosophy and Poetry* (Cambridge: Cambridge University Press, 2011), 54.

[26]Desmond, *Is There a Sabbath for Thought?*, 137.

to the scalpel of postmodern suspicion.[27] In an ironic return to skepticism, deconstructionism eroded confidence that imagining had any ground in some originating source. Instead all we have are signs referring to other signs, and it is signs "all the way down." In postmodern philosophy, Richard Kearney writes, we find a *parodic imagination*, manifesting in the ironic play of endless intertextuality. The parodic imagination is the inversion of mimesis, denying any original source beyond our imaginative reproductions. The imaginative mirror has been revealed to be just one more carnival mirror, endlessly reflecting and refracting perspectives in intentional or unintentional parody. In an age of screens, selfies, and social media saturation, we feel the force of the postmodern critique.

So where does the imagination go after the postmodern turn? Is there a way to move beyond the play of parody? Kearney himself offers a way forward: the recognition of *presence*. The presence of embodied others who are not reducible to myself furnishes me with an ethical imperative. When I encounter someone who is not myself, coping must also make space for care. In the spirit of Emmanuel Levinas, Kearney writes, "Here and now I face an *other* who demands of me an ethical response." Here is an image with a concrete referent: "the ethical existence of the other as an *other*—the inalienable right to be recognized as a particular person whose very otherness refuses to be reduced to a mimicry of sameness."[28] Deconstruction may be a necessary step for exposing power, but we must do more than tear down imaginative pretensions. Eventually deconstruction's thunder must fall silent before the face of the other, whose presence demands to be taken seriously. Indeed, Kearney suggests that the role of the imagination in hypermodernity is precisely this: to respond to presence, to negotiate "the relationship between the self and the other."[29] To put it technically, Kearney's solution focuses the phenomenological lens in a personalistic way. Once concerned with connecting to and representing reality, now the imagination's constructive function is oriented

---

[27] As Kearney notes that in postmodern philosophy the imagination is "subjected to suspicion or denigrated as an outdated humanist illusion spawned by the modern movements of romantic idealism and existentialism." Kearney, *Wake of Imagination*, 251.

[28] Kearney, *Wake of Imagination*, 361.

[29] Kearney, *Wake of Imagination*, 363.

toward social coping and cooperation, enabling understanding and empathy in a fragmented and violent world.

Kearney's personalism highlights the necessity of human solidarity, and this is a good start. But we must also say more than this: flourishing requires more than just an account of social cohesiveness. In light of local and global crises, a theory of imaginative care is needed where negotiating "the relationship between the self and the other" includes not just economy but also ecology, our relationship to the physical environment that we inhabit. Furthermore, a theological account of the imagination concerns the role of the imagination in negotiating our sense of being addressed by the divine, the Wholly Other. In other words, there is a givenness to the world, full of an otherness "which flows through me without my being its author."[30] If we can find a way to make sense of this, we can also find a better ground for our profoundly felt responsibility to care for human persons and non-human creation.

Literary critic George Steiner helps us take this further step, arguing that our encounter with otherness has more than just social implications; it has aesthetic and theological implications. Steiner writes that art is essential to our humanity because it trains our imaginations in hospitality. For it is in great works of art that we encounter "real presence," an otherness that breaks in, interrupts, and confronts us with an invitation we cannot ignore. Steiner writes: "The voice of intelligible form . . . asks: 'What do you feel, what do you think of the possibilities of life, of the alternative shapes of being which are implicit in your experience of me, in our encounter?'"[31] Aesthetic experience is generative: by its very nature it forces us to make sense of surprising new possibilities. As the poet Rilke reminds us, aesthetic encounters make a claim on us: "You must change your life."[32]

Perhaps we have all experienced this. A spark of insight when composing a song, a flash of wonder beneath the stars, a smile from a child

---

[30]Merleau-Ponty, *Phenomenology of Perception*, 224.

[31]George Steiner, *Real Presences* (Chicago: University of Chicago Press, 1989), 142.

[32]Rainer Maria Rilke, "Archaic Torso of Apollo," Poets.org, accessed October 4, 2018, www.poets .org/poetsorg/poem/archaic-torso-apollo.

that seizes us with an overwhelming sense of the goodness of existence. In such moments we feel that we are receiving something that we know is not of our making, not reducible to ourselves. Aesthetic experience, Steiner argues, calls us to imaginative hospitality. It calls us to respect and receive the otherness of the presence that knocks on the door of our hearts, to allow it to become our teacher. Steiner writes that we must "allow ourselves to touch or not to touch, to be touched or not be touched by the presence of the other. . . . The issue is that of civility . . . towards the inward savour of things."[33] Aesthetic experiences rarely fit neatly within our philosophical frameworks. They are saturated phenomena where the experience exceeds our categories to contain it.[34] Yet our inability to grasp completely what is confronting us does not limit its ability to affect us. Steiner's example is the power of music: "How music possesses us is a question to which we know no credible, let alone materially examinable answer. All we have are further images. And the defiant self-evidence of human experience."[35] The succession of images need not be parodic, especially when their cumulative effect shapes us in ways that enlarge our souls.

Steiner's most provocative argument, however, is his central one: that we must assume the presence of a transcendent Other in order to have meaning at all. God may or may not be there, he says, but we must suspend disbelief and wager God's existence in order to experience meaning. In other words, works of imagination stand on their own as phenomena full of felt meaning in search of a ground, even if we cannot empirically prove its ground. Though we may feel the contingency of meaning, we speak and create because we implicitly believe that meaning and feeling can be adequately conveyed. Every time we communicate, much less create or encounter art, we take the wager that our efforts are meaningful. To take the wager on transcendence is to believe that our intuitive sense that imaginative works have ultimate meaning is not a lie. These works are

[33]Steiner, *Real Presences*, 148.
[34]The idea of saturated phenomena comes from Jean-Luc Marion, *In Excess: Studies of Saturated Phenomena* (New York: Fordham University Press, 2002).
[35]Steiner, *Real Presences*, 198.

meaningful because reality is meaningful, grounded in the presence and address of God.

Steiner goes on to argue that "everything we recognize as being of compelling stature in literature, art, music is of a religious inspiration or reference,"[36] as is the category of meaningfulness itself. In every civilization our artifacts testify to the way that humans create imaginative works, not just to cope with their place in the world, or to cooperate with their neighbors, but to connect with and respond to the address of the divine. This inescapably religious consciousness must be taken seriously. Indifference to the divine (either divine presence or divine absence) suffocates artistic ability: "Where God's presence is no longer a tenable supposition and where His absence is no longer a felt, indeed overwhelming weight, certain dimensions of thought and creativity are no longer attainable."[37] Notice that Steiner is not arguing that only theists can be creative; great creativity comes as well from the recognition of divine absence. What shuts down creativity is a *closed* mind, a posture of indifference toward possibilities that linger outside the empirical frame.

It is not necessary to agree with Steiner on every point to feel the force of his argument. Regardless of the contested status of the imagination in postmodern philosophy, we have the experience of beauty, goodness, and truth emerging meaningfully from the realm of the imagination. This experience must be respected. Works of imagination create space for surprising encounter with the other, and if Steiner is correct, an Absolute Other. I will pause here to note that this is a key rationale for selecting novelists as my case studies in part two of this book. Artists, poets, and writers regularly traffic in the realm of imagination, training our powers of perception to see and feel things that we would not normally see and feel. If our habits of engagement have become narrow, works of imagination can reopen our horizons.

We can also extend Steiner's argument beyond our encounter with works of human creativity to our encounter with the world around us. The experience of sky and sea as beautiful and meaningful, the provocation of

---

[36]Steiner, *Real Presences*, 216.
[37]Steiner, *Real Presences*, 229.

gratitude or artistic response, suggests the ethical imperative of stewardship if not hospitality. To quote Steiner again: "The voice of intelligible form . . . asks: 'What do you feel, what do you think of the possibilities of life, of the alternative shapes of being which are implicit in your experience of me, in our encounter?'"[38] The creative impulse in the midst of creation makes sense if our physical environment is in some sense *authored*, addressed to our perception, meant to evoke our desire, hospitality, and participation. Indeed, as we will see below, a theological account of the imagination understands human imagining as a reflection of humanity's encounter with divine presence and action. This means that no matter how fallen or agonistic our creative acts may be, the very impulse to create follows our creational structure; we cannot help but create. As Paul Fiddes writes, "The reaching of the imagination towards a new world is the result of God's reaching towards us."[39] If this is correct, every act of creativity unwittingly continues the conversation that God is having with creation.

My use of Steiner is an imaginative provocation: my purpose is not so much to prove the Christian ground of imagination in terms acceptable to all but rather to suggest that the questions raised by our aesthetic sense of the gravity and goodness of being—the experience of *presence* in human relationships, art, and nature—are sufficient motivation to consider the ground for meaning offered by Christian theology. It is a further conviction that this exploration of meaning is primarily an affair for the imagination in the aesthetic realm, and only secondarily for the intellect in the realm of ratiocination. The imagination, after all, enables more than mere exploration; it facilitates *participation* in the mystery to which theology testifies, grasping the surplus of meaning that cannot be fully expressed in language ("this is my body"). Complete understanding of divine address is impossible, but the art of understanding can be cultivated through a disciplined imagination, and this is precisely what works of art invite.[40]

[38]Steiner, *Real Presences*, 142.
[39]Paul S. Fiddes, *Freedom and Limit: A Dialogue Between Literature and Christian Doctrine* (New York: St. Martin's, 1991), 30.
[40]This point is made eloquently by Trevor Hart in Trevor Hart, "Imagining Evangelical Theology," in *Evangelical Futures: A Conversation on Theological Method*, ed. John G. Stackhouse (Grand Rapids: Baker, 2000), 193.

Presence and participation: these terms highlight the Christian conviction of a God who moves toward humanity in communicative action, addressing human imagination with new possibilities of being in the world. Having defined the imagination as concerned with exploring possibility and defended the imagination as concerned with discerning presence, let us consider how the Scripture directs the imagination toward participation in the biblical theodrama. How does God engage, sin impair, and grace renew this faculty of presence and possibility?

DIRECTING THE IMAGINATION: SCRIPTING PARTICIPATION

Imagination in Scripture: The eyes of the heart. Running parallel with developments in philosophy, the imagination has been a topic of great theological interest in recent years.[41] Yet a search through Scripture for the word *imagination* may yield less than promising results. This is especially the case for the King James Version, which held sway in the English-speaking world for three hundred years. Though three different Hebrew words are translated, in every instance the translators render the word in a negative context. Genesis speaks of the pre-flood imagination [*yēṣer*] of humanity as "only evil continually" (Gen 6:5). The prophetic hope in Jeremiah is that one day the nations will be gathered at the throne of Yahweh and no longer walk "after the *imagination* [*šərrirût*] of their evil heart" (Jer 3:17). Proverbs tells us that one of the seven things that God hates is a heart that devises "wicked imaginations [*maḥăšābāh*]" (6:18). The New Testament seems to give us more of the same: three different Greek words (*dianoia* [Lk 1:51], *dialogismos* [Rom 1:21], *logismos* [2 Cor 10:5]) are rendered "imagination" with consistently negative connotations.[42] In modern translations like the NIV, "imagination" continues to appear in

---

[41]For a representative sample see Trevor Hart, *Between the Image and the Word: Theological Engagements with Imagination, Language and Literature* (Burlington, VT: Ashgate, 2013); Alison Searle, *"The Eyes of Your Heart": Literary and Theological Trajectories of Imagining Biblically* (Colorado Springs: Paternoster, 2008); Garrett Green, *Imagining God: Theology and the Religious Imagination* (Grand Rapids: Eerdmans, 1998).

[42]See the discussion in John McIntyre, *Faith, Theology, and Imagination* (Edinburgh: Handsel, 1987), 5-6.

consistently negative settings, as a stand in for either "foolish speculation" or "self-reliant thinking" (Ps 73:7; Ezek 13:17; Is 65:2). Does this mean that any attempt to validate the imagination using Scripture is doomed to fail?

Quite the contrary. The biblical authors are not objecting to the created structure of the imagination as I have been describing it, but only to its fallen direction. They are objecting to imagining, thinking, devising, arguing, prophesying, and living without reference to God. Autonomy, not creativity, is in view. Indeed, rather than trivializing the imagination, these passages treat the imagination as a faculty to be reckoned with! In Scripture, the evil use of the imagination results in idolatry, and idolatry is always accompanied by injustice. Imaginings have consequences, and vain imagination results in real-world wickedness.

Positively, we might note the close connection in these passages of imagination and heart: a vain imagination comes together with a foolish heart.[43] In the biblical usage "heart" is the control center for the human person, including the "personality and the intellect, memory, emotions, desires and will."[44] In view of this connection, Garrett Green goes so far as to argue that the biblical "heart" and what he calls "the paradigmatic imagination" are the same faculty.[45] But this runs the danger of losing the surplus of the meaning of "heart" in the associated freight of "imagination." A better solution is proposed by Alison Searle, who writes that the close connection leads us to incorporate "imagination" into the "richly suggestive semantic field" of the biblical concept of "heart" without identifying the two.[46] Drawing from Ephesians 1:18 ("I pray that the eyes of

---

[43]This is most apparent in older translations, such as the KJV. See Romans 1:21: "Because that, when they knew God, they glorified *him* not as God, neither were thankful; but became vain in their imaginations, and their foolish heart was darkened." This may be the case for two possible reasons. First, older translations predate the modern categories of reason and imagination. Second, older translations may reflect the classical bias against the imagination as a less reliable mode of perception. Thus, the translators appear to use "imagination" as reasoning gone awry, even as their vision of reasoning is more holistic that Cartesian calculation. Later translations are both more likely to move toward a more positive conception of the imagination but also to narrow the range of cognition from "imagination" to "thinking." For a survey of this reduction, see Searle, *"The Eyes of Your Heart,"* 35–36.

[44]Leland Ryken, James C. Wilhoit, and Tremper Longman III, eds., "Heart," *Dictionary of Biblical Imagery* (Downers Grove, IL: InterVarsity Press, 1998).

[45]Green, *Imagining God*, 108.

[46]Searle, *"The Eyes of Your Heart,"* 35.

your heart may be enlightened"), Searle proposes that the imagination is better understood as the "eyes of your heart," connecting vision with volition. She writes:

> Imagination is shown biblically to be both corrupt like every aspect of human nature since the Fall and thus intimately connected to intellectual and volitional acts of disobedience against God; but also necessary to a right application of the Word of God, as in the command to "love your neighbor as yourself" (Matthew 22:39), which implies a degree of empathetic identification.[47]

We should also notice that imagination is necessary in making sense of the pluriform shape of Scripture, which comes to us just as often in stories, songs, and parables as it does in letters and law. To take the imagination as seriously as Scripture requires, we must move beyond the fallen direction that the imagination may take to explore its creational structure more carefully. This will enable us to seek a redeemed direction for the imaginative work in which we are already engaged. I will sketch an account of imagination within the biblical story to highlight three primary aspects of creaturely imagining: seeing, sensing, and shaping.

Imagination and imago dei: *Seeing, sensing, shaping.* Although the word *imagination* does not appear in the Genesis account, there is more than just a lexical link between image and imagination. George MacDonald asserts a theological connection: "The imagination of man is made in the image of the imagination of God."[48] This claim is striking for two reasons: the identification of imagining as something God does, and the identification of imagination (rather than rationality, morality, or relationality) as central to the divine image.[49] We do not need to displace these other aspects; we only need to recognize how imagination is vitally connected to each of them. As humans reflect God's image, it is the

---

[47]Searle, *"The Eyes of Your Heart,"* 39.

[48]George MacDonald, *A Dish of Orts* (Whitethorn, CA: Johannesen, 1996), 3. This may seem like a characteristically Romantic claim, reminiscent of Coleridge. But as I will argue in an upcoming chapter, MacDonald avoids the Romantic "will to power" by making the Reformed distinction between creaturely and divine creativity.

[49]See discussion in McIntyre, *Faith, Theology, and Imagination,* 14.

imagination that explores possibilities in order to fulfill the mandate of care and cultivation, unleashing the potentialities of creation for its own good to the glory of God.

Pascal Bazzell corroborates this interpretation of the divine image, arguing that the pronouns in Genesis 1:26 ("Let *us* make humankind in *our* image,") are plurals of "deliberation,"[50] and that what is being highlighted in the Genesis account is the reflexive capacity of divine image bearers "to see and to talk to themselves." This reflexivity is foundational to human identity and ethical action: "Every human being has a reflexive capacity, which means that people perceive themselves and live out their lives according to that perception."[51] We can see how imaginative reflexivity enables other aspects of the image like rationality, morality, and relationality. Rooted in the created world, the imagination enables us to navigate our position in the world amid the rational, relational, and moral possibilities that exist. William Dyrness makes this connection in an evocative way:

> A world that offers the conditions for growth into obedience and maturity also offers the opportunity to exercise genius and creativity. In such a world, humans wonder: what if we could find a way to ride those horses, or let that dog come and lie by our fire? What if we crossed this daisy with that one; what would that be like? This reflexive spark lies behind all creativity, all culture making.[52]

Thus, imagination is essential for imaging God in cultivation of creation, and any discussion of the divine image ought to include the imaginative capacity to say, "what if we did this?"[53]

[50]See also Claus Westermann, *Genesis 1-11: A Continental Commentary* (Minneapolis: Fortress, 1994), 145.

[51]Pascal Daniel Bazzell, "Toward a Creational Perspective on Poverty," in *Genesis and Christian Theology*, ed. Nathan MacDonald, Mark W. Elliott, and Grant Macaskill (Grand Rapids: Eerdmans, 2012), 233-34.

[52]William A. Dyrness, "Poised Between Life and Death: The Imago Dei After Eden," in *The Image of God in an Image Driven Age: Explorations in Theological Anthropology*, ed. Beth Felker Jones and Jeffrey W. Barbeau (Downers Grove, IL: InterVarsity Press, 2016), 51-52.

[53]To be a human person, as Ingolf Dalferth has argued, is to be a "creature of possibility," defined not simply by what we are or are not but also by what we *might* become. Ingolf U. Dalferth, *Creatures of Possibility: The Theological Basis of Human Freedom*, trans. Jo Bennett (Grand Rapids: Baker Academic, 2016).

It is because of this creaturely reflexivity that we are, as Taylor puts it, "self-interpreting animals,"[54] always seeking to understand ourselves. We ask the question that other animals do not: Who are *we*? There are multiple layers to our self-interrogation. First, there is an aspect of *seeing*, the apprehension of our position in the world: Where are we? Next, there is an aspect of *sensing*, the way desire is evoked particular directions: What is worth pursuing? Finally, there is an aspect of *shaping*, the creative activity of culture making: What will we make of our situation?[55] The imaginative faculty moves us forward by facilitating three things: (1) an orienting vision *for* the world, (2) an aesthetic experience *of* the world, and (3) poetic participation *in* the world. The lives we lead in response to these questions are our lived interpretations of God's creative address.

Let us briefly examine each of these dimensions. Imaginative seeing occurs when the imagination projects an image toward the world that is connected to belief or desire that something be the case. Projected belief is successful when belief matches the world; projected desire is successful when the world matches the desired state of affairs. This is the most basic level of intentional imaginative activity, including the simplest forms of imagining like speculation ("I imagine it will rain today").

Whereas *seeing* projects an image on the world, *sensing* moves in the opposite direction and occurs when an image impresses itself on the mind. Instead of me using my imagination, my imagination uses me, captivating me with a felt sense that translates spontaneously into a physiological response. The image that impresses itself spontaneously evokes fear or gladness, anxiety or anticipation, consistent with my desires.

Finally, *shaping* is the most creative exercise of the imagination, a multi-dimensional constructive project in which a person clears a generative space to facilitate a perspectival shift. Counterintuitively, this

---

[54]Charles Taylor, "Self-Interpreting Animals," in *Philosophical Papers*, vol. 1 (Cambridge: Cambridge University Press, 1985), 45-76.

[55]Seeing, sensing, and shaping correlate to Amy Kind's analytic categories: she calls them propositional, sensory, and creative imagining. Kind, "Exploring Imagination," 5-6.

means pursuing imaginative tension, even stirring up unpleasant emotions, for the sake of some greater imaginative payoff.[56]

An illustration may be helpful. When I read *Harry Potter* to my children, their imagination is engaged at multiple levels.[57] First, when my children imagine that Voldemort is chasing Harry, their minds are projecting an image for the sake of the story. This is the first layer of imagining: seeing. The image allows the story to be believable on its own terms, even if my children willingly suspend their disbelief about Voldemort's existence in the "real" world. They are seeing things that are not physically present, and they are able to distinguish between the truth-value of their imaginings in terms of the story from the truth-value of the imagining in terms of the real world. Furthermore, they desire that Voldemort *not* exist in the real world, even as they desire that he exist in the world of the story; both imaginative desires seem to be satisfactory to them. When we close the book and they try to go to sleep, they find that the image of Voldemort continues to impress itself on their consciousness. This is the second layer of imagining: sensing. They still see images of things that are not present, but what they see is evoked contrary to their desire (they don't want to see it). Yet their imagination has been taken captive, and they feel that they are still on the inside of the story. Thus they spontaneously feel Harry's fear as the imaginative impulse evokes their desire for safety. The image has *captivated* their imagination so that they are not able to wish it away by sheer force of will. Finally, even if the feeling of fear evoked by the images that linger is unpleasant, they continue to ask for the story each night. When they play, they integrate the narrative of the story into their games, acting out the adventure together in a mash-up of other stories they have heard, seen, or invented. This is the third layer of imagining: shaping. The story creates tension, but it also situates the difficult emotions in a larger narrative. Playing with the elements of the story creates a space where they can process the difficult emotions they encounter in the primary world. In the scenario, all three kinds of imagining are active at the same time. The

---

[56]Gregory Currie and Ian Ravenscroft, *Recreative Minds: Imagination in Philosophy and Psychology* (Oxford: Clarendon, 2003), 187.
[57]Here I am adapting and expanding an illustration from Kind, "Exploring Imagination," 5-6.

first moves from mind to world, the second reciprocally from world to mind, and the third creates a space in which the two can be negotiated in a satisfying manner. Throughout the process, they are engaged in the larger project of exploring possible ways of being in the world.

But if human imagination is meant to image God in unfolding the potentialities of creation, it follows that our seeing, sensing, and shaping find their fullness in *being, loving,* and *doing,* the "essence of ethical life."[58] The imagination projects possible visions, draws out our desire, and seeks creative space. But as we move toward ethical fullness, seeing must lead to *integrity*: the visions we project must become true of us. Sensing must lead to *commitment*: properly elicited desires, rightly ordered by love. And shaping must lead to *care*: taking responsibility for the world in which we are embedded (see fig. 1).

Figure 1: Organizing the Imagination

Aspect of Imagining	*Seeing:* imagination as orienting vision	*Sensing:* imagination as aesthetic sense	*Shaping:* imagination as poetic participation
Operative Question	Where are we?	What is worth pursuing?	What will we do?
Kind's Taxonomy	*Propositional* Imagining Mind → World	*Sensory* Imagining World → Mind	*Creative* Imagining Intermediate Space
Ethical Dimension	Being	Loving	Doing
Ethical Concern	Integrity	Commitment	Care

We become more fully human as we use our imagination to image God. The image of God gives the imagination structure, but it also provides direction, a destiny. To follow and fulfill this destiny, our imaginations— what we see, what we sense, and what we shape—must become more fully responsive to the work of God in creation and new creation, which directs us to a fuller and deeper humanity.

---

[58]Taylor writes, "If we give the full range of ethical meanings their due, we can see that the fullness of ethical life involves not just doing, but also being; and not just these two but also loving (which is shorthand here for being moved by, being inspired by) what is constitutively good. It is a drastic reduction to think that we can capture the moral by focusing only on obligated action, as though it were of no ethical moment what you are and what you love. These are the essence of ethical life." Charles Taylor, *Sources of the Self: The Making of the Modern Identity* (Cambridge: Harvard University Press, 1992), 15.

Imagination and creational constraints: The limiting structures of creation. Human imagining reflects the imagination of God, but always in a creaturely way. To be a creature is to be limited, and so there are always limits for human imagination. In the Genesis narrative, Adam and Eve are given extensive freedom ("You may freely eat of every tree of the garden," Genesis 2:16 NLT) but always within particular constraints. These constraints are not meant to diminish human beings. They are intended rather to guide them into flourishing proper to the kind of creatures that they are meant to become. Some of the limits in the Genesis story are structural, reflecting their embodiment (the need to eat and to rest), while others are aesthetic (the cultivated garden over against uncultivated creation). The most significant limit is moral: the prohibition of the tree of the knowledge of good and evil. Although the imagination is able to suspend actuality to explore possibility, it remains constrained by and grounded in created limits. The imagination can help us discover truths about the world only because our embeddedness in the world sets the parameters for our engagement. As we learned from Merleau-Ponty, if our imaginings are to be intelligible, they must take root in embodied experience, and this is true even in our wildest fantasies.

Some of the structural features of imagining are inescapable: we are unable, for example, to imagine logical contradictions (like a square circle). But imagination is also constrained by natural laws. We *are* able to imagine ourselves resisting gravity (as in the case of superheroes), but under normal conditions we do not take this flight of fancy as an actual option. When it comes to enacting the possibility, imaginative play gives way to profound imaginative resistance ("I imagine that if I jump off this building, things will not go well"). Things are a bit more complicated when it comes to moral constraints, but a moral structure does exist. Whatever we imagine automatically triggers our moral intuitions. We may find it possible to imagine a state of affairs where evil is conflated with good, but we resist imaginative identification with the conflation.[59] For example, imagine a world in which all baby girls are killed at birth.

---

[59]Neil Van Leeuwen, "The Imaginative Agent," in *Knowledge Through Imagination*, ed. Amy Kind and Peter Kung (Oxford: Oxford University Press, 2016), 104.

Now imagine a world in which it *feels* virtuous to kill them. We can quite easily fulfill the first proposal, but we feel incredible resistance to the "countermoral proposition" in the second.[60] Perhaps it is possible to justify such a world, but only through a tragic failure of imagination. When the imagination functions correctly, it follows moral intuition, what Paul called "the law written on our hearts" (Rom 2:15). Similarly, when it comes to aesthetic judgments, our imaginations seek space and resist sterility. Imagine life in a cell. Now imagine life in a garden. Now imagine a world where life in a cell is better than life in a garden. It is almost impossible without the addition of constraints. We simply have the *sense* that the garden affords greater possibility, a greater opportunity to grasp and make meaning in the world. Our embodied desire to have a "maximal grip" on our situation means that the imagination seeks the best possible conditions for achieving it.[61] The imagination must have limits in order for it to navigate between real possibilities for life in the world. These limits, the most important of which is the body, reflect the structure of creation and are meant to lead to fruitfulness rather than sterility.

Imagination and sin: Life outside limits. God created the human imagination to aid us in our cultural task, unfolding the potentialities of creation. This creative obedience is meant to take place within the physical, rational, moral, and aesthetic limits of created order. The imagination simultaneously tests the boundaries of these limitations in search of new possibilities even as it is grounded in them. But the Genesis story shows humanity's ability—on the serpent's supposition—to imagine and enact behaviors outside the limits of divine design. The tempter encourages humanity to overstep the limits set for them by God, proposing a way of being in the world in which humans refuse their creaturely vocation, reaching for autonomy. To return to Bazzell, the serpent's temptation exploited Adam and Eve's reflexive capacity, their ability to imagine

[60]Kengo Miyazono and Shen-yi Liao, "The Cognitive Architecture of Imaginative Resistance," in *The Routledge Handbook of Philosophy of Imagination*, ed. Amy Kind (London: Routledge, 2016), 368-79.

[61]Hubert L. Dreyfus, *Skillful Coping: Essays on the Phenomenology of Everyday Perception and Action* (Oxford: Oxford University Press, 2014), 117.

themselves living outside God's limits.[62] Once the limits are overstepped, and humanity rejects the Creator's rule, entropy is unleashed. Denied vocation begets distorted vision. As Calvin writes, "The natural order was that the frame of the universe should be a school in which we were to learn piety and from it pass over to eternal life and perfect felicity. But after man's rebellion, our eyes—wherever they turn—encounter God's curse. This curse, while it seizes and envelops innocent creatures through our fault, must overwhelm our souls with despair."[63]

The result of the curse is that wherever we turn, rather than being led to worship we are beset by anxiety. Sin disorients what we see (we encounter God's curse) and what we sense (we are overwhelmed with despair). This in turn skews what we shape. A diseased imagination traffics in idolatry, injustice, and what Bazzell calls "reflexive oppression," the misperception of who I am and the possibilities that are available to me. All aspects of fallen imagination conspire in futility, sensing, seeing, and shaping projects that are distorted, deceitful, and destructive.

The creative freedom of the human imagination remains significant, and in a fallen world this is a frightening fact. It is the distortion of reflexive freedom that leads Cain to say to his brother, "Let's go out to the field" (Gen 4:8) and the Babelites to say, "Come, let us build ourselves a city and a tower" (Gen 11:4 KJV). Rather than participating in divine blessing, human imagination unleashes divine curse. Indeed, to the biblical writers there is no greater horror than a world in which people fail to see themselves and the world in light of God, a world where everyone does as they see fit (Judg 21:25).

Yet despite human rebellion, creaturely limits continue to exert their gravity on us. While the human imagination can resist and rebel, it can never function fully outside of created structures, since those limits make possible our making sense of the world. Thus, the imagination, though cut off from the source of virtue, is nevertheless pulled back toward creational norms. These norms reflect the structure of creation, but we can

---

[62]Bazzell, "Toward a Creational Perspective," 233.
[63]Jean Calvin, *Institutes of the Christian Religion*, ed. John T. McNeill, trans. Ford Lewis Battles (Louisville, KY: Westminster John Knox, 2001), 2.6.1.

choose whether we will live into them or against their grain. Violation is possible but destructive. Robert Goudzwaard explains:

> The purpose of norms is to bring us to life in its fullness by pointing us to paths which safely lead us there. Norms are not straitjackets which squeeze the life out of us. . . . the created world is attuned to those norms; it is designed for our willingness to respond to God and each other. If man and society ignore genuine norms, such as justice and restitution of rights, respect for life, love of neighbor, and stewardship, they are bound to experience the destructive effects of such neglect. This is not, therefore, a mysterious fate which strikes us; rather, it is a judgment which men and society bring upon themselves.[64]

When norms are broken, they break us; when followed, they move us toward greater flourishing. Even in our rebellion we feel the provocations of beauty and justice, norms reflecting the grooves of creation, and God's continuing commitment to a world that though badly broken, still belongs to God. We will return to this in a moment.

Nevertheless, apart from further divine intervention fallen imagination leads to an earth full of violence. In the days of Noah, human imaginings are described as "only evil continually," turning creativity toward corruption (Gen 6:5 KJV). Divine judgment in the form of a flood arrests the destructive work of human imagination, stopping the spread of evil across the face of the earth. Yet all is not lost. God's redemptive project continues: "God remembered Noah" (Gen 8:1), and God works within the fallen situation to bring creation into the fullness intended from the beginning. Both image and imagination find their renewal through divine action: God chooses a covenantal people, and through this people gives the redeeming gifts of the Son and the Spirit. As the Son renews the image of God through the Spirit's power, grace grants renewed possibilities for human imagining, for what we see, sense, and shape. But how exactly does this happen?

Imagination and renewal: The liberating spirit of new creation. Only the light of revelation, made effectual by the Spirit, is able to open the eyes of the heart (Eph 1:18). This revelatory light comes through the law of the

---

[64]Robert Goudzwaard, *Capitalism and Progress: A Diagnosis of Western Society*, trans. Josina Van Nuis Zylstra (Carlisle: Paternoster, 1997), 243.

Lord (Ps 19:8; 119:105) and finds its ultimate expression in Jesus Christ, "the true light, which enlightens everyone" (Jn 1:9 NRSV). Christ comes as the atoning sacrifice for sin, and the gospel gives us new eyes to see creation.[65] The curse that caused us to look on creation with despair is reversed. Creation becomes doxological again, as the Spirit grasps us with a renewed sense of our place in God's world. We now find ourselves "in Christ," captivated by visions of his kingdom, a kingdom of "justice, peace, and joy in the Holy Spirit" (Rom 14:17 NTE). Restored vision serves our restored vocation. As God's workmanship, we seek to do good work, shaping possibilities that anticipate the kingdom that is to come (Eph 2:10).[66] This imaginative renewal, the healing of our seeing, sensing, and shaping, takes place in union with Christ; as we contemplate the glory of the Lord, the Spirit transfigures us with ever-increasing glory (2 Cor 3:18).[67] This is good news!

And yet more must be said concerning the work of the Spirit in the imaginings of those *outside* the covenant community. This is especially relevant since Christian witness invites us to engage outsiders hospitably with a reason for our hope. Indeed, what hope do we have that the gifts of the Son and Spirit have bearing on those outside the walls of the church?

There is plenty of hope. Made in God's image, inhabiting God's world, and living before God's face, every human being is always already responding to God's revelatory initiative. As we saw in the previous chapter, Calvin developed this responsiveness in terms of the sense of the divine (*sensus divinitatis*) and the seed of religion (*semen religionis*), an inward capacity to perceive God's presence that results in the religious impulse to reach for God.[68]

---

[65]Todd Billings writes, drawing from Calvin, "Only through the eyes provided through the gospel of Jesus Christ can one discover that 'he accepts us as his children and heirs.'" J. Todd Billings, *Calvin, Participation, and the Gift: The Activity of Believers in Union with Christ* (Oxford: Oxford University Press, 2007), 161.

[66]A wonderful model of this is found in the work of Kevin Vanhoozer. Vanhoozer describes how the Spirit directs believers by giving them an imaginative sense of the "theodrama" to which Scripture testifies, grasping them with its imaginative force, and guiding them in imaginative skill to continue the action in new situations. See Kevin J. Vanhoozer, *Drama of Doctrine: A Canonical-Linguistic Approach to Christian Theology* (Louisville: Westminster John Knox Press, 2005).

[67]Billings writes that for Calvin justification is not "simply about a legal decree, but about *an entrance into a new way of being and acting* through union with Christ." Billings, *Calvin, Participation, and the Gift*, 114.

[68]Neither is the result of rational deduction; they are intuitive and inescapable, to use Alvin Plantinga's phrase, "properly basic." Alvin Plantinga, *Warranted Christian Belief* (New York: Oxford

Calvin is expressing the deep Christian conviction (which of course he draws from the Scriptures and tradition) that everything good is a divine gift, having its source in God rather than in humanity. The corollary to this is that if we find beauty, goodness, and truth in human imaginings, we can look nowhere else for their source.[69] For his part, Calvin was convinced that the droplets of divinity given to fallen humanity lead to idolatry rather than piety.[70] The "bright lights" of creation fail to bring clarifying vision apart from further illumination by the Spirit.[71] And yet a tension remains in Calvin's thought. He emphasizes that despite the distortion of sin, God daily discloses his grace and glory through everything, "so that men cannot open their eyes without being compelled to see him . . . upon his individual works he has engraved unmistakable marks of his glory, so clear and so prominent that even unlettered and stupid folk cannot plead the excuse of ignorance." He continues:

> Yet, in the first place, wherever you cast your eyes, there is no spot in the universe wherein you cannot discern at least some sparks of his glory. You cannot in one glance survey this most vast and beautiful system of the universe, in its wide expanse, without being completely overwhelmed by the boundless force of its brightness. The reason why the author of The Letter to the Hebrews elegantly calls the universe the appearance of things invisible [Heb 11:3] is that this skillful ordering of the universe is for us a sort of mirror in which we can contemplate God, who is otherwise invisible.[72]

God's glory continues to shine, giving off such "sparks" that fallen humanity cannot escape the "boundless force of its brightness."

University Press, 1999). Van der Kooi notes that Calvin makes it clear that the *sensus divinitatis* "is not something which can wear away; it is constantly renewed. . . . God 'constantly sends down new droplets of it.'" Cornelius Van der Kooi, *As in a Mirror: John Calvin and Karl Barth On Knowing God* (Leiden: Brill, 2005), 71. Cf. Calvin, *Institutes* 1.3.1

[69]To be fair, this is only half the story. As I will develop in chapter six, this (Protestant) theological tradition also requires an antithesis, the refusal of idolatry in light of the image of God in Jesus Christ.

[70]On this point, Van der Kooi writes: "Calvin is, we can say, well aware of the creativity inherent to human consciousness. However, according to him, this creativity has only negative results. In his imagination sinful man, caught up in himself, cannot rise above his own measure. . . . He designs an image of God according to the things which he encounters in his own world. In his creativity man "manufactures" idols. Van der Kooi, *As in a Mirror*, 72.

[71]Calvin, *Institutes*, 1.5.4.

[72]Calvin, *Institutes* 1.5.1.

Why does Calvin so emphasize the inescapability of revelation if it does not lead to faith? There seems to be an extra-cognitive apprehension of God's presence that Calvin cannot rightly call knowledge (since all true knowledge leads to piety).[73] Nevertheless this apprehension is ineradicable. The imagination is impaired by sin, in need of enlightenment in order to see clearly again. And yet there remains a deeply felt sense of divine presence and address, to which humanity responds in all our cultural and imaginative endeavors.[74]

Many of the imaginative models and cultural products that fallen humanity makes manifest reflexive oppression, proliferating idolatry and injustice, resembling Babel (Gen 11) or Babylon (Rev 20). But this is not the whole story. As Bavinck reminds us, though the descendants of Cain seem outside God's covenantal line, God graciously allows them to live, multiply, and develop culture. This can never be done in God's absence, and Bavinck writes, "There is thus a rich revelation of God even among the heathen—not only in nature but also in their heart and conscience, in their life and history, among their statesmen and artists, their philosophers and reformers. There exists no reason at all to denigrate or diminish this divine revelation." Bavinck emphasizes that this is not merely a leftover presence of God; it "is always a positive act on the part of God." This means that the difference between religions is not revelation; rather, all religion is a response to revelation: "All that is good and true has its origin in grace, including the good we see in fallen man. The light still does shine in darkness. The spirit of God makes its home and works in all the creation."[75] This is the hallmark of a truly Christian imagination, the conviction that every good and

---

[73]See the discussion on the extra-cognitive aspects of human awareness of the divine in Nathaniel Gray Sutanto, "Neo-Calvinism on General Revelation: A Dogmatic Sketch," *International Journal of Systematic Theology* 20, no. 4 (2018): 495–516.

[74]As Van der Kooi writes, "What can conceptually be described as a continuing field of tension pushes itself to the surface in Calvin's texts: only someone who himself was strongly impressed by the givenness and irresistibility of God's presence could write about the world around us as he does." Van der Kooi, *As in a Mirror*, 83. This sense that humanity is constantly confronted with divine presence and address will be taken up again with reference to the work of Marilynne Robinson in later chapters.

[75]Herman Bavinck, "Common Grace," *Calvin Theological Journal* 24, no. 1 (1989): 51.

perfect gift—every impulse of faith, every inkling of virtue, even the idea of the beautiful—comes from above (Jas 1:17).

There is mystery here, to be sure. Calvin himself acknowledged that God's Spirit must be at work outside the covenantal community, encountering them with grace so that God's "goodness can be felt without the Spirit of adoption."[76] These are real encounters with God's Spirit, even if those encounters do not result in regeneration. Such a conclusion is entailed by the unity of divine revelation. Listen to Bavinck: "Revelation, while having its center in the Person of Christ, in its periphery extends to the uttermost ends of creation. It . . . does not resemble an island on the ocean, nor a drop of oil upon water. . . . The world itself rests on revelation; revelation is the presupposition, the foundation, the secret of all that exists in all its forms."[77] God's revelation in creation, conscience, and culture is comprehensible because "to objective general revelation there corresponds an illumination of Logos (John 1:9) or of the Spirit of God in understanding and conscience, in heart and mind of man, whereby he can understand the general revelation of God in nature and history."[78] The point is that whatever imaginings orient our life in the world, they are always in some way (however diminished) responsive to the revelatory initiative.

---

[76]Calvin, *Institutes* 3.2.11. Van der Kooi highlights the way that Calvin's focus on the Holy Spirit safeguards the mystery of divine action: "The mysterious working of God's Spirit is the vital ground of being for all that exists. . . . The realization that there is a secret working of God in all things defines [Calvin's] symbolic universe." Van der Kooi, *As in a Mirror*, 78.

[77]Bavinck, *The Philosophy of Revelation*, 19. Intriguingly, Willem de Wit argues that we should understand *The Philosophy of Revelation* as an apologetic work. Willem J. De Wit, *On the Way to the Living God* (Amsterdam: VU University Press, 2011), 64-70.

[78]Bavinck, *Reformed Dogmatics*, 1:323. In his *Philosophy of Revelation*, Bavinck expounds multiple dimensions of the Spirit's revelatory activity. First, the Spirit illuminates creation, enabling humanity to accurately access the world. Second, the Spirit instills within humanity a lingering sense of God's nearness, and a hunger for God, an "ineradicable metaphysical need" composed of a sense of dependence and a sense of freedom. Third, the Spirit continues God's revelatory work, so that the effects of sin are restrained, and creation is preserved for re-creation. Fourth, the Spirit applies the redemptive work of Christ in order to renew humanity and all of creation, which has been prepared and preserved by general revelation. It is this fourth movement that we are apt to designate as "special revelation," and certainly revelation pulls us with centripetal force toward Christ, the source and root of revelation. But the first three movements remind us that revelation stands behind all human culture, and that non-Christians are given an ineradicable, extensive, and positive sense of the divine, even if further revelation is needed to heal the effects of sin.

The critical issue, of course, is discernment.[79] Imagination leads people not just to build and create but also to tear down and destroy. Human depravity reminds us to be cautious in our celebration of imaginative meaning making. The difficulty with the resource of common grace/general revelation is that we can make hasty pronouncements of where God is at work. The Barthian "nein" came as a result of a German church so overjoyed and astonished at human progress that they were unable to see a difference between the march of the violent armies and the footprints of God. But this caution should color rather than collapse our critical engagement.

Whether we call God's initiating action "general revelation" or "common grace," we need some way to speak about God's nonsalvific, revelatory movement toward creation, to which human imagining and human culture is a response. To deny the true, good, and beautiful outside the covenantal community, Bavinck writes, "would not only be in conflict with experience but would also entail a denial of God's gifts and hence constitute ingratitude to him."[80] This does not mean that fallen humanity has been given a universal upgrade or that we can give a blanket affirmation to all human imaginings. Both common grace and general revelation remain *ad hoc* and mysterious, a matter of careful and discerning identification, of saying, "Perhaps this is" or "What else could this be?"[81] Such divine overtures, when we encounter them, may not always bring about individual salvation, and yet they give a foretaste of cosmic salvation, the healing of all creation. This eschatological perspective might make further sense of times when the imaginative sense projected or

---

[79]As criteria of discernment, we could do worse than to follow Amos Yong's criteria for discerning the Spirit in the world of religions: "fruits of the Spirit, works of the kingdom, salvation understood in various dimensions, conversion in various human domains, and holiness." These criteria are "abstract in the extreme," but discernment requires a spirit of recognition, which prevents a more specific list. Amos Yong, *The Spirit Poured Out on All Flesh: Pentecostalism and the Possibility of Global Theology* (Grand Rapids: Baker Academic, 2005), 256.

[80]Richard J. Mouw, *He Shines in All That's Fair: Culture and Common Grace* (Grand Rapids: Eerdmans, 2002), 50.

[81]Robert Johnston has argued that a wider view of general revelation is required, in which God encounters humanity, enjoying and inspiring the true, beautiful, and good for their own sakes. Robert K. Johnston, *God's Wider Presence: Reconsidering General Revelation* (Grand Rapids: Baker Academic, 2014). I want to extend this and say that God enjoys and inspires these things because they are representative of the kind of God that God is and the kind of place that God is making the world to be.

provoked by a cultural product is deeply resonant with the theodramatic imagination of Scripture.[82] The Holy Spirit continues to guide human imagining toward instantiating a taste of God's kingdom. This is the theological ground for us to anticipate God's work in human imaginings outside the walls of the church.

CONCLUSION

Our larger project is a reimagined apologetic, or an apologetic that takes the role of the imaginative mode of "feeling the way in" to faith much more seriously. This chapter sought clarity on the imagination itself, defining the imagination as an embodied faculty concerned with possibility. It is able to suspend actuality for the sake of reality, exploring proposals of belief (seeing), experiencing evocations of desire (sensing), and expanding a space where tensions can be made manifest and managed (shaping). It is precisely through this embodied, emotive, imaginative engagement with the world that we integrate experience, belief, and desire to make meaning of our lives. I next sought to defend the imagination against its skeptical despisers, arguing that the experience of meaning in imaginative works suggests its ground in some originating presence. Finally, I sketched a theological account of how God engages, sin impairs, and grace renews human imaginings. I further argued that this imaginative activity never takes place in God's absence. God, through the Holy Spirit, encounters humanity in mysterious ways, casting new visions, drawing out and deepening desire, and creating spaces of possibility for human identity and community. This is one aspect of the image of God that remains in fallen humanity. As Dyrness writes, "To image God is also to imagine a better future—a new way of being in the world. To image God is to ask, 'What if my life, our life together, could be like this?'"[83] As I will argue in the remainder of the book, it is precisely in this space of possibility that a reimagined apologetic seeks to work.

---

[82]See this argument in Justin Bailey, "The Theodramatic Imagination: Spirit and Imagination in the Work of Kevin Vanhoozer." *International Journal of Public Theology*. 12 (2018), 455–470.

[83]Dyrness, "Poised Between Life and Death," 62.

What might this look like? For help we will turn to listen to those whose work regularly draws them into the realm of imagination: artists, poets, and writers. In the next section I explore two case studies of imaginative engagement in the midst of a secular age. As I have argued, the postromantic ethic of authenticity invites an approach that takes our imaginative sensibilities seriously. I offer an example of a reimagined apologetic at the dawn of modern secularity (George MacDonald) and an example of a reimagined apologetic once the age of authenticity is in full flower (Marilynne Robinson).

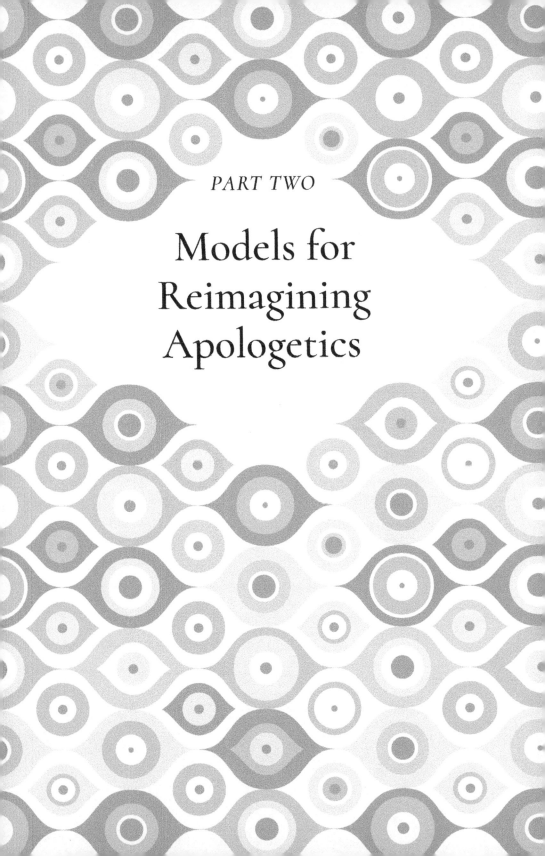

PART TWO

Models for Reimagining Apologetics

– four –

Waking Things Up

George MacDonald's Reimagined Apologetic

The best thing you can do for your fellow, next to rousing his conscience,

is not to give him things to think about, but to wake things up

that are in him; or say, to make him think things for himself.

<small>GEORGE MACDONALD, *A DISH OF ORTS*</small>

GEORGE MACDONALD'S CONTEXT:
THE VICTORIAN CRISIS OF FAITH

The sixty-three years of Queen Victoria's reign (1837–1901) fit within the boundaries of George MacDonald's life (1824–1905) and represent the imaginative context for his writing. In scholarly literature the story of Victorian Christianity is frequently framed as a crisis, marked by growing doubt and disbelief. That story is overstated, but a shift had certainly occurred.[1] In the prior century, religious skepticism had been expressed

---

<small>[1]The literature tends to give the impression that the most important characteristic of Victorian Christianity is its decline, and that we see among the Victorians a specter of the secularity that would grow to encompass the Western world. Timothy Larsen has shown that the decline thesis is overblown, ignoring contradictory data that does not fit its narrative. Although there were</small>

cautiously. But now agnosticism was growing in respectability, and public break-ups with the Christian faith became more common.

The Victorian crisis is most evident in memoirs narrating deconversion.[2] Among the doubts enumerated in these autobiographical accounts we find intellectual, moral, and social reasons for rejecting the Christian faith. But one of the most striking critiques is aesthetic: the accusation that Christianity shrunk the world, suppressing the human spirit and diminishing the joys of life.[3] This postromantic complaint is put poignantly by one commentator:

> Anyone who undertakes a prolonged course of reading in autobiographies of the nineteenth and early twentieth century will emerge dazed with a sensation of listening to a jangling, long-drawn-out and infinitely lugubrious lament. "They told us," it seems to say, "that it was wicked to play on Sundays, that cleanliness was next to godliness, that England was God's chosen race, that foreigners were wicked, that Catholics were idolaters, that the Bible was to be interpreted literally, but that we must on no account take the slightest notice of large parts of it. . . . We can no longer accept this narrow and illogical conglomeration of myths, fallacies and half-truths. We are very desolate and what are we to do? Most terrible of all, we have nothing to love."[4]

The phrase "nothing to love" is a quotation of Victorian luminary John Ruskin.[5] Raised in a devout Calvinist household, Ruskin's narrow vision

---

legitimate crises of faith during the Victorian era, there were also "crises of doubt," wherein prominent secularists and freethinkers reconverted to Christianity, or to theosophy, or to some form of spiritualism. See Timothy Larsen, *Crisis of Doubt: Honest Faith in Nineteenth-Century England* (Oxford: Oxford University Press, 2009). A revised account of Victorian Christianity recognizes that the condition of secularity does not mean diminished religious interest; rather, it recognizes the new conditions of belief: the immanent frame. Charles Taylor's term *fragilization* is a better word for Victorian faith. Fragilization applies pressure in both directions, leading to a spectrum of live options, rather than a simple binary of belief or unbelief.

[2]See Susan Budd, *Varieties of Unbelief: Atheists and Agnostics in English Society, 1850-1960* (London: Heinemann, 1977).

[3]Barbour calls this the "aesthetic critique" of Christianity and defines it as a pattern "of revulsion against the aesthetic limitations of the middle-class English sensibility." John D. Barbour, *Versions of Deconversion: Autobiography and the Loss of Faith* (Charlottesville: University of Virginia Press, 1994), 57. To use Taylor's term, the critique shows an overidentification between Christianity and "polite society."

[4]A. O. J. Cockshut, *The Art of Autobiography in 19th and 20th Century England* (New Haven: Yale University Press, 1984), 187-88. Originally cited in Barbour, *Versions of Deconversion*, 57.

[5]John Ruskin, *Praeterita*, ed. Francis O'Gorman (Oxford: Oxford University Press, 2012), 28.

of the world was punctured during a childhood trip to Rome. There he became convinced "how guiltily and meanly dead the Protestant mind was to the whole meaning and end of mediaeval Church splendour."[6] Cleansing him of anti-Catholicism, the trip also opened his heart to the power of art, leading him to publish five widely acclaimed volumes of *Modern Painters* from 1843 to 1860. His earlier volumes celebrated art as a vehicle for religious experience. But the contrast between the way that art seemed to expand the soul and the way that religion seemed to diminish it plagued Ruskin. In 1858, he "un-converted."[7] Though critical of organized religion for the rest of his life, Ruskin experienced the loss of faith as traumatic and yearned to believe again.

I make special note of Ruskin's deconversion for two reasons. In the first place, Ruskin is a paradigmatic example of the aesthetic dimension of Victorian doubt. But Ruskin is also significant because he would become one of George MacDonald's dearest friends. This friendship was to play a major role in MacDonald's life and the development of his imaginative project. MacDonald shared with Ruskin the conviction that Victorian Christianity suffered from an impoverished imagination. But MacDonald's body of work aimed to address precisely the kinds of doubts and difficulties articulated by his friend. MacDonald was convinced that the resources for a more generative vision would be found, not outside the faith of his fathers, but further in.

GEORGE MACDONALD AS "NEW APOLOGIST"

MacDonald and traditional apologetics. It is uncommon to think of George MacDonald as an apologist in the contemporary sense, a "public defender of the faith." Apologists of this sort did exist during MacDonald's time.[8] But MacDonald shows little interest in reviewing

---

[6]Ruskin, *Praeterita*, 185.

[7]"Un-converted" is Ruskin's word, and Hansen uses "unconversion" as a technical term for "refugees from religious orthodoxy," those who lost faith yet remained "nostalgic for the promises of a former, more heroic religious vision." Lesley Alan Hansen, "The Frightful Reformation: Victorian Doubt and the Personal Novel of Religious Unconversion" (PhD diss., Columbia University, 1984), 74-75.

[8]See Bernard M. G. Reardon, *Religious Thought in the Victorian Age: A Survey from Coleridge to Gore* (London: Longman, 1971), 293.

or defending the proofs for God, such as his contemporary William Paley's argument from design.[9] He shows rather Reformed sensibilities when he argues that the project of proving God's existence "implies that you could go all around him, and buttress up his being with your human argument that he should exist."[10] MacDonald rejected the Enlightenment posture that put God in the dock; for him the nearer analogy of our situation is that of "a child on his mother's bosom, looking up into his mother's face, [writing] a treatise on what a woman was, and what a mother was."[11] In contrast to the deism of the earlier century, for MacDonald, God is too *close* to be proved, upholding our very life and being. This sensitivity suggests a wholly different conception of God's presence and how God's presence might be shown to others and thus a very different kind of apologetic.

This is not to say that argumentation plays no role in MacDonald's work. He notes, for example, the value of arguments in disquieting the believer's anxiety enough to allow her to give attention to her duty.[12] The arguments he offers, however, are intuitive ones in the mouths of common characters rather than analytical arguments in the mouths of philosophers. Even in MacDonald's fairy tales, the narrator sometimes weighs in with trenchant critiques of the narrowness of materialism. He describes, for example the kind of person who is afraid to believe in what cannot be empirically demonstrated, who is "more and more afraid of being taken in, so afraid of it that he takes himself in altogether, and comes at length to believe in nothing but his dinner: to be sure of a thing with him is to have it between his teeth."[13] To borrow an image from Lewis, a person

---

[9]Paley famously argued that just as the design of a watch implies a watchmaker, so too the design of the natural world implies a designer. MacDonald writes: "We are not satisfied that the world should be a proof and varying indication of the intellect of God. That was how Paley viewed it. He taught us to believe there is a God from the mechanism of the world. But, allowing all the argument to be quite correct, what does it prove? A mechanical God, and nothing more." MacDonald, *A Dish of Orts* (Whitethorn, CA: Johannesen, 1996), 246.

[10]George MacDonald, *God's Words to His Children: Sermons Spoken and Unspoken* (New York: Funk & Wagnalls, 1887), 116. Elsewhere he remarks, "As well ask a fly, which has not yet crawled about the world, if he can prove that it is round!" George MacDonald, *Thomas Wingfold, Curate* (Whitethorn, CA: Johannesen, 1997), 78.

[11]MacDonald, *God's Words to His Children*, 116.

[12]George MacDonald, *The Seaboard Parish* (Whitethorn, CA: Johannesen, 1995), 450.

[13]George MacDonald, *The Princess and Curdie* (Whitethorn, CA: Johannesen, 2000), 22.

may be so afraid of being taken in that it is impossible for him to be taken out of his narrow vision of the world.

We can also see in MacDonald shades of Thomas Reid's common-sense realism, which was dominant in the Scottish educational system for much of the late eighteenth and early nineteenth century.[14] Reid argued for the reliability of our creaturely faculties: "There are many things which it concerns us to know, for which we can have no other evidence. The Wise Author of nature has planted in the human mind a propensity to rely upon this evidence before we can give a reason for doing so."[15] In MacDonald, Reid's philosophy takes on a more poetic sensibility; indeed, one of his earliest biographers describes MacDonald as a "common-sense mystic."[16] For MacDonald as for Reid, the existence of God is a common-sense intuition rather than the result of calculated intellection.

Nevertheless, MacDonald shows incredible sympathy with those who doubt. As he says in a sermon: "I question if there is a doubt or a sense of difficulty that prevails now that has not passed through my own mind. . . . It is natural that we should doubt." He encourages honest wrestling with the difficulties of belief and cautions that at best intellectual arguments will often result in a draw: "Not all the intellect or metaphysics of the world could prove that there is no God, and not all the intellect in the world could prove that there is a God." At the same time, he refuses to allow doubters to shut down the search because of the ambiguity of the evidence. Genuine faith is found, he argues, not in bare intellectual assent but in doing God's will. Disordered desire fuels doubt, and what is needed is not proofs but purity of heart. He asks,

> Are you fit to believe? I have just said that I believe it to be the loftiest exercise of the human being and of human nature. How can you expect to believe? Are you like Nathaniel—an Israelite indeed, a man without guile?

---

[14]As discussed in chapter two, Reid writes that a man who doubts that there is a material world external to his senses because he cannot prove it is like a man who worries that he might be made of glass.

[15]Thomas Reid, *Essays on the Intellectual Powers of Man*, ed. James Walker (Cambridge: John Bartlett, 1852), 395.

[16]Joseph Johnson, *George MacDonald: A Biographical and Critical Appreciation* (London: Pitman, 1906), 126.

What are your ways? What have you been about? What are your desires in life? How have you been ordering yourself? If it may be that although the power of God upon you makes you feel that you ought to believe, that you are such that you cannot believe, and it is your own fault.[17]

Or as Mr. Raven will say to Mr. Vane in *Lilith*, "What you call riddles are truths, and seem riddles because you are not true."[18] Our first responsibility in seeking the truth is to become trustworthy. The failure of vision is often a failure of virtue; in order to wake the one, you must wake the other.

When MacDonald's character, Thomas Wingfold, experiences a crisis of faith, Wingfold seeks refuge among classic and contemporary Victorian thinkers: Paley, Butler, Leighton, Neander, Coleridge, and Liddon. But he finds no compelling consensus among these intellectuals. It seems rather that what "one man received, another man refused; and the popular acceptance was worth no more in respect of Christianity than of Mahometanism."[19] Merely studying "Christian evidences" might mollify the intellect but not the hunger of the soul for truth "in the inward parts."[20]

For this reason, MacDonald claims that apologetic argumentation is frequently counterproductive since it primarily aims at the intellect instead of the heart. He writes, "When I am successful in any argument, my one dread is of humiliating my opponent. . . . When a man reasons for victory and not for the truth in the other soul, he has just one ally—the devil. The defeat of the intellect is not the object of fighting with the sword of the Spirit, but rather the acceptance of the heart."[21] He elsewhere warns of coercive attempts at conversion, which he describes as "gapings of the greed of power over others . . . hungerings to see self reflected in another

---

[17]MacDonald, *God's Words to His Children*, 116.

[18]George MacDonald, *Lilith: First and Final* (Whitethorn, CA: Johannesen, 1998), 65.

[19]MacDonald, *Thomas Wingfold, Curate*, 51-52.

[20]As MacDonald will later comment: "To explain to him who loves not, is but to give him the more plentiful material for misinterpretation. Let a man have truth in the inward parts, and out of the abundance of his heart let his mouth speak." MacDonald, *Thomas Wingfold, Curate*, 346.

[21]George MacDonald, *Annals of a Quiet Neighborhood* (Whitethorn, CA: Johannesen, 2004), 46-47. Or again: "To get people's hearts right is of much more importance than convincing their judgments. Right judgment will follow." MacDonald, *Seaboard Parish*, 470.

convinced."[22] MacDonald is cautious lest the goal of opening up the heart to God give way to ideological conquest. It is not, after all, the intellect but the heart that is the site of the spiritual struggle, and thus he sought to wake the "eyes of the heart," the imagination.

The apologetic aim of MacDonald's novels. It is no surprise that MacDonald's primary mode of apologetic engagement is imaginative. He tells fantastic stories in which the beauty and goodness of the truth can be experienced. He tells realistic stories that create a space in which doubt can be negotiated. But identifying apologetic aims for MacDonald's writing runs the risk of compromising the literary integrity of his work in service of an ulterior aim. Indeed, here we encounter the need to rehabilitate Mac-Donald's legacy against perhaps his greatest admirer: C. S. Lewis. Lewis's praise for MacDonald in *Surprised by Joy* has sent countless readers to Mac-Donald's works. Yet Lewis also seems to discount MacDonald as barely a "second rank" writer of novels, anthologizing him not "as a writer but as a Christian teacher."[23] This reputation has been hard to shake. Following Lewis's assessment, MacDonald continues to be painted as a "writer of mor-alizing novels whose style is ornate and clumsy." Lewis deserves due credit for the ongoing popularity of MacDonald's fantasy writings. But he is also largely responsible for the relegation of MacDonald's realistic fiction to the margins. Literary critic John Pennington's comment is worth repeating: "Ironically, Lewis is simultaneously MacDonald's savior and his albatross."[24]

Lewis suggests that the prolificacy of MacDonald's fiction was driven primarily by financial need. But though it is certainly the case that Mac-Donald (with eleven children!) had significant expenses throughout his life,

---

[22]George MacDonald, *There and Back* (Whitethorn, CA: Johannesen, 1991), 225.

[23]C. S. Lewis, *George MacDonald: An Anthology* (New York: Macmillan, 1947), xxiv. Kirstin Jeffrey Johnson helpfully notes that Lewis's statement is not necessarily a condemnation, since to Lewis, the "first order" writers were Dante, Milton, and Shakespeare. She goes on: "While Lewis did not grant MacDonald such laurelled status, he nonetheless rates MacDonald's influence upon his own life as higher than any of these." Unfortunately, Lewis's statement is almost always read as a deprecation of MacDonald. Kirstin Jeffrey Johnson, "Rooted in All Its Story, More Is Meant Than Meets the Ear: A Study of the Relational and Revelational Nature of George MacDonald's Mythopoeic Art" (PhD diss., University of St. Andrews, 2011), 7.

[24]John Pennington, "A 'Wolff' in Sheep's Clothing: The George MacDonald Industry and the Dif-ficult Rehabilitation of a Reputation," in *George MacDonald: Literary Heritage and Heirs* (Wayne, PA: Zossima, 2008), 241-42. Sadly, this has been my personal experience as well in encountering the popular assessment of MacDonald's works.

it is just as likely that the choice to write so many novels was strategic. MacDonald is remembered for his fairy tales, but in his realistic fiction he hoped to awaken his readers to the wonder and the enchantment at the heart of everyday life.[25] Indeed, MacDonald problematizes the standard distinction between his realistic novels and his fairy tales, because his entire project consists in alerting readers to deeper layers of reality. He was convinced that the most important dimensions of reality are not apprehensible by the senses without relational transformation. This meant that the lines between fantasy and reality quickly begin to blur. His fantasies have the feel of reality; as Chesterton wrote of *The Princess and the Goblin*, "Of all the stories I have read it remains the most real, the most realistic, in the exact sense of the phrase, the most like life."[26] Conversely, his realistic novels have the feel of fairy tales; in the words of one literary critic, we must "read the full-length novels . . . to discover the fairy tales within them."[27] This was the aim of MacDonald's writing in all its forms: to "wake things up," to create a hospitable space in which creative movement could occur.

MacDonald's writing fuses story and spiritual direction, in which the narrator pauses the action to address the reader. Modern readers have found this obtrusive—the mark of an inferior storyteller—but a better assessment comes from one of his contemporaries, the literary critic John Dyer. Dyer casts MacDonald as "the first of a new school of fiction . . . a theological novelist," and if this is the case, then it is unfair to judge his work by the standards of modern storytelling. MacDonald was trying to tell a different kind of story, one that breathed with the theology that animated his life.[28] MacDonald's genius was found in painting believable

---

[25]MacDonald's description of one of his characters might be taken as a self-portrait: "In his commitment to follow Jesus, he worked to make apparent the presence and love of the transcendent God in all aspects of life, and so to offer 'real vision: for instead of making common things look commonplace, as a false vision would have done, it had made common things disclose the wonderful that was in them." George MacDonald, *The Gifts of the Child Christ and Other Stories and Fairy Tales*, Glen Edward Sadler, ed. (Grand Rapids: Eerdmans, 1996), 168. Originally cited in Kerry Dearborn, *Baptized Imagination: The Theology of George MacDonald* (Burlington, VT: Ashgate, 2006), 120.

[26]Greville MacDonald, *George MacDonald and His Wife* (Whitethorn, CA: Johannesen, 1998), 1.

[27]Robert Trexler, "George MacDonald: Merging Myth and Method," *The Bulletin of the New York C. S. Lewis Society* 34, no. 4 (August 2003): 7.

[28]Dyer captures MacDonald's primary theological theme well: "Man as a son of his Father in heaven, prospering in his life while he respects that relation, and the other human and divine

characters of remarkable purity and goodness. When asked whether his portrayals were overly idealistic, MacDonald replied, "I will try to show what we might be, may be, must be, shall be—and something of the struggle to gain it."[29] For MacDonald, his novels were spaces in which to pull his readers toward the full possibilities of their humanity.

Accordingly, the danger of describing MacDonald's work as apologetic is similar to the danger of describing MacDonald—as Lewis did—primarily as a Christian teacher rather than as a writer. It makes MacDonald's mythopoeic art instrumental to some other narrow aim (e.g., evangelism, moralism, etc.). Let us be clear: MacDonald was supremely a writer before he was a teacher, preacher, or apologist, even if he was all these as well. MacDonald certainly hoped that his art, like the best preaching, would bring about a transformative effect. But this means expanding the boundaries of art to include preaching, rather than reducing art to its homiletical value. He did not set out to preach but to write stories that were deeply true. If his stories "preached," it was not because his aim was primarily homiletic, but because they brought mythopoeic truth to bear on his readers' souls. MacDonald's creative work flowed from his love for God and God's world; he reasoned that he could not help but imitate the Creator's work in responsive love. But as MacDonald sought to serve his readers in their lived situation of doubt and disbelief, a profoundly pastoral and therefore apologetic impulse emerged. MacDonald led his readers along, challenging narrow visions of the world and inviting them into larger ones. We could thus adapt Dyer's assessment and call MacDonald not just a "new novelist" but also a "new apologist," one who is responsive to the postromantic sensibilities of the Victorian age.

THE DOUBTS AND DESIRES OF JOHN RUSKIN

I want to situate MacDonald's apologetic project in terms of the concrete complaints of Ruskin, a doubting friend he loved deeply. Ruskin "found

---

relations that grow out of it, ruining his life and its good by living under the spiritual restraints of no spiritual household, of no filial and fraternal love." John Dyer, "The New Novelist," in *The Penn Monthly* (Philadelphia: University Press Company, 1870), 221.

[29]Rolland Hein, *George MacDonald: Victorian Mythmaker* (Whitethorn, CA: Johannesen, 1999), 22.

himself unconverted from his old Evangelical faith" in 1858, five years before being introduced to MacDonald.[30] Upon being introduced, the two formed such an intimate friendship that Greville lists Ruskin as one of his father's four closest friends.[31] A moving précis of their disagreement on matters of faith can be seen in Ruskin's 1868 response to MacDonald's *Unspoken Sermons*. In the short letter, Ruskin praises the beauty of MacDonald's writing, expresses his own objections, and anticipates his friend's response:

> Thank you exceedingly for the book. They are the best sermons—beyond all compare—I have ever heard or read—and if ever sermons did good, these will. Pages 23-34 are very beautiful—unspeakably beautiful. If they were but true! . . . But I feel so strongly that it is only the image of your own mind that you see in the sky! And you will say, "And who made the mind?" Well, the same hand that made the adder's ear—and the tiger's heart—and they shall be satisfied when they awake—with *their* likeness?[32]

In an earlier letter (1866), composed after the death of their common friend A. J. Scott, Ruskin writes that in contrast to MacDonald, who is able to believe whatever he likes, Ruskin counts himself as one of those "poor, wicked people, who sternly think it our duty to believe nothing but what we know to be fact."[33] If Ruskin rejected his evangelical upbringing for its impoverished aesthetic vision, these were his stated objections to MacDonald's more capacious version: (1) that there was no way of proving the truth of it, (2) that it seemed mere wish-fulfillment, and (3) that it was more a reflection of MacDonald's own goodness than of any supernatural reality.[34]

---

[30]Ruskin describes the experience that sealed his loss of faith, when on a Sunday morning in Turin "from before Paul Veronese's *Queen of Sheba*, and under quite overwhelmed sense of his God-given power, I went away to a Waldensian chapel, where a little squeaking idiot was preaching to an audience of seventeen old women and three louts, that they sweere the only children of God in Turin; and that all the people in Turin outside the chapel, and all the people in the world out of sight of Monte Viso, would be damned. I came out of the chapel, in sum of twenty years of thought, a conclusively un-converted man." John Ruskin, *Fors Clavigera: Letters, to the Workmen and Labourers of Great Britain*, vol. 4 (New York: Greenwood Press, 1968), 9-10.

[31]MacDonald, *George MacDonald and His Wife*, 192.

[32]MacDonald, *George MacDonald and His Wife*, 337.

[33]MacDonald, *George MacDonald and His Wife*, 334-35.

[34]Here we see shades of Ludwig Feuerbach, whose influence on the British literati was mediated through Marian Evans (George Eliot), who in 1854 translated Feuerbach's *Essence of Christianity*

Yet underneath these objections lurked a more painful and personal question, which surfaces in the Scott letter: "Now—if it were possible for me to go to my Father in a direct personal way—(which it is not) the very first thing I should say to him would be—'What have you been teasing me like this for?—Were there *no* toys in the cupboard you could have shown me—but the one I can't have?'"[35] Here Ruskin is referencing his storied and tragic love for the beautiful Rose la Touche, who had recently rejected his marriage proposal.[36] To engage Ruskin's doubts, MacDonald would need to respond, not simply to the more common objections, but also to the deep personal pain of thwarted desire. In the section that follows, I chart the contours of MacDonald's engagement with Victorian unbelief in general, and Ruskin in particular, by offering a reading of MacDonald's Wingfold trilogy. The trilogy is notable for its central themes of faith and doubt. Multiple interpreters, starting with Greville, draw connections between characters in the trilogy and Ruskin.[37] Nevertheless, an apologetic examination of the trilogy has not, to my knowledge, been undertaken. Below I seek to offer such a distillation. I want to pay special attention to the way that MacDonald engages his character's doubts and desires, as emblematic of his engagement with fragilized Victorian faith.

Reimagining apologetics in the Wingfold trilogy. Throughout the Wingfold trilogy, MacDonald creates characters inhabiting various spaces along the spectrum of doubt. The character that unites all of the stories is Thomas Wingfold. Wingfold is a clergyman whose initially unexamined

---

(1841). See Philip Davis, *The Oxford English Literary History, 1830-1880: The Victorians* (Oxford: Oxford University Press, 2002), 147.

[35]MacDonald, *George MacDonald and His Wife*, 334-35.

[36]Rose was the daughter of Maria la Touche, who had introduced MacDonald and Ruskin. Ruskin fell in love with her and proposed in 1866, when she was eighteen and he was forty-seven. Her parents opposed the match, and Rose asked him to wait until 1869, yet even then she was unable to consent due to concerns over Ruskin's unbelief. The MacDonalds were close to both parties and helped bring them together at their home in Hammersmith. However, the two never were able to settle the matter, and Rose died in 1875, nearly crushing Ruskin with grief. For an account of the Rose la Touche affair, see Derrick Leon, *Ruskin, the Great Victorian* (Hamden, CT: Archon, 1969), 390–417. For an account of MacDonald's literary engagement with Ruskin's story in his fantasy *Lilith* see Johnson, "Rooted in All Its Story," 195-206.

[37]See MacDonald, *George MacDonald and His Wife*, 340-41; Jocelyne Slepyan, "'With All Sorts of Doubts I Am Familiar': George MacDonald's Literary Response to John Ruskin's Struggles with Epistemology," in *Rethinking George MacDonald: Contexts and Contemporaries* (Glasgow: Scottish Literature International, 2013).

faith grows through deep doubt into a generative confidence that is able to minister to doubting others. In telling a story about an Anglican churchman entertaining doubt but resolving it in the direction of authentic faith, MacDonald is offering a counter-narrative to other well-known Victorian novels in which clergymen renounce their faith.[38] Like the other novels, MacDonald takes as his protagonist a churchman whose faith is shaken by the upheavals of the century, but unlike the others MacDonald finds faith sufficient to the challenge. MacDonald is less interested than the other authors in the status of the Anglican Church or the unique pressures of being a clergyman. He is engaged in finding a faith that is capacious enough to continue undaunted by the doubts of the elite as well as the doubts of the common person. Along Wingfold's journey, clergy and laity of all stations are drawn up into honest encounter with faith and doubt: Mr. Bevis, the rector of the parish; Mr. Drake and Dorothy, a nonconformist minister and his doubting daughter; Mr. Drew, a cloth dealer; Paul and Juliet Faber, an atheist physician and his mysterious wife; Richard Tuke, a bookbinding prodigy; and Barbara Wylder, an orphaned heiress.[39] Not all of these characters end their story in a place of secure faith, but all of them are forced to wrestle with reality and are led to greater openness in their search for truth. It is only the self-assured characters—the atheist lawyer George Bascombe and the Christian crank Ms. Ramshorn—whose convictions remain static and unexamined.

Space does not permit an examination into the intricacies of each character's struggle for faith. I rather want to highlight three kinds of doubters in order to explore MacDonald's apologetic response: the enlightened scoffer (corresponding to the truth of Christian faith), the humane atheist (corresponding to the goodness of faith), and the unbelieving aesthete (corresponding to the beauty of faith). Uniting them all is Wingfold,

---

[38]See Pamela Lee Jordan, "Clergy in Crisis: Three Victorian Portrayals of Anglican Clergymen Forced to Redefine Their Faith" (PhD diss., Ball State University, 1997).

[39]Yamaguchi argues the trilogy is conversant with two seventeenth century works on faith and doubt: Thomas Hooker's *Poor Doubting Christian* (1629) and John Hart's *Ms. Drake Revived* (1649). Indeed MacDonald's characters Magistrate Hooker and Minister Drake seem to be something of an homage to these books. Miho Yamaguchi, "Poor Doubting Christian: An Exploration of Salvation, Love, and Eternity in MacDonald's Wingfold Trilogy," *North Wind* 23 (2004): 1-12.

whose journey toward a more genuine and generative faith begins when his creed is called into question.

Truth: *the enlightened scoffer* (Thomas **Wingfold, Curate**). The lawyer George Bascombe is mostly a foil, but his portrait is important because he represents the kind of bold disbelief that had become fashionable among the Victorian elite. MacDonald highlights the fact that Bascombe's bold atheism is a novel phenomenon of his generation: "In the last century, beyond a doubt, the description of such a man . . . would have been incredible because unintelligible." Bascombe not only prides himself on his ability to see through the "humbug" of belief but also feels a special calling "to destroy the beliefs of everyone else."[40] Whereas in Bascombe's estimation Christians have "no courage to face the facts of existence," he believes that materialistic utilitarianism equips him to face the hard facts of reality.[41]

MacDonald does not attempt a refutation of Bascombe's worldview; he is interested in serving a different sort of doubter. Yet he places a short criticism in the mouths of Bascombe's acquaintances:

> They said also that he inveighed against the beliefs of other people, without having ever seen more than a distorted shadow of those beliefs—some of them he was not capable of seeing, they said—only capable of denying. Now while he would have been perfectly justified, they said, in asserting that he saw no truth in the things he denied, was he justifiable in concluding that his not seeing a thing was a proof of its non-existence—anything more, in fact, than a presumption against its existence?[42]

Here MacDonald signals two lines of response to which he will return throughout the novels. First, that the inability to see a thing is no proof of its nonexistence. Second, that there are certain truths that must be first seen by the imagination, the eyes of the heart. There are certain things that cannot be seen until the heart is adequately prepared and awake.

Bascombe's unbelief, MacDonald wants us to see, is in part a failure of imagination. Bascombe mistakes the imagination for a faculty of mere

---

[40]MacDonald, *Thomas Wingfold, Curate*, 31.
[41]MacDonald, *Thomas Wingfold, Curate*, 23.
[42]MacDonald, *Thomas Wingfold, Curate*, 32.

amusement. Since he did not realize that "imagination had been the guide to all the physical discoveries which he worshipped," he could not entertain the possibility that "she might be able to carry a glimmering light even into the forest of the supersensible."[43] Indeed, it is obvious that Bascombe's vision of reality is claustrophobically narrow. In his enlightened reverie he is coldly Malthusian, suggesting to his cousin Helen that the dwarves who keep the grounds of a nearby estate should have been strangled at birth, and that there should be laws and penalties to prevent their procreation, for the sake of the race. He is too blind to see that the dwarf Polwarth is actually the wisest person in town, and thus Bascombe is the only character who fails to be enriched from Polwarth's acquaintance.[44]

It is Bascombe's relentless focus on the *facts* that prevents him from discovering the *truth*. The distinction was necessary because MacDonald's understanding of truth was nearer to the Middle English understanding of *troth*—a relational and covenantal concept—rather than the bare facticity of the Enlightenment. For MacDonald, truth suggested a covenantal relationship between humanity and ultimate reality. Truth as *troth* implies a trustworthy source, the "public expectation of constancy."[45] Here we see shades of Ruskin's objection that he belonged to those "poor, wicked people, who sternly think it our duty to believe nothing but what we know to be fact." Greville opines that Ruskin's unbelief was due in part to the Victorian tendency to "overvalue the fast-breeding facts of science," and he imagines his father's response to this overestimation: "Since when have

---

[43]MacDonald, *Thomas Wingfold, Curate*, 32.

[44]It is possible that in the dwarf Polwarth MacDonald is inverting and embodying a statement from chapter thirteen of *Biographia Literaria*, where just before his famous definition of the imagination, Coleridge writes: "Those whom I had been taught to venerate as almost super-human in magnitude of intellect" to actually be "grotesque dwarfs." Samuel Taylor Coleridge, *Biographia Literaria, or, Biographical Sketches of My Literary Life and Opinions*, ed. James Engell and Walter Jackson Bate (London: Routledge, 1983), 301. Bascombe, who prides himself on his intellect is in moral terms a dwarf; Polwarth, a giant.

[45]Helen Bromhead, *The Reign of Truth and Faith: Epistemic Expressions in 16th and 17th Century English* (Berlin: Walter de Gruyter, 2009), 139. Bromhead distinguishes troth from faith, where the former has an exclusively human reference, but MacDonald, following his Calvinist upbring-ing, does not make this distinction, writing: "In its deepest sense, the truth is a condition of heart, soul, mind, and strength towards God and towards our fellow—not an utterance, not even a right form of words; and therefore such truth coming forth in words is, in a sense, the person that speaks." George MacDonald, *Unspoken Sermons: Series I, II, III in One Volume* (Whitethorn, CA: Johannesen, 1999), 103.

your devitalized facts, O Man of Science, found such paramount authority? Have you forgotten that Alpine revelation of which you would so often tell me?"[46] Facts were the province of the intellect, not to be feared. But the imagination was required to harmonize them with truth, which could be imbibed intuitively as well, as MacDonald believed Ruskin had done during an epiphanic visit to the Alps, which he references above.[47]

In addition to showing the narrow aperture of the materialistic lens, MacDonald also points out scientific pretensions of honesty and humility. Writing in a time when writers would speak of the vice of "blind faith" in contrast to the virtue of "honest doubt," MacDonald wants to show that honesty does not dwell necessarily in either the province of belief or disbelief. Bascombe prides himself on his honesty; his early confrontation of Wingfold turns on this apparent virtue: "Now, I am going to be honest with you. . . . A man ought to speak out what he thinks. So here goes! Tell me honestly—do you believe one word of all that?"[48] And yet, the readers can see that Bascombe's unbelief is every bit as unexamined as Wingfold's faith. Bascombe only has seen "a distorted shadow of those beliefs." Bascombe is honest in the sense that he says what he thinks, but he is not honest in that he has never really wrestled with reality, nor considered how much of his life is lived trusting things he cannot see.[49]

For MacDonald, honesty requires the admission of finitude rather than certitude. In *There and Back*, Barbara challenges Richard on the need to acknowledge the limitations of his own mind:

---

[46]MacDonald, *George MacDonald and His Wife*, 335. As Juliet says to Paul Faber: "It seems to me that enjoying a thing is only another word for believing in it. If I thought the sweetest air of the violin had no truth in it, I could not listen to it a moment longer." What kind of truth? "It pretends that something it gives birth to in the human mind is also a true thing." George MacDonald, *Paul Faber, Surgeon* (Whitethorn, CA: Johannesen, 1992), 78.

[47]In Polwarth's words we see part of MacDonald's response: "The truth conveyed is the revelation. I do not deny that facts have been learned in dreams, but I would never call the communication of a mere fact a revelation. Truth alone, beheld as such by the soul, is worthy of the name. Facts, however, may themselves be the instruments of such revelation." MacDonald, *Thomas Wingfold, Curate*, 173.

[48]MacDonald, *Thomas Wingfold, Curate*, 22.

[49]We see shades of this enlightened mentality in MacDonald's description of Richard Tuke in, for whom "Whatever was not to him definite—that is, was not by him formally conceivable, must not be put in the category of things to be believed; but he had not a notion how many things he accepted unquestioning . . ." George MacDonald, *There and Back* (Whitethorn, CA: Johannesen, 1991), 148.

"Tell me honestly then," said Barbara, "—for I do believe you are an honest man—tell me, are you sure there is no God? Have you gone all through the universe looking for him, and failed to find him? Is there no possible chance that there may be a God!"

"I do not believe there is."

"But are you sure there is not? Do you know it, so that you have a right to say it?"[50]

MacDonald's strongest pushback against the enlightened scoffer is the recognition of finitude. This is the one thing, he writes, that seems to lie beyond the reach of a person's imagination, that "requires the purest faith . . . a man's own ignorance and incapacity."[51] In contrast to an honesty that prides itself on questioning everything not established as fact is the honesty that allows every aspect of the self to be called into question. This is the kind of honest doubt that Wingfold finds, and it leads him to search for God all the more diligently:

Was there—could there be a living heart to the universe that did positively hear him—poor, misplaced, dishonest, ignorant Thomas Wingfold, who had presumed to undertake a work he neither could perform nor had the courage to forsake, when out of the misery of the grimy little cellar of his consciousness he cried aloud for light and something to make a man of him? For now that Thomas had begun to doubt like an honest being, every ugly thing within him began to show itself to his awakened probity.[52]

These, MacDonald writes, are doubts of "good parentage"—doubts that call into question one's own honesty and integrity. Under the guidance of Polwarth, Wingfold takes his struggle into the pulpit, giving his congregation a vicarious experience of his wrestling, scandalizing some, but provoking others to wake as well. As MacDonald writes elsewhere, "Doubts are the messengers of the Living One to wake the honest. . . . Doubt must precede every deeper assurance."[53] Far from wanting to bring doubting

---

[50]MacDonald, *There and Back*, 161.

[51]MacDonald, *There and Back*, 263.

[52]MacDonald, *Thomas Wingfold, Curate*, 54.

[53]MacDonald, *Unspoken Sermons*, 354-55.

Christians cheap assurance, MacDonald wants his readers to move through the gauntlet of doubt. The willingness to be called into question and to step into the light of self-examination is the necessary condition for vision-enabling virtue. As Wingfold will later say to his wife, "It's a big thing to say, *I am honest*."[54] Bascombe's fashionable unbelief has no such honesty, but neither does the fashionable belief of Ms. Ramshorn, who prizes the respectability of her faith above all else.

The heart of MacDonald's response to the enlightened scoffer is a call to true humility, the engine of the imagination. To do this he must make a distinction between facts and truth, calling comfortable certainties into question. This opens the door for doubt but also for faith. God, as the source of life and being, is not a *thing* to be proved like other things in the universe, but in the absence of definitive proof against God's existence, we are freed to entertain the overtures of belief. In *There and Back*, Barbara asks Wingfold how a person can be "sure of a thing you can't prove?" Wingfold responds,

> What you love, you already believe enough to put it to the proof of trial. My life is such a proving; and the proof is so promising that it fills me with the happiest hope. To prove with your brains the thing you love, would be to deck the garments of salvation with a useless fringe. Shall I search heaven and earth for proof that my wife is a good and lovely woman? The signs of it are everywhere; the proofs of it nowhere.[55]

Although the open question of God with relationship to proofs of God's existence will lead some to reject God, MacDonald counsels an imaginative receptivity to hope.[56] We can see this in Polwarth's assessment of Bascombe's skepticism:

> Still, and notwithstanding, if the facts of life are those of George Bascombe's endorsing—*and he can prove it*—let us by all means learn and accept them, be they the worst possible. Meantime there are truths that ought to be facts, and until he has proved that there is no God, some of us

---

[54]MacDonald, *Paul Faber, Surgeon*, 111.
[55]MacDonald, *There and Back*, 195.
[56]Greville writes: "Ruskin lacked this prophetic hope; his honesty *seemed* destructive to his faith." MacDonald, *George MacDonald and His Wife*, 330.

will go feeling after him if haply we may find him, and in him the truths we long to find true. . . . And if he be such as their idea of what we think him, they *are* better without him. If, on the contrary, he be what some of us really think him, their not seeking him will not perhaps prevent him from finding them.[57]

Here is a remarkably hopeful sentiment! Indeed, if God was as great as MacDonald believed, then he could hold out hope even for the most self-assured, like Bascombe, as well as for the most skeptical, like Ruskin. And in the same way that humility opens the door for imaginative hope, virtue could prepare the way for vision.

Goodness: The humane atheist (Paul Faber, Surgeon). In contrast to Bascombe, the surgeon Paul Faber is an atheist of much greater complexity. Whereas Bascombe is self-satisfied, Faber is self-sufficient. He feels no *need* of God and is content simply to observe the "lower but equally in-dispensable half of religion—that, namely, which has respect to one's fellows."[58] This leads everyone to respect him, despite his public atheism. In Faber, MacDonald endeavors to explore a riddle of human virtue: Why is it that Faber, an ostensibly good character, cannot seem to see the goodness of God? Faber's service toward humanity complicates things: it is simultaneously the thing that puts him in direct contact with God (since he unintentionally performs God's will in loving his neighbor) and the source of the pride that deludes him into self-satisfaction (since he congratulates himself on his benevolence).

This benevolent impulse is at the heart of Faber's greatest objection to faith. As a doctor, he has seen so much suffering that he cannot bring himself to believe in a God who oversees, permits, or ordains such a world. He is unwilling to believe in a God who is less humane than himself. Faber, MacDonald tells us, is one who does philosophy "by the troubled light of wrong and suffering, and that is not the light of the morning, but of a burning house."[59] We should pause to note that it is this phrase that

---

[57]MacDonald, *Thomas Wingfold, Curate*, 171.

[58]MacDonald, *Paul Faber, Surgeon*, 6. Faber's religious impulse is wholly immanent, concerned with the duty of universal benevolence that emerges in Taylor's "modern moral order." See the discussion in chapter one.

[59]MacDonald, *Paul Faber, Surgeon*, 80.

Greville picks from his father's works to describe Ruskin.[60] It depicts a person, who upon experiencing the beauty and brutality of the world, cannot help but see brutality as the truer reality. To quote Chesterton, "Bad is so bad, that we cannot but think good an accident; good is so good, that we feel certain that evil could be explained."[61] MacDonald did not shrink back from the brutality of the world, from the "troubled light of wrong and suffering." But he was convinced that the light of the morning would bring greater light.

To return to Faber: MacDonald's response to such humane self-sufficiency runs primarily along two lines. First, he wants to show that Faber is not as good as he thinks he is; indeed, that no one is as good as they think. Second, he suggests that the real God is better than Faber believes. Once again, we see virtue fueling the imagination's search for God. Wingfold, who has become Faber's friend, knows that Faber's objections are not the kind that can be answered with good arguments. Instead, he hopes "to cause the roots of those very objections to strike into, and thus disclose to the man himself, the deeper strata of his being."[62] When Faber objects, "Why don't I desire him then?" Wingfold simply responds, "That is for you to find out. . . . But it may *have* to be in a way you will not like."[63] MacDonald is navigating between two poles. He wants to demonstrate the individual nature of the quest for God, and yet he also wants to show the perils of unchecked individualism. On the first count, MacDonald wants no one simply to stand on the shoulders of another's confidence. An interior journey is required, and no two journeys are quite the same.

And yet, on the second count, MacDonald wants to show that Faber's self-sufficiency is part of the problem. He writes that Faber's humane atheism "veiled the pride behind it all, the pride namely of an unhealthy conscious individuality, the pride of self as *self*, which makes a man the center of his own universe."[64] The journey to truth might be an individual

[60]MacDonald, *George MacDonald and His Wife*, 340-41.
[61]G. K. Chesterton, *The Annotated Thursday: G. K. Chesterton's Masterpiece, The Man Who Was Thursday* (San Francisco: Ignatius, 1999), 246.
[62]MacDonald, *Paul Faber, Surgeon*, 6.
[63]MacDonald, *Paul Faber, Surgeon*, 155.
[64]MacDonald, *Paul Faber, Surgeon*, 98-99.

and interior quest, but it is not isolated, either from the rest of created reality, or from the creator. True individuality will only be realized inter- dependently, in relationship to the larger whole.[65] MacDonald's essay on the imagination expresses this memorably: "No man is capable of seeing for himself the whole of any truth: he needs it echoed back to him from every soul in the universe."[66] It is only in opening the door hospitably to the reality beyond yourself that it becomes possible for the soul to realize its true individuality and its full humanity.[67] On his own, Faber cannot be as good as he could be; indeed, as the story shows, he is not as good as he believes.[68]

MacDonald also aims to show that the real God is better than Faber imagines. Throughout his writing, MacDonald grants the problem of evil to have great force. And yet he wants to press materialists like Faber to consider the cold implications of their unbelief. Faber recounts an oc- casion when, upon hearing a young, bereaved husband submit to the will of God, the doctor could not keep from scorning the existence of such a God. Upon hearing this, the young man "turned white as death." Wingfold reminds Faber, "You were taking from him his only hope of seeing her again."[69] For the young man, more horrible than there being a God who would allow such bereavement to occur is a universe in which there is no God to put things right again, no God to raise the dead. Here we are brought back to the fundamental choice: Is brutality or beauty the deeper reality? Either existence is, as Polwarth puts it, "a chaos with dreams of a

---

[65]To use the language introduced in the first two chapters, MacDonald is after a thicker authenticity.

[66]MacDonald, Dish of Orts, 22.

[67]As Polwarth tells Wingfold: "God is in every man, else how could he live the life he does live? But that life God keeps alive for the hour when he shall inform the will, the aspiration, the imagination of the man. When the man throws wide his door to the Father of his spirit, when his individual being is thus supplemented—to use a poor miserable word—with the individual- ity that originated it, then is the man a whole, healthy, complete existence." MacDonald, Thomas Wingfold, Curate, 295.

[68]Faber falls in love with one of his patients, Juliet. At first, she rebuffs his advances. But slowly he overcomes her resistance, both in matters of love and faith; she begins to feel the persuasiveness of his arguments against God as well. But once both have given up faith, no Savior remains for them save the other. Thus, when Juliet confesses her darkest secret and Faber is unable to forgive her, the emotional weight of guilt nearly crushes them both.

[69]MacDonald, Thomas Wingfold, Curate, 367.

world," or it is the work of the "Father of lights who suffers himself that he may bring his many sons into the glory."[70] This is MacDonald's major response to the problem of evil, not just a soul-making theodicy but a cosmos-making theodicy, in which even suffering is meant to birth an ever-growing glory in individual souls and in the larger universe.[71] In the meantime,

> It comes to this, that the suffering you see around you, hurts God more than it hurts you, or the man upon whom it falls; but he hates things that most men think little of, and will send any suffering upon them rather than have them continue indifferent to them. Men may say, "We don't want suffering! we don't want to be good!" but God says, "I know my own obligations! and you shall not be contemptible wretches, if there be any resource in the Godhead."[72]

To such a framing of things, Faber responds: "Your theory has but one fault: it is too good to be true." Wingfold laughs and argues by contrast: "The only possibility of believing in a God seems to me to lie in finding an idea of a God large enough, grand enough, pure enough, lovely enough to be fit to believe in."[73] The prior issue is not whether one can prove that there is a God but whether one can find a God worthy of belief, which is to say that the crisis is imaginative before it is intellectual. It is a matter of love before it is a matter of knowledge.

And yet, Faber's longing for goodness—to be and to do good—is an indication for MacDonald that Faber is already unwittingly moving in the right direction. MacDonald writes,

> It is better to be an atheist who does the will of God, than a so-called Christian who does not. . . . The thing that God loves is the only lovely thing, and he who does it, does well, and is upon the way to discover that he does it very badly. When he comes to do it as the will of the perfect Good, then is he on the road to do it perfectly—that is, from love of its

---

[70]MacDonald, *Thomas Wingfold, Curate*, 88.

[71]"Say then, that he might be both strong and good, and have some reason for allowing, or even causing it, which those who suffer will themselves one day justify, ready for the sake of it to go through all the suffering again." MacDonald, *There and Back*, 229.

[72]MacDonald, *There and Back*, 230.

[73]MacDonald, *Thomas Wingfold, Curate*, 369.

own inherent self-constituted goodness, born in the heart of the Perfect. The doing of things from duty is but a stage on the road to the kingdom of truth and love. Not the less must the stage be journeyed; every path diverging from it is "the flowery way that leads to the broad gate and the great fire."[74]

Faber's goodness is far from sufficient; he must be shown just how deficient it is. But MacDonald believes that the hunger for goodness, when met with the will to do what is right, is the path that God paves to his presence: "It is by acting upon what he sees and knows, hearkening to every whisper, obeying every hint of the good, following whatever seems light, that the man will at length arrive."[75] Indeed, for MacDonald, every such provocation to act is sourced not in the human ingenuity but in the work of the Holy Spirit.

Faber, for his part, does *not* arrive at faith by the end of the story. Yet we are told that his heart is open and growing, "and that is all we can require of any man."[76] In any case he finds that he is beginning to entertain thoughts heretofore foreign to his mind, finding himself "actually wondering whether the story of the resurrection *could* be true."[77] The impulse to believe the unspeakably beautiful, as the impulse to be unreservedly good, is for MacDonald to be on the very doorstep of truth. Both represent the presence of God-wrought virtue, which prepares the way for revelatory vision. This is displayed most powerfully in the final book of the *Wingfold* trilogy, *There and Back*. In the love story of Richard Tuke and Barbara Wylder, we see MacDonald's most direct engagement with his friend Ruskin's doubts.

Beauty: *The unbelieving aesthete* (There and Back). In Richard we see shades of Bascombe's intellectual and Faber's moral doubts. But the primary site of Richard's struggle with reality is in the aesthetic realm, where he—like Dante—is led by his love for a woman into love for God. Indeed, Dante's *Commedia* receives multiple citations throughout the

---

[74]MacDonald, *Paul Faber, Surgeon*, 24.
[75]MacDonald, *There and Back*, 264.
[76]MacDonald, *Paul Faber, Surgeon*, 396.
[77]MacDonald, *Paul Faber, Surgeon*, 393.

story, and its publication date (1891) corresponds to latter years of MacDonald's life, which were steeped in a fascination with Dante.[78] Thus it is no surprise that the protagonist is guided to faith through engagement with the Beatrician character of Barbara. In this story MacDonald's response to the aesthetic crisis is to show the way that beauty—and the love of the beautiful—enlarges the soul, making space for revelatory encounter.

Richard has been raised by a religious aunt and an agnostic uncle; although his uncle agrees not to steer Richard away from a faith, "subtle effluences are subtle influences."[79] Richard finds himself neither believing in God nor seeing any beauty in the idea. On the contrary, to him religion "was an evil phantom, with a terrible power to blight; [it was] a miasm that had steamed up from the foul marshes of the world, before man was at home in it."[80] Where Richard does find beauty is in books; as a bookbinder Richard is enamored both with the bodies of the books as well as their souls. Yet his maturity has begun to lead him astray; his imagination has begun to give way to a purely intellectual admiration, "for he had begun to think truth attainable through the forces of the brain, sole and supreme."[81] The character of Richard recalls other bookish characters throughout MacDonald's writings, especially Anodos in *Phantastes* and Mr. Vane in *Lilith*, who are taught that their fascination with books must prepare the way for sacrificial love in the primary world.[82] Richard's bookishness parallels Faber's benevolence. It is an opening for revelation,

---

[78] After years of residence in Italy (where he spent much of the latter part of his life for his health), MacDonald began lecturing on Dante in 1889. *There and Back* was published two years later; even the title has Dantean suggestiveness. By the time of publication, which corresponds to the writing of *Lilith*, Dante's influence had worked its way, as Spina puts it, "into the very marrow of MacDonald's narrative." Girogio Spina, "The Influence of Dante on George MacDonald," trans. Paul Priest, *North Wind* 9 (1990): 25-26.

[79] MacDonald, *There and Back*, 29.

[80] MacDonald, *There and Back*, 42.

[81] MacDonald, *There and Back*, 28.

[82] As MacDonald writes in *Lilith*, "A book is a door in, and therefore a door out." MacDonald, *Lilith*, 58. Johnson explains Mr. Raven's statement: "In *Phantastes* there had been an explicit emphasis on learning vicariously through Story, now [in *Lilith*] MacDonald ensures that the reader does not mistake Story—still of grave importance—as more important than the acting out of what is learned from stories in one's relationship with actual people." Johnson, "Rooted in All Its Story," 223.

but apart from a disorienting relational encounter, Richard's books will limit his horizon rather than liberate it. Nevertheless, the important site of Richard's spiritual awakening is a library, which he has been commissioned to repair at the baron's estate.

Upon meeting Barbara, he is instantly entranced, though his belief that he is below her station prevents the immediate effusion of love. Barbara is described with Beatrician suggestiveness: "He soon discovered that, not her beauty, but her heavenly vivacity, was the more captivating thing about her. At once her very soul seemed to go out to meet whatever object claimed her attention. She must know all about everything, and come into relations with every live thing! . . . So small and so bright, the little lady looked a very diamond of life."[83]

Barbara, the heiress of a neighboring estate, is a character of common creativity; she thinks "like a poet, but had never read a real poem."[84] Richard offers to share with Barbara his love of books and poetry, but Barbara's effect on Richard is far more profound, and he falls hopelessly in love with her.[85]

Barbara's faith is awakened earlier than Richard's; despite her irreligious upbringing, she is beset by a haunting sense of *Sehnsucht*. Indeed, it is on discussing Coleridge's *Rime of the Ancient Mariner* with Richard that her faith begins to bud. Richard opines that the mariner is freed from his curse by his love of beauty: beauty for beauty's sake. But on hearing the end of the poem, "He prayeth best that loveth best all thing both great and small, For the dear God who loveth us, He made and loveth all," Barbara exclaims, "That's it! The love of everything is the garden-bed out of which grow the roses of prayer!—But what am I saying! . . . I love everything, at least everything that comes near me, and I never pray!" Richard responds that prayer is pointless and that we simply are meant to love living things. But Barbara reasons that our sense that life is to be loved betrays a conviction that it is a gift, and therefore we should look for a giver. The

---

[83]MacDonald, *There and Back*, 45.
[84]MacDonald, *There and Back*, 77.
[85]The "fairy tale" element in the story, which results in the eucatastrophic ending, is that Richard is actually the lost heir to the baron's estate.

loveliness of the world is enough to cause us to imagine a generous and supremely lovable God:

> "Just fancy!" she said, "—if God were all the time at our backs, giving us one lovely thing after another, trying to make us look round and see who it was that was so good to us! Imagine him standing there, and wondering when his little one would look round, and see him, and burst out laughing—no, not laughing—yes, laughing—laughing with delight—or crying, I don't know which! If I had him to love as I should love one like that, I think I should break my heart with loving him—I should love him to the killing of me! What! all the colours and all the shapes, and all the lights, and all the shadows, and the moon, and the wind, and the water!—and all the creatures—and the people that one would love so if they would let you![86]

Materialism suffers from a profound inability to account for beauty, and Richard's conviction of meaningless beauty also entails meaningless barbarity. Not only is there no one to thank for the joys of life, but there is no one to whom we can turn in the midst of suffering. While suffering leads Richard to reject the cruel god of popular consciousness, it leads Barbara to search for a better and more beautiful God. Under Wingfold's care, Barbara finds faith.

In Dantean fashion, Barbara gazes at heaven, and Richard gazes at Barbara. He shares with her a love of beauty, but the reality of suffering leads him to doubt the presence of any ultimate Artist: "He's well enough for the wind and the stars and the moonlight! but for human beings . . . for creatures dying of hunger, what a mockery! If he were there, it would be a sickness to talk of him! Beauty is beauty, but for anything behind it—pooh!"[87] Nevertheless, after spending time with Barbara, he finds that the world feels bigger, and that Nature seems "more alive than she ever had been." As Richard looks at the world alongside Barbara, her apprehension of the world seeps into his own. Soon it seems "that the idea of a God worth believing in, was coming a little nearer to him, was becoming to him a little more thinkable."[88] Again, the first movement of

---

[86]MacDonald, *There and Back*, 137.
[87]MacDonald, *There and Back*, 155
[88]MacDonald, *There and Back*, 140.

MacDonald's imaginative apologetic is to find a God *worthy* of belief, one whose presence accounts not just for truth and goodness but also for beauty.

Wingfold knows that Richard does not believe in God, but he does not confront his unbelief head-on. Wingfold is confident that Richard is on the right track and that his burgeoning love of Barbara is auspicious for his awakening, for "next to the worship of God, the true worship of a fellow-creature, in the old meaning of the word, is the most potent thing for deliverance."[89] The heart of virtue is a love that centers not on the self but on the well-being of the beloved. In loving this way humans are most like God, harmonizing their souls with reality. MacDonald rejects the idea that "the higher love demands suppression of the lower," calling it "the most fearful of all discords . . . the house divided against itself."[90] Rather, lower loves, as they become rightly ordered, will lead us into the higher ones, closer to the heart of God.

The description of Richard's expansive apprehension of the world parallels the way that MacDonald describes his own conversion in an 1847 letter to his father:

> One of my greatest difficulties in consenting to think of religion was that I thought I should have to give up my beautiful thoughts and my love for the things God has made. But I find that the happiness springing from all things not in themselves sinful is much increased by religion. God is the God of the Beautiful—Religion is the love of the Beautiful, and Heaven is the Home of the Beautiful—Nature is tenfold brighter in the Sun of Righteousness, and my love of Nature is more intense since I became a Christian—if indeed I am one.[91]

For MacDonald as for almost all of his characters, it is the beauty of the gospel that leads him into its truth rather than the other way around, and

---

[89]Here MacDonald may be referencing the old English marriage liturgy from the 1559 Book of Common Prayer: "with my body I thee worship," which signifies wholehearted devotion to the other.

[90]George MacDonald, *Robert Falconer* (Whitethorn, CA: Johannesen, 1995), 91. Timothy Larsen terms this approach to earthly desires the "Romantic Road" to salvation. See Timothy Larsen, *George MacDonald in the Age of Miracles* (Downers Grove, IL: IVP Academic), 62-65.

[91]MacDonald, *George MacDonald and His Wife*, 108.

MacDonald is convinced that the love of anything that is beautiful can draw us centripetally toward its source.

It is Richard's love for Barbara, and his desire to see her again (and he believes the only possibility of this will be after death), that keeps the door of his soul open in a way that books and poetry could not: "Everything beautiful turned his face to the more beautiful, more precious, diviner Barbara. With each new sense of loveliness, she floated up from where she lay, ever ready to rise, in the ocean of his heart." Knowing that Barbara is in the world makes it more beautiful to him. Richard considers that there are others who have no Barbara to make things lovely and yet find that the loveliness of things suggests some other maker: "If man and Nature came both out of nothing, why should they not be nothing to each other?"[92] Why does humanity find beauty so full of meaning, as if blessed by an unseen presence?

All of these musings move Richard closer to faith; he even begins to offer desperate prayers that God might exist. With a more attentive soul, he begins regularly attending the concert hall at St. James: "It was his church, the mount of his ascension, the place whence he soared—no, but was lifted up to what was as yet his highest consciousness of being."[93] One night as he listens to the music, he is startled to find Barbara (whom he never expected to see again in this life) present in the hall. The experience is revelatory, as the beauty of the music and the beauty of Barbara become one intermingled, synesthetic gift: "Barbara was the music, and the music was Barbara. He saw her with his ears; he heard her with his eyes."[94] In this Dantean moment, "Hell became purgatory, for there was hope in it."[95]

Lovesick over Barbara, and feverish from anxiety for suffering loved ones, Richard has a near mental breakdown. And it is in the recognition of his inability to make life work on his own that he is able faintly to entrust himself to God. Perhaps God could take "all the endeavours of all his children, in all their contrarieties, and out of them bring the

---

[92]MacDonald, *There and Back*, 260.
[93]MacDonald, *There and Back*, 278.
[94]MacDonald, *There and Back*, 280.
[95]MacDonald, *There and Back*, 390.

right thing. . . . If there were such a splendour, he would either make him well, and send him out again to do . . . what he could, or he would let him die and go where all he loved would come after him—where he might perhaps help to prepare a place for them!"[96]

Richard's hope is the faintest spark of faith, but, as MacDonald writes, "One better thought concerning [God], the poorest desire to draw near him, is an approach to him."[97] As Richard recovers, he is able dimly to profess faith to his aunt: "I think I do—a little—in a sort of a way—believe in God—but I hope to believe in him ten thousand times more!"[98] Richard is led by beauty into truth; MacDonald suggests that love for God is found by deepening rather than displacing human desire. It is precisely on this line that MacDonald is engaging Ruskin's deepest doubts and desires.

Responding to Ruskin: Too good to be true? Richard's doubts are the most Ruskin-like of the Wingfold trilogy. As Ruskin with MacDonald, Richard tolerates Barbara's God-talk about God because the God she believes in is so lovable, like herself. But we can hear shades of Ruskin's objection: "I feel so strongly that it is only the image of your own mind that you see in the sky!" For Ruskin, MacDonald's God was beautiful but too good to be true. And so MacDonald responds in Wingfold's speech:

> Why should he be able to think anything too good to be true? Why should a thing not be true because it was good? It seems to me, if a thing be bad, it cannot possibly be true. If you say the thing is, I answer it exists because of something under the badness. Badness by itself can have no life in it. But if the man really thought as you suggest, I would say to him, "You cannot know such a being does not exist: is it possible you should be content that such a being should not exist? If such a being did exist, would you be content never to find him, but to go on for ever and ever saying, *He can't be! He can't be! He's so good he can't be!* Supposing you find one day that there he is, will your defense before him be satisfactory to yourself: 'There

[96]MacDonald, *There and Back*, 294.
[97]MacDonald, *There and Back*, 295.
[98]MacDonald, *There and Back*, 297.

he is after all, but he was too good to believe in, therefore I did not try to find him'? Will you say to him—'*If you had not been so good, if you had been a little less good, a little worse, just a trifle bad, I could and would have believed in you?*'[99]

MacDonald's point is that until God has been definitively disproved, it is reasonable to go on searching for as beautiful a God as possible. The very beauty of the idea suggests a near relation to truth, which should lead to openness and hope rather than slamming the door in despair.

Moreover, to love anyone deeply, as Ruskin loved Rose, is to awaken to the hope of eternity, the desire of never being parted from them. As Richard's half-sister remarks, "He thinks there's no life after this one! He can't have loved anybody much, I fear, to be able to think that!"[100] It will not be until Richard is sent away from the estate, prevented from seeing Barbara, that he begins to think that his only hope of seeing her again is if there is indeed "life after this one." The desire to never be parted from those we love is no proof of immortality and may be written off as wishful thinking, but MacDonald wants us to consider the source of the wish.

The question of the source of human desire appears often in MacDonald's work. In the final chapter of *Lilith*, Mr. Vane wonders whether he is really awake or still in a dream, and if the Dantean vision of harmony and beauty he has seen is too good to be true. In his internal struggle he invokes the language of his earlier essay on the imagination regarding the source of his dreams:

In moments of doubt I cry,

"Could God Himself create such lovely things as I dreamed?"

"Whence then came thy dream?" answers Hope.

"Out of my dark self, into the light of my consciousness."

"But whence first into thy dark self?" rejoins Hope.

"My brain was its mother, and the fever in my blood its father."

---

[99]MacDonald, *There and Back*, 196-97.
[100]MacDonald, *There and Back*, 182.

"Say rather," suggests Hope, "thy brain was the violin whence it issued, and the fever in thy blood the bow that drew it forth. But who made the violin? And who guided the bow across its strings? . . . Whence came the fantasia? And whence the life that danced thereto? Didst thou say, in the dark of thy own unconscious self, "Let beauty be; let truth seem!" and straightway beauty was and truth but seemed?"

Here MacDonald shows a Victorian concern to keep the imagination connected to the empirical body (the brain and the blood) but not to regard them as its ultimate source. MacDonald is convinced that the true imagination, which enables good dreams and draws out the desire, moves in response to divine initiative. As he goes on to write, "When a man dreams his own dream, he is the sport of his dream; when Another gives it him, that Other is able to fulfill it."[101]

Bascombe speaks for the skeptic, disdaining the idea that the longing of some for immortality is a "proof that immortality is their rightful inheritance." Immortality is not a universal desire, for he himself does not feel it. Thus, hope serves merely to bring artificial warmth to cold reality. But Helen muses that to take such a position is to deny hope simply because it brings comfort: "What if the warm hope denied should be the truth after all? What if it was the truth in it that drew the soul towards it by its indwelling reality?"[102] In other words, the generativity of the hope, the vitality it fosters, suggests its near relation to truth. Hope that the beautiful God exists and is engaged in the healing of creation is generative. Indeed, hope seems to forge the most beautiful thing in all of creation: saints.

But there is for MacDonald a deeper ground of hope than its generativity. When Wingfold tells Faber that he is searching for "an idea of a God large enough, grand enough, pure enough, lovely enough to be fit to believe in," Faber asks him if he has found one. Wingfold replies, "I think I am finding such." "Where?" "In the man of the New Testament."[103] So too when Richard is pressed by his agnostic father to explain his newfound

[101]MacDonald, Lilith, 357–58.
[102]MacDonald, Thomas Wingfold, Curate, 162-63.
[103]MacDonald, Thomas Wingfold, Curate, 369.

faith, he says, "Father, do you know Jesus Christ! . . . he said God was just like him, and in the God like him, if I can find him, I will believe with all my heart and soul—and so would you, father, if you knew him."[104] This is the substance of the Christian argument: not a proof, but a person. So Wingfold preaches to his congregation in the midst of his struggle with doubt:

> If . . . we could prove there is a God, it would be of small avail indeed: we must see him and know him, to know that he was not a demon. But I know no other way of knowing that there is a God but that which reveals WHAT he is—the only idea that could be God—shows him in his own self-proving existence—and that way is Jesus Christ as he revealed himself on earth, and as he is revealed afresh to every heart that seeks to know the truth concerning him."[105]

This is the final foundation of MacDonald's faith, the captivating vision that dissolved all false imagining of God. Throughout the Wingfold series, the hunger for beauty, goodness, and truth finds its most concrete ground in the incarnate Christ, whose truth is not meant first to be debated but beheld.[106]

"WAKE THEM UP": SUMMARIZING MACDONALD'S APOLOGETIC APPROACH

We are now in a position to offer a summary of MacDonald's apologetic approach. MacDonald's primary method for engaging doubt is not to supply facts for the intellect but food for the imagination. He seeks to show that an approach to life that insists on "nothing but the facts" limits the horizon of possibility and shuts down the generativity of hope and desire. In his essay titled "The Fantastic Imagination," MacDonald writes, "The best thing you can do for your fellow, next to rousing his conscience, is not to give him things to think about, but to wake things up that are in him; or say, to make him think things for himself."[107] So we might call

---

[104]MacDonald, *There and Back*, 328.
[105]MacDonald, *Thomas Wingfold, Curate*, 88.
[106]MacDonald, *Dish of Orts*, 205.
[107]MacDonald, *Dish of Orts*, 319.

MacDonald's apologetic method "waking things up," opening the imagination to formerly unexamined possibilities.

Indeed, MacDonald's description of the pastoral office through the asthmatic dwarf Polwarth could be taken as a précis for MacDonald's apologetic strategy: "to wake them up lest their sleep turn to death; next, to make them hungry, and lastly, to supply that hunger."[108] This is resonant with the counsel that Wingfold gives to Barbara in *There and Back:*

> Talk to Richard of the God you love, the beautiful, the strong, the true, the patient, the forgiving, the loving; the one childlike, eternal power and Godhead, who would die himself and kill you rather than have you false and mean and selfish. . . . Make his thoughts dwell on such a God as he must feel would be worth having. Wake the notion of a God such as will draw him to wish there were such a God. . . . Set in Richard's eye a God worth believing in, a God like the son of God, and he will go and look if haply such a God may be found.[109]

In these quotations we find the basic shape of MacDonald's strategy. He begins with the assumption that the things we love have a source beyond themselves, that our deepest longings are not lies. Next, he wakes the imagination to consider what kind of a God would be worth having, worth believing in. Next, he aims to fill the heart with hope that such a God actually exists. For MacDonald, the beauty of a thing—including one's idea of God—suggests a near relation to its truth: a beauty that generates goodness must be closely connected to truth. This leads MacDonald to question the common phrase "too good to be true." Indeed, truth can only be found by those who acknowledge their own limitations in humble wonder. It can never be found by those who in certitude shut down the search. He makes space for honest (as opposed to unexamined) doubt, confident that authentic self-examination will further open the imagination to truth. Next, he shows how imaginative inquiry must always be grounded by the duties of creative love. Those who obey God in loving

---

[108]MacDonald, *Thomas Wingfold, Curate*, 73.
[109]MacDonald, *There and Back*, 226-27.

their neighbor (even if they do not consider their duty to be directed toward God) have already placed themselves "on God's creative lines" and cannot help, in some sense, to engage with God.[110] Virtue and vision are connected: waking the imagination will wake the conscience, and waking the conscience will wake the imagination. Finally, the substance of MacDonald's imaginative appeal is to direct the doubter not to proofs but to the person of Jesus Christ. The ground of Christian hope is not the creative imagination but the concrete person and work of Jesus Christ. Jesus fulfills the human desire for a beautiful God, reshaping our image of God to resemble the face of Jesus.

We get a glimpse of MacDonald at his best in the letter he wrote to Ruskin after Rose's death in 1875. Ruskin was disconsolate with grief, and I will quote MacDonald's letter in full, since it embodies the pastoral tenderness, undaunted hope, and imaginative apologetic that MacDonald exemplified:

> My very dear Ruskin,
>
> I want just to speak a word in your ear. I do not know what it shall be. I only want you to know it is my voice. Do not turn your head to look at me, or stop what you are doing to think a moment about me. Go on. But the Psyche is aloft, and her wings are broad and white, and the world of flowers is under her, and the sea of sunny air is around her, and the empty chrysalis—what of that?
>
> Now we are all but Psyches half awake, who see the universe in great measure only by reflection from the dull coffin-lid over us. But I hope, I hope. I hope infinitely. And ever the longer I live and try to live, and think, and long to live perfectly, I see the scheme of things grow more orderly and more intelligible, and am more and more convinced that all is on the way to be well with wellness to which there was no other road than just this whereon we are walking.
>
> Let us then call a word now and then through the darkness as we go. There is a great sunrise behind the hill. But that hill Death alone can

---

[110] As one of MacDonald's characters finds, "The world might be divided into those who let things go, and those who do not . . . those who are always doing something on God's creative lines, and those that are always grumbling and striving against them." George MacDonald, *Home Again and The Elect Lady* (Whitethorn, CA: Johannesen, 1993), 23-24.

carry us over. I look to God to satisfy us all. It cannot be but that he will satisfy you to your hearts content. You have fought a better fight, I think, than you yourself know, and his gentleness will make you great in the kingdom of love. For Rose, is there anything fitting but gladness? The growing weight is gone; the gravestone heaved from off her; the fight with that which is as and yet was not herself is over. It may be she haunts you now with ministrations. Anyhow the living God does. Richter says it is only in God that two souls can meet. I am sure it is true. My wife's heart is with you in your loss. She sends her love. If we could do anything for you!

Your friend ever

George MacDonald[111]

Fueled in part by the hope of seeing Rose again, Ruskin returned to Christian faith later that year. His faith remained tentative, more a fragile hope than a firm confidence, but preferable to the malnourishment of materialism.[112]

MacDonald responded to the Victorian crisis of faith by forging an apologetic approach in which the primary goal is to wake the imagination, and in which virtue opens the way for vision, leading to a generative Christian faith. In chapter six I will return to the theological ground of MacDonald's approach. But first I want to turn to a second model for reimagining apologetics from a contemporary writer. For although the

---

[111]George MacDonald, *An Expression of Character: The Letters of George MacDonald*, ed. Glenn Edward Sadler (Grand Rapids: Eerdmans, 1994), 243. Johnson notes that both MacDonald and Ruskin loved the multivalent imagery of the Greek word *psyche*, which meant butterfly as well as soul, and that the transformation of the mythical figure Psyche was one of MacDonald's and Ruskin's favorite images. For a masterful exposition of the letter in the context of their relationship see Johnson, "Rooted in All Its Story," 152-55, 199-203.

[112]From a letter to Charles Norton in March 1876: "I have no *new* faith, but am able to get some good out of my old one, not as being true, but as containing the quantity of truth that is wholesome for me. One must eat one's faith like one's meat, for what's good in it. But modern philosophy for the most part contents itself in the excremental function and rejoices in that: absolutely incapable of nourishment." John Ruskin and Charles Eliot Norton, *The Correspondence of John Ruskin and Charles Eliot Norton*, ed. John Lewis Bradley and Ian Ousby (Cambridge: Cambridge University Press, 1987), 380. Ruskin's doubts and desires will be discussed in further detail below. For a more comprehensive survey of Ruskin's faith, see George P. Landow, *Aesthetic and Critical Theory of John Ruskin* (Princeton: Princeton University Press, 1971), 243-317.

nineteenth century was decidedly postromantic, the age of authenticity was just beginning to dawn. The masters of suspicion had not yet sown widespread doubt about the reliability of human consciousness itself. Thus, it will be fruitful to examine the work of the American novelist Marilynne Robinson.

– five –

Revealing a Wider World

Marilynne Robinson's Reimagined Apologetic

I do not intend this as a defense of religion. I do not share
the common assumption that religion is always in need of defending.

MARILYNNE ROBINSON, *THE DEATH OF ADAM*

IN A 2014 COLUMN FOR THE *SUNDAY TIMES*, British journalist
Bryan Appleyard wrote glowingly about the novels of Marilynne Robinson. Robinson's novels, he writes, seem to "some British readers wildly
exotic, because what is going on here is religion. . . . Many, probably most
British people—artists, writers, audiences—will find this exotic because
to them, religion has been embarrassed out of existence."[1] And yet,
Appleyard notes, Robinson's artistry compels readers to take religion seriously. What readers are encountering is what Robinson has called the
"ravishment of revelatory perception." Her writing is an invitation to meet
"the Calvinist soul . . . full of Calvinist wonder."[2]

---

[1]Bryan Appleyard, "He Is Risen," *The Sunday Times*, November 2, 2014, www.thetimes.co.uk
/article/he-is-risen-2t9hsgl7gv9.
[2]Marilynne Robinson, *John Calvin: Steward of God's Covenant: Selected Writings*, ed. John F. Thornton (New York: Vintage, 2006), xxvi-xxvii. For an excellent collection of essays reflecting on

What might it mean to commend the Christian faith in secular settings like the one Appleyard describes, among those for whom religion has been "embarrassed out of existence"? Robinson shows us a possible way forward. And yet, like MacDonald, Marilynne Robinson may seem an unlikely candidate for the title of apologist. At best, she regularly expresses ambivalence toward faith's defenders throughout her writing. Nevertheless, few public intellectuals have responded so vociferously to the "new atheists."[3] Robinson's favorite foil seems to be the social Darwinist or Freudian who wants to dismiss religious experience. Yet even as she contests their arguments, she makes it clear that her aim is not to provide a positive defense of religion in general, or Christianity in particular. This is because for Robinson, religious experience—which she takes as the beating heart of religion—is simply a given of existence. To rule it out because it cannot be standardized, or to feel the need to defend it with proofs, is to cede the game to positivism, as if the revelatory riches of human culture and history could somehow be ignored. Using traditional distinctions, we might say that Robinson engages in negative apologetics (demonstrating epistemic permission) while eschewing positive apologetics (demonstrating epistemic obligation).

The burden of this chapter, however, is to argue that Robinson's fiction inhabits the imaginative space between permission and obligation. It allows her readers to get a sense of what it feels like to live within the Christian imaginary. If MacDonald's aim is to awaken his readers with goodness, Robinson plunges her readers into a vicarious vision. She ravishes with revelatory perception. Her writing invites

---

Robinson's work through a theological lens, see Timothy Larsen and Keith L. Johnson, eds., *Balm in Gilead: A Theological Dialogue with Marilynne Robinson* (Downers Grove, IL: IVP Academic, 2019).

[3]The "new atheists" are a contingent of contemporary thinkers distinguished both by the caustic tone with which they dismiss religion, and the bestselling books in which they do so. Four of the most well-known works are Christopher Hitchens, *God Is Not Great: How Religion Poisons Everything* (New York: Twelve, 2009); Daniel C. Dennett, *Breaking the Spell: Religion as a Natural Phenomenon* (New York: Penguin Books, 2007); Sam Harris, *The End of Faith: Religion, Terror, and the Future of Reason* (New York: W. W. Norton, 2005); Richard Dawkins, *The God Delusion* (Boston: Mariner, 2008). Robinson interacts with Dennett throughout her essays and has published reviews of Harris and Dawkins. See for example Marilynne Robinson, "Hysterical Scientism—the Ecstasy of Richard Dawkins," *Harper's Magazine*, November 2006; Marilynne Robinson, "What Unitarians Know (and Sam Harris Doesn't)," *Wall Street Journal—Eastern Edition* 256, no. 79, October 2, 2010, C5.

outsiders to see the world through the shocked eyes of wonder, even as it invites insiders to a posture of generous love. Only such a posture enables the possibility of understanding. To both, she commends imaginative hospitality, the skill of making room for the other by providing a generative imaginative space.

DEFENDING THE RELIGIOUS IMAGINATION

Against parascience and paratheology. Though primarily known as a novelist, Robinson has published more pages of social criticism than fiction. Her essays are self-consciously "contrarian in method and spirit," asserting that the prevailing view of things, as well as its opposite, are both mistaken, and that "there are other ways of thinking, for which better arguments can be made."[4] This contrarian spirit can be seen clearly in Robinson's vocal rejection of what she calls *parascience.*[5] Parascience teaches us to distrust the reliability of our minds on the most fundamental questions of human existence. It tells us that our noblest impulses are little more than masks for unconscious urges (to procreate, to dominate, etc.). The triumph of parascience, she writes, has had disastrous ethical and cultural consequences, cutting us off from the harvest of human imagination, inwardness, and culture making. Centuries of rich reflection on human nature and ethics—grounded on the conviction of human dignity—have been eclipsed by "tooth and claw" economic calculation: everything now can be explained in terms of self-interest and competition.[6]

---

[4]Marilynne Robinson, *The Death of Adam: Essays on Modern Thought* (New York: Picador, 2005), 1.
[5]This defense takes place most incisively in *Absence of Mind*, an adaptation of her Terry lectures at Yale University. Marilynne Robinson, *Absence of Mind: The Dispelling of Inwardness from the Modern Myth of the Self* (New Haven: Yale University Press, 2011). In a later essay, she makes it clear that her defense of mind against materialistic reductions might also be understood as a defense of the human soul. She writes: "We have no current language for the culture of the mind, which another generation might have called the care of the soul." Marilynne Robinson, *What Are We Doing Here?: Essays* (New York: Farrar, Straus and Giroux, 2018), 208.
[6]Robinson affirms the compatibility of science and Christianity; indeed, one of Robinson's favorite topics is the way that quantum theory is compatible with Christian metaphysics. What she rejects is scientism: Darwinism as a grand narrative, significant for its Promethean achievement in unmasking religion as an illusion. Distinct from the theory of evolution, Darwinism purports to "refute religion and to imply a personal and social ethic which is, not coincidentally, antithetical to the assumptions imposed and authorized by Judaeo-Christianity." Robinson, *Death of Adam*, 30-31.

Parascience seeks to colonize the mystery of reality, teaching humanity to speak a single tongue: positivism. In this way of seeing, only that which is scientifically verifiable may be admitted as real. Since we are aware that we have been "optimized by competition and environment" (Darwin), "shaped by economic forces and means of production" (Marx), "inheritors of primal guilt" (Freud), and "molded by experiences of frustration and reinforcement" (Skinner), we may reduce the rich complexity of human experience to the sum of its parts.

Though these models disagree with one another, they are united in distrusting our ability to reliably access the world. Works of human imagination can be explained away with the hermeneutics of suspicion. Regardless of what an artist might think about her own motivation, Robinson writes, the modern thinker knows that it is really all about "attracting mates," or a "sublimation of forbidden impulses." Indeed, "the first thing to know about art . . . is that its maker is self-deceived." Robinson grants that each of the modern models of mind may be on to something; nevertheless, "To acknowledge an element of truth in each of these models is to reject the claims of descriptive sufficiency made by all of them."[7] Such overreaching claims result in thin descriptions. Here one slice of reality is taken for the whole, and the testimony, not just of religion but also of culture and history, is excluded. The core assumption, which Robinson seeks to combat, is "that the experience and testimony of the individual mind is to be explained away. . . . In its place we have the grand projects of generalization, solemn attempts to tell our species what we are and what we are not."[8]

For example: the primary critique she levels against new atheist writer Daniel Dennett is that he has defined religion primarily as a social system held together by "belief in supernatural agents," which Dennett then sets out to disprove. But Robinson argues that collective expressions of religion cannot be separated from religious subjectivity, the way each of us

---

[7]Robinson, *Absence of Mind*, xvi-xvii.

[8]Robinson, *Absence of Mind*, 22. Alexander Engebretson puts it well: "She does not want to do away with science so much as humble it." Alexander John Engebretson, "'The Dear Ordinary': The Novels of Marilynne Robinson" (PhD diss., City University of New York, 2013), 27.

experiences the world. Religion cannot be understood simply from detached observation, she writes, "without reference to the deeply pensive solitudes that bring individuals into congregations and communities to be nurtured by the thought they find there."[9] In other words, religious faith is less about extracted beliefs in supernatural agents and more about an imaginative vision, a tradition of perceiving the world. These traditions not only discern God's presence in the world but also wrestle with God's absence.[10] Robinson puts this argument in more ordinary language in *Gilead*:

> But if the awkwardness and falseness and failure of religion are interpreted to mean there is no core of truth in it—and the witness of Scripture from end to end discourages this view—then people are disabled from trusting their thoughts, their expressions of belief, and their understanding, and even from believing in the essential dignity of their and their neighbors' endlessly flawed experience of belief.[11]

While granting human fallibility, Robinson's burden is to defend the general reliability of the individual human experience, as well as the collective perceptual experience of the world embodied in culture, which seems to be inescapably religious as well.

While leveling her attack at parascience, Robinson also takes issue with its mirror image, what we might call paratheology. Paratheology gives in to parascience by attempting to play its game. It seeks to legitimize the Christian faith by advancing undeniable proofs for religion's truth. She writes, "People have always tested these claims of ultimate truth against their own models of reality. Nothing is proved by the fact that these two things never align, except when religion is wrenched into conformity with human understanding and effectively ceases to be religion."[12] Robinson finds paratheology as potentially meaningless as the parascience it claims to defeat. Apologetic defense, she argues, is prone to a category error—an attempt to place God within our conceptual

---

[9]Robinson, *Absence of Mind*, 9.
[10]Robinson, *Absence of Mind*, 15.
[11]Marilynne Robinson, *Gilead* (New York: Picador, 2006), 146.
[12]Robinson, *What Are We Doing Here?*, 210.

grasp—as if we could build a ladder to the moon.[13] In *Gilead*, she has John Ames tell his young son, "In the matter of belief, I have always found that defenses have the same irrelevance about them as the criticisms they are meant to answer." He goes on: "So my advice is this—don't look for proofs. Don't bother with them at all. They are never sufficient to the question. . . . And they will likely sound wrong to you even if you convince someone else with them."[14]

It is not that Robinson thinks that theistic arguments (such as those of Anselm or Aquinas) are without value. Anselm's ontological argument, after all, was framed in the form of a prayer. Rather, her sensitivity is to the posture in which theistic proofs are pursued. If God is God, she reasons, then we can neither validate nor invalidate him by our intellectual ingenuity. So Robinson has little patience for "justifying faith in terms that might seem reasonable to skeptics."[15] She writes,

> But the point to be stressed is that religious people—by definition, I would say—do not look for proof of the existence of God, or understand God in a way that makes his existence liable to proof or disproof. . . . That attempts at proofs of God's existence have been made from time to time, under the influence of Aristotle, or of early science, does not mean that religious belief has sought or depended on that kind of affirmation, as any reader of theology is well aware. Faith is called faith for a reason.[16]

Religious proofs, she argues, tend to confirm believers in their belief even as they confirm skeptics in their skepticism.[17] Faith cannot be grounded on defensive proof, she believes. This is because faith is not just willful assent in light of evidence but also responsive trust to the wonder of the world and its Creator.

---

[13]This is reminiscent of Barth's rejection of apologetics, and though Robinson does not cite him directly, she often expresses her admiration, writing to Hesselink that she has read a "large sliver of *Church Dogmatics.*" John Hesselink and Marilynne Robinson, "Hesselink and Robinson: An Exchange of Letters," *Perspectives*, March 1, 2001, 12.

[14]Robinson, *Gilead*, 178.

[15]Marilynne Robinson, *Givenness of Things: Essays* (New York: Farrar, Straus and Giroux, 2015), 155.

[16]Robinson, *Death of Adam*, 39.

[17]She writes: "I do not propose to argue for the truth of religion by storming the heavens, by arguing from design or offering ontological proofs. These things are meaningful only to those who are predisposed to find them meaningful." Robinson, *What Are We Doing Here?*, 215.

It is for this reason that Robinson tends to see contemporary apologetics (apologetics that seeks to ground God's existence in evidential proof) as a betrayal of its subject matter. In her estimation, both sides subscribe to the positivist assumption that proof is required for belief. This fuels an unceasing ideological battle that is intransigent because it misses the very heart of faith. Robinson also notes the irony that despite their apparent disagreement, both sides align to co-sign a social and political economy that gives blessing to the forces of competition that displace the weak.[18]

I should note at this point that although I agree with Robinson's basic conviction (about the significance of experience), I am less pessimistic about the value of traditional apologetic defenses. As I wrote in the introduction, contemporary apologetics does not need to cease but to be reinvigorated by attention to the imagination. Apologetics needs to be expanded once again to include a wider view of the human person, sensitive to the subjectivity that Robinson prizes. But for many skeptics, it is precisely their inability to countenance Christian belief that shapes their religious experience (or lack thereof). So all sorts of provocations are needed to prepare the way for faith. Traditional proofs remain part of the apologetic mix so long as they are placed in a larger context and so long as the human person is conceived as a complex individual with hopes, desires, and imaginings, and not just a "brain on a stick."

In any case, what Robinson wants us to see is that the failures and betrayals of Christians to defend their faith do not diminish the vitality of the Christian vision. As Ames puts it in *Gilead*, "I felt, as I have often felt,

---

[18]Robinson's critique is that conservative defenders have created a caricature of Christianity in which the text of Genesis is defended but its theological vision is not. The powerless are thus left to the forces of competition, which are rejected in accounting for human origins but given free rein in ordering human society. Robinson, *Death of Adam*, 40. To be fair, Robinson is not necessarily saying that a literalistic reading of Genesis necessitates market absolutism. She is arguing that focus on the wrong things has made "religion seem foolish while rendering it mute" with relationship to larger ethical issues. Robinson acknowledges in another essay that sincere believers hold what seem to be intractable differences on what justice entails, "mulling other texts": "Some, in the fear of God, could never knowingly vote against the interests of the poor or of those who suffer discrimination, while others, in the fear of God, are content that the poor should be with us always, and would never vote for marriage equality." Robinson, *Givenness of Things*, 94.

that my failing the truth could have no bearing at all on the Truth itself, which could never conceivably be in any sense dependent on me or on anyone."[19] Robinson is clearly disturbed over the way that Christian theology has ingested the parascientific worldview. And yet she argues that theology's resilience is a testimony to its legitimacy: "Theology persists, even when it has absorbed as truth theories and interpretations that could be reasonably expected to kill it off. This suggests that its real life is elsewhere, in a place not reached by these doubts and assaults."[20]

There are other essential ways of knowing, Robinson wants to say, which is why humanity needs poetry, literature, art, and theology. Theology, like poetry, "earns its authority by winning assent and recognition . . . with the difference that the assent seems to be to ultimate truth, however oblique or fragmentary the suggestion of it."[21] Robinson has a fundamentally aesthetic interest in theology, rooted in the vision of the world it facilitates. Her goal is to reopen space for wonder at the miracle of existence. This brings us to what Robinson believes is the heart of theology, "awe at the entire phenomenon of Being . . . that embraces thought, and error, and the work the mind does in its sleep."[22] Untouched by the assaults of the most militant atheists, and unexamined by the most militant apologists, is the key phenomenon for which we must account: religious experience.[23] Faith is found, not primarily by intellection but by feeling the way in.

The centrality of religious experience and perception. In *Gilead*, John Ames tells his young son, "It is religious experience above all that authenticates religion, for the purposes of the individual believer."[24] This defense of religious experience is part of Robinson's larger defense of the legitimacy of human perception. Indeed, Robinson's central apologetic

---

[19]Robinson, *Gilead*, 172.
[20]Robinson, *Absence of Mind*, 35.
[21]Robinson, *Death of Adam*, 117. Here we see a parallel to David Tracy's notion of the religious classic, noted in chapter three.
[22]Robinson, *What Are We Doing Here?*, 35.
[23]In her celebration of religious experience, Robinson reminds us of Schleiermacher, the first to attempt an apologetic of authenticity (as noted in chapter two). And yet, Robinson rarely if ever cites Schleiermacher, sourcing her approach in Calvin's Reformational humanism instead. The sources of Robinson's theological vision will be explored in chapter six.
[24]Robinson, *Gilead*, 145.

given—defended and celebrated in almost every novel and essay—is the miracle and mystery of human consciousness. This depth dimension of human inwardness is the inexhaustible source of art and culture. These are the riches she fears are being lost with the advance of the parascientific worldview, and thus she spends the majority of her energy holding the line against cultured despisers of the religious imagination.

Robinson claims that any model of human consciousness must account for two givens of human nature: "that we are brilliantly creative and brilliantly destructive."[25] The only way to account for these givens is to begin with a "very high estimate of human nature" capable of containing our worst impulses and liberating our best impulses."[26] She states that this high estimate is a foundational assumption (we might call it properly basic), something that must be reasoned from rather than reasoned to. She does not want to argue for it but to take it as a given, just as parascience takes an opposite view as a given. Both sides work from a position of faith, "a loyalty to a vision of the nature of things despite its inaccessibility to demonstration."[27]

Similarly, she argues for the validity of the human sense of a soul, "a richly individual history of experience, perception, and thought," which is legitimized not by argument but by experience. The soul is "that haunting I who wakes us in the night wondering where time has gone, the I we waken to, sharply aware that we have been unfaithful to ourselves."[28] The ruminations of that "I," when taken together with the collective ruminations of others who feel similarly haunted, are something to be taken seriously.

We can sum up Robinson's apologetic defense in her nonfiction work thus. First, she endeavors to show the inadequacy of positivist systems to make sense of our experience. Second, she draws on the deep history of religious experience throughout culture and history as an irrefutable given. Third, she appeals to the felt experience of our life in the world, which we

---

[25]Robinson, *Absence of Mind*, xi.
[26]Robinson, *Absence of Mind*, 32. As a Calvinist, Robinson believes in original sin, but the pessimism of original sin is mitigated by the original goodness and dignity of creation.
[27]Robinson, *Death of Adam*, 39.
[28]Robinson, *Absence of Mind*, 110.

intuitively tend to take as disclosive and meaningful. Indeed, as John Ames opines, the religious experience of a group of worshipers exceeds the religious reflections of our best theologians: "When this old sanctuary is full of silence and prayer, every book Karl Barth ever will write would not be a feather in the scales against it from the point of view of profundity."[29]

This does not mean, however, that Robinson is an emotivist mystic who believes that theology is irrelevant. Just the opposite: she finds the ground for this vision of the centrality of human perception in the tradition stemming from her favorite theologian, John Calvin.[30] The following chapter will explore the theological roots of Robinson's vision. For now, it is enough to say that she places her own work in a Calvinist literary stream. In keeping with that tradition, she celebrates epiphanies of the ordinary. If the world is truly the theater of God's glory, then everyday life holds revelatory potential. Robinson depicts John Ames in awe of the prairie at dawn, astonished at being "allowed to witness such a thing." This leads to the sort of epiphany we find in the closing pages of *Gilead*:

> It has seemed to me sometimes as though the Lord breathes on this poor gray ember of Creation and it turns to radiance—for a moment or a year or the span of a life. And then it sinks back into itself again, and to look at it no one would know it had anything to do with fire, or light. . . . But the Lord is more constant and far more extravagant than it seems to imply. Wherever you turn your eyes the world can shine like transfiguration. You don't have to bring a thing to it except a little willingness to see. Only, who could have the courage to see it?[31]

Epiphanic vision is not abolished by fallenness, though it does require "a little willingness to see," itself a gift of grace.[32]

---

[29]Robinson, *Gilead*, 173.

[30]In fact, just after dismissing the value of traditional theistic arguments, she writes, "There is a much stronger argument to be made, beginning with Calvin's descent into the self, where, he says, one will find unmistakable marks of divinity." Robinson, *What Are We Doing Here?*, 215.

[31]Robinson, *Gilead*, 245. "Wherever you turn your eyes the world can shine like transfiguration" is a clear paraphrase of Calvin: "wherever you cast your eyes, there is no spot in the universe wherein you cannot discern at least some sparks of his glory." John Calvin, *Institutes of the Christian Religion*, ed. John T. McNeill, trans. Ford Lewis Battles (Louisville: Westminster John Knox, 2001), 1.5.1.

[32]Ames goes on to say that just as there is a prevenient grace that enables our acceptance of grace, so too there is a prevenient courage that enables our courage to see. Robinson, *Gilead*, 246.

Robinson's nonfiction, too, is full of wonder at the miracle of existence. She expresses delight, for example, at "the enormous number of English words that describe the behavior of light. Glimmer, glitter, gliste, glisten, glow, glare, shimmer, sparkle, shine, and so on." The surplus of language, she argues, reflects an aesthetic attentiveness to the range of conscious experience. This allows us to make "pleasing distinctions, between a candle flame, the sun at its zenith, and the refraction of light by a drop of rain."[33] Such sensitivity to the particularity of our felt experience brings about a larger sense of wonder at existence itself. Indeed, Ames tells his son that existence itself is "the most remarkable thing that could ever be imagined." It is when we love the sheer being of people and things that we are most like God.[34] In her most recent collection of essays, Robinson names this wonder at the particularity of existence a delight in "the givenness of things."

Robinson's most powerful argument for revelatory perception, however, is not found in her essays. It is rather in her novels where she constructs a fictional world in which revelatory perception actually occurs. In her fiction, those separated by divergent viewpoints can be drawn together in the common experience of seeing. In building this literary world, Robinson creates a nondefensive space where her readers can inhabit her Christian imagination. This imaginative hospitality, I argue, is precisely what is needed in crossing the seemingly untraversable gaps between worlds of belief and unbelief.

ROBINSON'S APOLOGETIC ART:
INHABITING HER IMAGINATIVE UNIVERSE

Imaginative identification: Robinson as philosophical novelist. The contrast between Robinson's nonfiction and her fiction is striking. While her essays can be acerbic, polemical, and contrarian, her fiction is exquisite, meditative, and capacious. Perhaps this is appropriate to the genre: fiction invites literary analysis and appreciation rather than counterargument. To

---

[33]Marilynne Robinson, *When I Was a Child I Read Books: Essays* (New York: Picador, 2013), 22.
[34]As John Ames narrates to his son: "[Your mother] has watched every moment of your life, almost, and she loves you as God does, to the marrow of your bones. . . . You see how it is godlike to love the being of someone. Your *existence* is a delight to us." Robinson, *Gilead*, 53.

put it another way, discursive argument has real but limited apologetic value. Even if you can persuade a person of the validity of your argument, it does not follow that the most significant gaps of understanding have been crossed. Literary critic Amy Hungerford describes Robinson's fiction as an "American revival of the philosophical novel." Hungerford explains that the philosophical novel "imagines fiction as a way of taking thought beyond philosophy proper, beyond proposition and argument (while including those things) and into a sense of what it is like to live with and through philosophical—or in Ames's case, theological—reflection."[35]

To speak of Robinson's art as apology is not to signify an ulterior motive in her fiction, as if to sneak ideas past the imagination that would not have been able to make it past the intellect. Rather, it reveals how Robinson's fiction allows readers to inhabit a theological perspective. A parallel might be drawn on the relationship of her novels and her social criticism. She comments: "I want my fiction to be world-creating, so I don't intentionally insert my social criticism in my novels. It comes through anyway."[36] Similarly, demonstrating a Christian experience of mind and world, grounded in a metaphysic of divine encounter, is not the intentional aim of her fiction, but "it comes through anyway." Indeed, it is in her fiction that these twin passions, her social criticism and her religious wonder, come together most profoundly.[37]

Robinson's belief in the power of fiction to cultivate more than imagination is the direct fruit of her many hours spent in world and character building. She argues that imaginative identification with the other is, in fact, the basis of community:

> I would say, for the moment, that community, at least community larger than the immediate family, consists very largely of imaginative love for people who we do not know or whom we know very slightly. This thesis

---

[35] Amy Hungerford, *Postmodern Belief: American Literature and Religion Since 1960* (Princeton: Princeton University Press, 2010), 116-17.

[36] Marilynne Robinson, "Religion and the Arts Award Lecture" (Annual Meeting of the American Academy of Religion, Atlanta, Georgia, 2015).

[37] As Hungerford writes, "Her novels imagine belief made capacious, and aim to show us behavior within the life of belief that can heal both family and Republic." Hungerford, *Postmodern Belief*, 121.

may be influenced by the fact that I have spent literal years of my life lovingly absorbed in the thoughts and perceptions of—who knows better than I?—people who do not exist. . . . I think fiction may be, whatever else, an exercise in the capacity for imaginative love, or sympathy, or identification.[38]

Robinson is clearly "lovingly absorbed" in her characters. The gift she gives to her readers is to offer us the opportunity to share her vision and thus to grow the sensibilities of our own religious imaginations. My goal is not to summarize Robinson's novels exhaustively. Rather I want to trace key themes, with sensitivity to Robinson's larger apologetic logic throughout her body of work, building on the imaginative vision developed in the first section of this chapter.

Robinson's novels are philosophical insofar as they revolve around the mysteries of existence, contemplated by ordinary characters. As Lila asks John Ames, Why do things happen the way they do? Why are we? Where are we? And what does it mean to feel at home in this place? Robinson's characters are engaging and believable because they capture the sense of wandering and transience that our hypermodern situation makes all the more acute. Robinson would resist this hypermodern diagnosis as one more variety of the "nostalgic fallacy": it seems to assume that people in the past were without the anxieties of metaphysical homelessness.[39] The impermanence of things, she would argue, is quite enough to make a person feel deep anxiety. Nevertheless, the homelessness of hypermodernity is a trauma not merely of metaphysics, but of meaning.[40] The success of parascience in rooting itself in our social imaginary is a testimony to the seriousness of our condition. All of this is to say that Robinson's novels, rooted as they are in the psychic homelessness of her characters, have special resonance for contemporary readers.

Housekeeping. Robinson's first novel, *Housekeeping*, captures this sense of transience exquisitely. Pre-dating her discovery of Calvin, it is

---

[38]Robinson, *When I Was a Child I Read Books*, 21.

[39]Marilynne Robinson, "Writers and the Nostalgic Fallacy," *The New York Times*, October 13, 1985, www.nytimes.com/1985/10/13/books/writers-and-the-nostalgic-fallacy.html.

[40]Peter L. Berger, *Homeless Mind: Modernization and Consciousness* (New York: Vintage, 1974).

the least explicitly religious of her novels. Nevertheless, we see an implicitly Christian imagination at work, one that will come into full bloom in *Gilead*. *Housekeeping* is haunted by biblical imagery from the opening sentence: "My name is Ruth." This is a subtle homage both to the Scriptural heroine as well as to Melville's immortal opening to *Moby Dick*: "Call me Ishmael." Both biblical characters—Ruth and Ishmael—surface themes of loss, wandering, and homecoming that will continue throughout Robinson's body of work. Ishmael was expelled from Abraham's family, forced to survive with his mother Hagar in the wilderness. Ruth, by contrast, was an outsider welcomed in.

Robinson's Ruth struggles to find a sense of home, and the central conflict is in determining whom she should follow. This choice is catalyzed by tragedy: Ruth's mother drives her car off a cliff into a glacial lake, and Ruth and her sister Lucille are passed on to their grandmother, then to their great aunts, and finally to their peculiar aunt Sylvie. Sylvie, who has lived as a drifter, is ill-fit for settling down and keeping house in the small town of Fingerbone. Her eccentricities (sleeping on park benches, riding trains, and throwing ice at dogs) unsettle polite society and begin to drive a wedge between the sisters. While Lucille is embarrassed by and begins to avoid Sylvie, Ruth finds in Sylvie a kindred spirit.

In light of the trauma that these sisters have suffered, they employ two different strategies of coping with loss. Lucille, following society, strives for mastery. Ruth, following Sylvie, opts for mystery. Ruth wonders about all the fragmentary bits of conscious life that cannot be reduced to neat categorization. The contrast emerges profoundly when Lucille asks Ruth to look up "pinking shears" in their grandfather's dictionary so that she can help her cut a pattern for her dress. Upon opening the dictionary, Ruth finds herself distracted by the flower petals her grandfather has pressed in its pages. Lucile turns the book upside down, shaking all the petals to the ground. "What are they good for?" she asks Ruth.[41] To Lucille, a dictionary is for words, to be put in service of utilitarian projects. But for Ruth, the dictionary is a treasure trove full of the stuff of life, like her

---

[41]Marilynne Robinson, *Housekeeping* (New York: Picador, 1980), 126.

grandfather's flowers. It is wrong to harden one's heart against such things, even if they have been "smothered in darkness for forty years."[42] Robinson is pushing her readers to question reductive visions of the world that tie up too quickly the loose ends of existence.

Indeed, the glacial lake that swallowed both her grandfather (who died in a train crash) and her mother comes to represent the vast reservoir of meaning and memory of the humans that live on its shores. So many things have been lost to the depth of time, passing into the abyss of memory, and yet this does not mean that they are worthless or forgettable. Just the opposite: they make their presence known by means of conspicuous absence, their weightiness by means of displacement, their significance by the vacuum they leave. This is especially the case with those we love. As Sylvie says, "You feel them most when they're gone."[43]

This sense of presence by means of absence is the central aesthetic of the novel. Ruth asks, "When did I become so unlike other people?" Perhaps, she reasons, it was "when my mother left me waiting for her, and established in me the habit of waiting and expectation which makes any present moment most significant for what it does not contain."[44] Hungerford calls this an "anorexic aesthetic," because of how painfully the absence is felt.[45] The word *anorexic*, however, suggests starvation; what is nearer to the truth is renunciation. Sylvie, who seems free from the need for material comfort and stability, becomes a model for Ruth's growth through asceticism. When Fingerbone floods, threatening the town and covering the lower floor of the house, Ruth is drawn toward Sylvie's ability to accept and adapt to the new reality, free from attachment to things. Engebretson's analysis marks the flood as surfacing Ruth's spiritual problem:

> If everything physical is subject to flooding, isn't it better to assume a way of life that accepts this reality? The problem is not that time produces chaos, since, like the seasons, time in *Housekeeping* has order: the disorder of

---

[42]Robinson, *Housekeeping*, 127.

[43]Robinson, *Housekeeping*, 185.

[44]Robinson, *Housekeeping*, 214.

[45]Amy Hungerford, *The American Novel Since 1945: Lecture 16—Marilynne Robinson, Housekeeping*, Open Yale Courses, 2012, oyc.yale.edu/english/engl-291/lecture-16.

death necessarily circles toward a new order of things, the reassertion of "the dear ordinary." The problem for Ruth is framed as a spiritual problem: Given the reality of transience, how should one live? What kind of self should one cultivate?[46]

It is the question of absence, created by change and loss, and what it means to cope, that occupies *Housekeeping*, and to a lesser degree Robinson's other books. The answer seems to be the cultivation of a robust inwardness, an aesthetic posture toward the world. This posture is ascetic in its aim. It does not seek to control reality but to ascend through imaginative contemplation, in the manner of a mystic. Let us call this not an anorexic aesthetic, but an ascetic aesthetic, presence by means of absence.

To be clear, in *Housekeeping* Robinson is not yet engaged in anything like apologetics. *Housekeeping* pre-dates her discovery of Calvin and her self-conscious identification with the Calvinist metaphysical tradition. Indeed, the principal characters in this first novel have little patience or need for the respectable religion of the church ladies who come over to express their concern. Yet two things are important to note: Robinson is celebrating the power of the imagination, and the concept of imagination that she celebrates is haunted by the Christian mythos. Let us take each in turn.

First, Robinson celebrates the imagination as the only organ humans have with which to knit together such disparate strands of existence. It is the imagination that can somehow weave together past memories with present realities and future hopes, and that *ascertains* meaning in human existence. It is not just the best and brightest lights, Robinson wants to say, who are able to sense the gravity of existence. The driving assumption in all of her fiction, as Hungerford writes, is that "ordinary people have rich and complicated interior lives, that they embody a silent discourse of thought that, if we knew its voice, would astonish us." The idea that all ordinary people have this kind of rich interior life enacts, as Hungerford argues, a profoundly "Protestant understanding of inner life," because

---

[46]Engebretson, "Dear Ordinary," 48.

each person lives their life in direct encounter with ultimate reality, *coram deo*.[47] Robinson aims to give language to match consciousness, to give words for what we cannot find the words to say ourselves.

Second, Robinson's imagination is already working within the Christian mythos. This is especially clear insofar as Ruth reflects on the place of hope amid the trauma of loss. To the question of what living in the face of transience means, Ruth weaves together memory with hope, house-keeping with homecoming:

> There is so little to remember of anyone—an anecdote, a conversation at table. But every memory is turned over and over again, every word, however chance, written in the heart in hope that memory will fulfill itself, and become flesh, and that the wanderers will find a way home, and the perished, whose lack we always feel, will step through the door finally and stroke our hair with dreaming, habitual fondness, not having meant to keep us waiting long.[48]

"That the memory will . . . become flesh." This is the hope of some future resurrection, renewal, or restoration of what has been lost. Such things seem too good to be true, and yet Ruth permits herself to imagine them. She imagines the train that killed her grandfather leaping backward up out of the water. She imagines her mother being restored to give her strawberries from her purse. Near the end of the novel, Ruth makes a specifically theological connection between this kind of hope and the incarnation. For surely if "God Himself was pulled after us into the vortex," and if Jesus "even restored the severed ear of the soldier who came to arrest Him," then we are allowed to hope "the resurrection will reflect considerable attention to detail."[49] Only something like resurrection could make sense, could encompass and knit together all the ill-fitting fragments of human existence: "What are these fragments for," she asks, "if not to be knit up finally?"[50] Here human imagination meets the hope of divine intervention.

---

[47]Hungerford, *Postmodern Belief*, 114.
[48]Robinson, *Housekeeping*, 195.
[49]Robinson, *Housekeeping*, 194.
[50]Robinson, *Housekeeping*, 92.

Gilead. When Robinson writes *Gilead* two decades later, the implicitly religious imagination of *Housekeeping* has developed into a robustly theological vision. In *Gilead* Robinson takes up the voice of septuagenarian minister John Ames. Whereas Ruth's is a coming-of-age story, Ames writes in preparation for his death. Knowing that he will soon be gone, Ames writes his memoirs for his young son Robbie. Once again, we are led to contemplate absence and loss, though in this case it is the anticipation of absence that looms large. Writing self-consciously in the Calvinist tradition, her stripped-down style (relative to *Housekeeping*) reflects the aesthetic sensibility of her Calvinist narrator. *Gilead* is, as Engebretson writes, "the prose equivalent of a Congregationalist church, so barren of iconography and decoration that it even excludes the cross, a stark reductionism intended to suggest its aesthetic opposite: the beauty of God."[51] Indeed, now we find that the ascetic aesthetic, presence by means of absence, has been transposed into a Calvinist key. Now the lonely spaces of inwardness begin to be filled with the recognition of an absolute presence. As Robinson says in an interview, "This is something again that runs all through mysticism and also Calvinism—the sense that the smallness of the self is a celebration of the utter vastness of the other. Whatever happens, this difference cannot be mitigated. It's a feeling of discomfort, because what you're doing when you have that feeling is apprehending a certain grandeur."[52]

Ordinary human perception now leads to the possibility of apprehending not just the gravity of existence but the greatness of God. Of all Robinson's works, it is in *Gilead* that we are allowed to look at the world with the "ravishment and shock of revelatory perception"[53] that so characterizes Robinson's imagination.

Ames is not, however, one who sits at ease in Zion. With an older brother who has deconverted,[54] pulling his minister father along with

---

[51]Engebretson, "Dear Ordinary," 120.

[52]Thomas Gardner, *A Door Ajar: Contemporary Writers and Emily Dickinson* (Oxford: Oxford University Press, 2006), 57.

[53]Robinson, *John Calvin*, xxvii.

[54]When John Ames was young, his brilliant older brother Edward was sent to Germany to study theology, and returned an atheist. Edward, who has published a monograph on Feuerbach, gives

him, Ames is fully aware of the potency of doubt (and that doubt is about more than merely ideas).[55] Nevertheless, Ames feels little anxiety over the arguments for unbelief that he finds in his brother's books. He writes to his son, "Many of the attacks on belief that have had prestige for the last century or two are in fact meaningless."[56] The word *meaningless* is important: Ames does not challenge the arguments because they are mistaken but because they are unable to make sense of human experience.[57] This does not mean "anything goes" for the religious consciousness, come hell or high water. Rather it means, as Robinson argues in her essays, that a theological vision of the world earns its authority by winning aesthetic assent. It is discerned by a spirit of recognition just like great poetry.[58] The evocation of this spirit of recognition enables the readers not merely to appreciate Ames's religious imagination but actually to inhabit it.

Here we have one of the clearest pictures of the kind of apologetic art that Robinson offers. She does not simply assert the validity of religious experience on its own terms, apart from arguments, but also offers a compelling vision of what it is like to see the world through aging Christian eyes.[59] Ames anticipates his impending absence from the world that he so loves, charging every moment with heightened meaning.

---

his brother Feuerbach's *Essence of Christianity* (1848). John Ames reads the book cover to cover, giving this assessment to his son: "Feuerbach is a famous atheist, but he is about as good on the joyful aspects of religion as anybody, and he loves the world. Of course he thinks that religion could just stand out of the way and let joy exist pure and undisguised. That is his one error, and it is significant. But he is marvelous on the subject of joy, and also on its religious expressions." Robinson, *Gilead*, 24.

[55] As Hungerford puts it: "We might say that John Ames is a character fully imagined to be living within Charles Taylor's secular age: he emerges in Gilead as a believer profoundly aware of the possibility—even the plausibility—of unbelief." Hungerford, *Postmodern Belief*, 114.

[56] Robinson, *Gilead*, 144.

[57] As Hungerford argues, "To take them as meaningful is to rob of its meaning, and thus its holiness, 'everything else' Ames has told his son and his congregation." The access of religious belief to reality is valid on its own terms, "imagined as a religiously understood reality that is simply other to arguments against it." Hungerford, *Postmodern Belief*, 116.

[58] Robinson, *Death of Adam*, 117.

[59] As Laura Tanner writes, "The novel allows the reader not just to comprehend Ames's vision but to inhabit his experience of seeing, to occupy not only the porch, the prairie, and the pulpit but the psychic space of displacement." Laura E. Tanner, "'Looking Back from the Grave': Sensory Perception and the Anticipation of Absence in Marilynne Robinson's *Gilead*," *Contemporary Literature* 48, no. 2 (2007): 250.

Robinson excels at dazzling the reader with Ames's vision of the ordinary world. The eyes of his memory linger over the glory of everyday things like light and water. He recounts an epiphanic experience watching a young couple at play:

> The sun had come up brilliantly after a heavy rain, and the trees were glistening and very wet. On some impulse, plain exuberance, I suppose, the fellow jumped up and caught hold of a branch, and a storm of luminous water came pouring down on the two of them, and they laughed and took off running, the girl sweeping water off her hair and her dress as if she were a little bit disgusted, but she wasn't. It was a beautiful thing to see, like something from a myth. I don't know why I thought of that now, except perhaps because it is easy to believe in such moments that water was made primarily for blessing, and only secondarily for growing vegetables or doing the wash.

Notably, Ames places the practical purpose of water beneath a religious one. Before water can be used to wash or grow, it is there to pour over humanity in blessing. Ames underlies the glory of existence itself in this scene: "I could have written that the sun just shone, and the tree just glistened, and the water just poured out of it and the girl just laughed. . . . People talk that way when they want to call attention to a thing existing in excess of itself, so to speak, a sort of purity or lavishness, at any rate something ordinary in kind but exceptional in degree."[60] Ames's world is one in which ordinary things exist in excess of themselves and are always just on the verge of shining like transfiguration, requiring only a little willingness to see.

Yet the question of whether willingness alone is sufficient for sight is tested in the central conflict (and central apologetic encounter) of the book: Ames's conflicted relationship to his godson, John Ames Boughton, or Jack. Jack is introduced to readers of *Gilead* as the prodigal son returned. In his youth, Jack scandalized the community and brought disgrace to his family by impregnating a poor young woman, then abandoning her and his child. Ames resents Jack for this, as well as for the

---

[60]Robinson, *Gilead*, 27-28.

heartache he has brought to Boughton, Jack's father and Ames's best friend. Ames is suspicious about Jack's intentions and feels jealous anxiety when he sees how easily Jack connects to Lila and Robbie, his young wife and child. Ames struggles to engage his namesake with generosity and grace, to bless rather than curse Jack in his heart.

A professed atheist, Jack gingerly pursues his godfather. Finally, Jack and Ames have a series of apologetic conversations in which (as Ames believes) Jack expresses a desire to be convinced of the Christian faith. Ames believes that little can be done on this count, since Jack has no "sympathy" with theology. What Ames means by this is that Jack misunderstands the nature of faith and theology. To use Hungerford's language, theology for Ames is a "discourse of relationship," not a "discourse of answers." Ames believes that Jack mistakes theology "for a discourse that could produce individual belief rather than a discourse that *enacts* shared belief."[61] This leads Ames to relate to Jack defensively,[62] climaxing in a clumsy discussion about predestination in which Ames suggests that Jack read Karl Barth on the subject. Jack is incredulous: "Is that what you do when some tormented soul arrives on your doorstep at midnight? Recommend Karl Barth?"[63]

This, however, is not a complete description of Jack's unbelief. In Robinson's next novel, we receive more perspective on Jack.[64] We begin to see that Jack wishes he could believe but has never been able to see and feel what his minister father and godfather see and feel. Jack's sense of alienation is already apparent in *Gilead*, where Jack suggests that his unbelief is positive proof of his reprobation. Why is it, after all, that Jack sees the world the way he does? Is there any hope for him? This results in an illuminating conversation between Jack and Ames on the distance between their views:

> "Does it seem right to you," he said, "that there should be no common language between us? That there should be no way to bring a drop of water to

---

[61] Hungerford, *Postmodern Belief*, 118.

[62] Ames later muses: "Nothing true can be said about God from a posture of defense." Robinson, *Gilead*, 175.

[63] Robinson, *Gilead*, 153.

[64] Much to the delight of her readers, Robinson's fourth novel in the series—forthcoming as this book goes to print—tells Jack's story. Marilynne Robinson, *Jack* (New York: Picador, 2020).

those of us who languish in the flames, or who will? Granting your terms? That between us and you there is a great gulf fixed? How can capital-T Truth not be communicable? That makes no sense to me."

"I am not sure those are my terms. I would speak of grace in that context," I said.

"And never the absence of grace, which would in fact seem to be the issue here."[65]

Profound differences in vision emerge. For Ames, in absence of common language, grace is that which bridges the abyss between the two. But for Jack, grace is precisely the problem. It is grace that seems to have been withheld or denied from reprobates like him.

Jack's question is a good one. Without a common language, a definitive frame for interpreting our experiences, how can one experience of the world be privileged over another?[66] Indeed, Ames questions whether understanding, much less persuasion, is actually possible:

> In every important way we are such secrets from each other, and I do believe that there is a separate language in each of us, also a separate aesthetics and a separate jurisprudence. Every single one of us is a little civilization built on the ruins of any number of preceding civilizations, but with our own variant notions of what is beautiful and what is acceptable—which I hasten to add, we generally do not satisfy and by which we struggle to live. We take fortuitous resemblances among us to be actual likeness, because those around us have also fallen heir to the same customs, trade in the same coin, acknowledge, more or less, the same notions of decency and sanity. But all that really just allows us to coexist with the inviolable, untraversable, and utterly vast spaces between us.[67]

Coexistence is possible, but is communication, much less comprehension of the other, really possible in the face of such vast spaces?

Robinson wants to do full justice to the gaps in understanding and perspective. Yet she does not leave her readers at this impasse. In the

---

[65]Robinson, *Gilead*, 170.
[66]This is reminiscent of the question of incommensurability explored by Lindbeck in chapter two. The postliberal strategy is catechesis rather than translation, but there I argued for the possibility of vicarious vision enabled by imaginative works.
[67]Robinson, *Gilead*, 197.

clumsy discussion about predestination recounted above, Ames's and Boughton's best efforts have failed. But Lila interjects, asserting the possibility of hope: "A person can change. Everything can change." And Jack replies, "Thanks, that's all I wanted to know."[68] Jack, of course, is neither convinced nor converted. But the grace that Jack believes to have been withheld is the grace that Lila extends to him with her words. The space between God and humanity, and between human persons, though utterly vast, is not ultimately untraversable if divine grace is operative in the world.

Robinson's apologetic interest is less in achieving complete understanding of the other as it is in achieving gracious acceptance of the other. This posture of grace and blessing is what enables the possibility of understanding. This is perhaps the most important contribution of Robinson's imaginative apologetic: the conviction that it is grace that is able to traverse the gaps of understanding, vision, and belief. But as we saw with MacDonald, this grace can only be enacted through generous acts of sacrificial love. The goal is not necessarily understanding but rather the apprehension of and participation in a divine love that may be able to cover all.[69] The effort that Robinson asks of the reader is imaginative identification, the willingness to see through the eyes of the other, and the willingness to move toward the other in their difference, in generosity and blessing. It is in grace that understanding becomes possible. Nevertheless, reconciliation is never cheap; it is never a quick gloss over difference. To borrow a line, reconciliation in action is a harsh and dreadful thing, not like reconciliation in dreams.

Home. If Robinson had merely given us *Gilead*, then perhaps we might say that she offers us a beautiful but incomplete picture, an "apologetics

---

[68]Robinson, *Gilead*, 153.

[69]The desire for reconciliation, for the bridging of gaps, Hungerford argues, is Robinson's larger project in all her novels: "the narrative is designed to knit up a broken world into a whole, through simile and analogy, or through the idea that absence produces the present thing through the intensity of longing. . . . Just as Sylvie and Ruth finally cross the bridge that a doomed train spectacularly fails to cross in [Housekeeping's] opening scenes, the human effort, at great cost, is to bridge the gap, draw difference close, knit up the world." Hungerford, *Postmodern Belief*, 120.

of glory" without an "apologetics of the cross".[70] But the difficulty of participation in divine blessing receives full treatment in Robinson's third novel, *Home*. Published four years after *Gilead*, *Home* follows Jack's homecoming from the perspective of his sister Glory. Glory had returned home herself just before her brother to serve as her father's caretaker.[71] *Home* is startlingly minimalistic and mundane in its title as well as in its tone. Boughton, now a widower full of years, has one stated desire: that his son Jack would come home to stay. The book opens with the precipitating action of the prodigal's return. Yet Robinson quickly shows us that she is telling a different story than the one in Luke's Gospel. A better parallel is the return of Israel from exile, resettled in the land of promise, yet unable to feel at home. Robinson is exploring the question of what it means to come home, even while deep, almost intractable differences remain between loved ones. Jack returns home, but he remains a stranger, and he is ultimately unable to give his father the kind of satisfaction he desires. His words to Glory are full of pain: "Sometimes it seems as though I'm in one universe and you're in another."[72]

Indeed, the chasm between Jack and his family creates the central drama of the novel. Can it be transcended? Can forgiveness cross the divide? For years Boughton has preached to his congregation and to his family that "you must forgive in order to understand. Until you forgive, you defend yourself against the possibility of understanding. . . . If you forgive, he would say, you may indeed still not understand, but you will be ready to understand, and that is the posture of grace." Though this would be the theme of many sermons, Glory tells us, "the real text was Jack."[73] Boughton hopes to bridge the gap between himself and his son through blanket forgiveness and unconditional grace.

---

[70]James K. A Smith reviewed Robinson's *What Are We Doing Here?*, writing that her "apology of glory" is in need of a corresponding "apology of the cross." James K.A. Smith, "Marilynne Robinson's Apologia Gloriae," *Comment Magazine*, March 1, 2018, https://www.cardus.ca /comment/article/marilynne-robinsons-apologia-gloriae/. I will address this criticism with regards to my larger project in the concluding chapter.

[71]The fact that Glory, the novel's main character, barely registers in *Gilead* is a testament to the profound limitations of human subjectivity. For all his capacious vision, Ames scarcely notices her other than to take pity on her; and yet she is the chief instrument of grace in the novel.

[72]Marilynne Robinson, *Home* (New York: Picador, 2009), 267.

[73]Robinson, *Home*, 45.

But grace is always in danger of becoming a theological abstraction. Despite his best intentions and his desire to play the prodigal's father, Boughton is unable either to understand or welcome Jack without conditions: Boughton insists on saving Jack's soul. Jack is unable to embrace the Christian faith, especially the idea that his soul would be worth saving. In the end, despite the best intentions of both parties, the fracture remains. Jack leaves home unreconciled.

And yet, the possibility of understanding, if not reconciliation, remains in the growing intimacy between Jack and his sister Glory. Glory, who like her sisters Grace and Hope has been "named for theological abstractions,"[74] is anything but an allegory. As a character she stands on her own two feet. She is a self-conscious, complicated character who feels resentment toward both her father and her brother, and whose personal faith is almost inextricably bound up with her sense of filial duty. Glory knows her father's theology; she has heard him say that God "lets us wander so we will know what it means to come home."[75] But Glory, who has never really wandered, is no more at home in her childhood house than Jack:

> So she prayed, Lord, give me patience. She knew that it was not an honest prayer, and she did not linger over it. The right prayer would have been, Lord, my brother treats me like a hostile stranger, my father seems to have put me aside, I feel I have no place here in what I thought would be my refuge, I am miserable and bitter at heart, and old fears are rising up in me so that everything I do makes everything worse.[76]

The drama of redemption, this striving-to-feel-at-home in the place called home, is played out in Glory's life just as surely as it is in Jack's. Yet Glory displays Robinson's ability to put human flesh on the dry bones of theology and a human face on the abstractions of grace, hope, and glory.

If the theater of redemption is the Boughton home, Glory is the one who attends to the priestly duty of housekeeping. As she gardens, cooks,

---

[74]Robinson, *Home*, 82.
[75]Robinson, *Home*, 102.
[76]Robinson, *Home*, 69.

and cleans, she cultivates a space for relationship to occur among her quotidian acts of kindness.[77] The space Robinson devotes to detailing Glory's domestic work gives it a quiet dignity, suggestive of the Reformation's affirmation of ordinary life. Recall that the Reformers rejected the distinction between higher and lower vocations. As Charles Taylor summarizes the Puritan ideal: "The highest life can no longer be defined by an exalted *kind* of activity; it all turns on the *spirit* in which one lives whatever one lives, even the most mundane existence."[78] What Robinson wants her readers to discover, along with Glory, is "How oddly holiness situate[s] itself among the things of the world."[79] Here we see the same metaphysic that permeates *Gilead*, made all the more incandescent for being subsumed in ordinary, domestic work.

Indeed, it is as Glory goes about her mundane daily rhythms that Jack slowly begins to open his life up to her. When he happens upon her reading the Bible, Jack asks his sister if she is trying to save his soul. He nourishes "the suspicion that pious folk are plotting [his] rescue." This leads to his confession of "a certain spiritual hunger," alongside his misfortune of knowing "the great truths without feeling the truth of them." Glory's only reply is to say, "I think I like your soul the way it is."[80] This is little help to Jack, who really does feel that he is doomed to perdition, but it is an act of acceptance without conditions that opens the door for further disclosure. It prepares the way for greater friendship, though not complete understanding.

Indeed, Robinson shows that relational generosity is necessary because of the reality of sin, which derails human relationships. For Robinson, sin almost always begins with a failure of perception: it is because of our fallen and finite situation that what we intend to help ends up doing harm. This occurs, for example, when Ames happens to preach his sermon on Hagar, Ishmael, and the responsibility of parents to their children on the Sunday that Jack happens to come to church. It happens

---

[77]As Engebretson writes, the "the smallest gestures, the most minuscule kindnesses are what ultimately makes or breaks the feeling of home." Engebretson, "Dear Ordinary," 192.

[78]Charles Taylor, *Sources of the Self: The Making of the Modern Identity* (Cambridge: Harvard University Press, 1992), 224.

[79]Robinson, *Home*, 102.

[80]Robinson, *Home*, 104-5.

when Jack carries his sleeping father to his bed, unintentionally shaming him. As Engebretson writes:

> The idea that Robinson interprets Calvin's "fallen state" of humanity in epistemological terms in her essays—that human knowledge is conditioned by finitude—is placed into social-ethical terms in *Home*. "Sin" might be defined as meaning well and doing harm. It's woven into social relations, unable to be dislodged by any human will, a mysterious, almost metaphysical reality. "Grace" is that rare, holy moment of meaning well and doing well, which occurs by a strange harmony of intention, action, and receptivity, such as when Glory buys new clothes for Jack and for whatever reason he receives them gladly.[81]

Yet for all the growth that occurs in Glory and Jack's relationship, such moments of grace are rare in the book. The car that Jack painstakingly repairs throughout the early part of the novel—representative of Jack's attempts to rehabilitate his life—is ripped apart in an evening of drunken relapse that culminates in a failed suicide attempt. Jack departs before his father's death into a second self-imposed exile. Indeed, he leaves just before his wife and son arrive at the house looking for him. Grace, so necessary to bridge the gaps caused by human finitude and fallenness, seems always to linger just outside of Jack's grasp.

The anticlimax is profound, and yet it is tinged by hope, once again rooted in the power of the imagination. After meeting Jack's young son, Glory allows herself to imagine him arriving many years later, looking for his father's house. She imagines herself in the scene with newfound purpose, waiting to welcome him and to answer his questions about his father. She imagines knowing that her whole life has "come down to this moment" of reconciliation and return. It is in light of this hopeful vision of the future that the book ends with Glory taking up a favorite statement of her father's: "The Lord is wonderful."[82] The ending seems, at first, discordant with the anticlimax, lack of resolution, and despair that precedes it. As Engebretson puts it, in any other novel, it might feel sentimental, but in Robinson it is "in such disproportion to the brokenness and despair"

---

[81]Engebretson, "Dear Ordinary," 194.
[82]Robinson, *Home*, 325.

that it "reads like something preposterous, something absurd, something like grace."[83]

Lila. Robinson's fourth novel continues the fascination with the theme of grace, especially for outsiders, those who are invisible and forgotten by mainstream society. If *Home* is the story of an outsider who is unable to find his way in, *Lila* holds open the possibility of a wanderer finding a home. In a narrative that predates the events of *Gilead* and *Home*, Robinson tells the story of Ames's mysterious second wife, who is more than thirty years his junior. Here again readers will be astonished at the complexity of Lila's inner world, as well as the depth of her perspective compared to what we know of her from the prior two books. Lila reminds us immediately of Sylvie, a drifter who has never been completely at home. When the book opens, we meet Lila as a child, crying on a stoop in the dark. She is rescued and raised by Doll, a hardened older woman. We are introduced to the theme of loneliness early in the book: "Doll may have been the loneliest woman in the world, and [Lila] was the loneliest child, and there they were, the two of them together, keeping each other warm in the rain."[84] Lila, like Glory in *Home*, never really gets free of her loneliness. Yet, as Robinson reminds us in an interview,

> I am not sure religion is meant to assuage loneliness. Who was ever lonelier than Jesus? "Can you not watch with me one hour?" I think loneliness is the encounter with oneself—who can be great or terrible company, but who does ask all the essential questions. There is a tendency to think of loneliness as a symptom, a sign that life has gone wrong. But it is never only that. I sometimes think it is the one great prerequisite for depth, and for truthfulness.[85]

Furthermore, for Robinson, loneliness is also the prerequisite not only for depth but also for encounter with God, a space for recognition of the "constant, unmediated presence of God in human inwardness."[86]

---

[83]Engebretson, "Dear Ordinary," 215.

[84]Marilynne Robinson, *Lila* (New York: Picador, 2015), 5.

[85]Rebecca M. Painter, "Further Thoughts on a Prodigal Son Who Cannot Come Home, on Loneliness and Grace: An Interview with Marilynne Robinson," *Christianity & Literature* 58, no. 3 (2009): 492.

[86]McGregor reminds us: "For Robinson, to be alone is a religious experience, a simultaneously harrowing and comforting encounter with the divine in the self. The constant, unmediated

Indeed, in Lila we see Robinson integrating all three streams of her previous work: the theme of abandonment from *Housekeeping*, the theme of grace from *Gilead*, and the theme of belonging from *Home*. Lila is in many ways a sharp-edged version of Ruth, and yet in Lila's story Ruth's hopes of reconciliation are extended and, to some degree, realized and redeemed.

Doll raised Lila with a doctrine of self-reliance and survival. People in general, and men in particular, are not to be trusted: "You got to look after your *own* self. When it comes down to it, you're going to be doing that anyway."[87] Church folk are the enemy because they promise so much, meanwhile shackling those who believe them with ever-increasing obligation. It is better to kill desire at the root, and Lila repeats Doll's mantras when she begins to feel too entangled. "Don't go wanting things."[88] "Don't go hoping."[89] She even keeps herself from naming the loneliness she feels, since it "wasn't any different from one year to the next, it was just how her body felt," just the way that things were.[90] Even after marrying Ames, she struggles to know how to relate to him. She knows that he is always "thinking and praying about how to make her feel at home," but "she had never been home in all the years of her life."[91]

Lila strives to remain wild and free, unattached and unaffected by the harshness of the "world being the world." Yet ironically it is the experience of Doll's loyal love that keeps her from achieving isolation. She later conflates her rescue with Ezekiel 16 and identifies Doll with Yahweh's redeeming love. This is what makes it impossible to live without attachment: "If there had not been that time when she mattered to somebody, she could have been at peace with it. . . . It was Doll taking her up in her arms that

---

presence of God in human inwardness, which Robinson traces back to the doctrine of the *imago dei*, is the theological *sine qua non* of her art." Jonathan D. McGregor, "Sacred Loneliness and Sacred Comfort: A Review of Marilynne Robinson's 'Lila,'" Mere Orthodoxy, December 2, 2014, mereorthodoxy.com/sacred-loneliness-sacred-comfort-review-marilynne-robinsons-lila/.

[87]Robinson, *Lila*, 51.

[88]Robinson, *Lila*, 135.

[89]Robinson, *Lila*, 143.

[90]Robinson, *Lila*, 34.

[91]Robinson, *Lila*, 107.

way. Live. Yes. What then?"[92] Doll becomes the paradigm for being able to receive love from Ames and, by extension, from God.

This is not to say that Lila's embrace of either Ames or his faith is quick and easy. She finds her way into Ames's church to get out of the rain and happens to arrive to see a baptism. Lila is drawn in by the service and keeps coming back to church.[93] Eventually she asks Ames to baptize her, which he does. But Lila soon begins to believe that her decision was premature, and she goes to the river to wash the baptism off: "She put on her old dress, and she went to the river and washed herself in the water of death and loss and whatever else was not regeneration."[94] Baptism, it seems to her, means renunciation of everything in her former life, including all the people that she has lived with and loved.

Yet Lila is never more Christian than in her concern for the souls of other outsiders like herself: for the women in the whorehouse where she worked in St. Louis, for the band of migrants with whom she traveled, and above all, for Doll. At first, she loves the idea of resurrection, "because it would mean seeing Doll." Then she learns about the last judgment, and then she hates "the thought of resurrection as much as she had ever hated anything. Better Doll should stay in her grave, if she had one." As she discusses these things with Ames, Lila struggles to understand theology, and wonders out loud about its usefulness, since "lots of folks live and die and never worry themselves about it."[95] Lila doesn't believe she could be happy in a heaven without Doll, which leads to an important conversation with Ames, in which Ames cites the limitless nature of God's grace:

"If the Lord is more gracious than any of us can begin to imagine, and I'm sure that He is, then your Doll and a whole lot of people are safe, and warm, and very happy. And probably a little bit surprised. If there is no Lord, then things are just the way they look to us. Which is really much harder to accept. I mean, it doesn't feel right. There has to be more to it all, I believe."

[92]Robinson, *Lila*, 59.
[93]We can make a connection here to the church-oriented apologetic discussed in chapter two, in which the best way to understand the logic of Christian belief is to be immersed in the practices of Christian community.
[94]Robinson, *Lila*, 103.
[95]Robinson, *Lila*, 100-101.

"Well, but that's what you want to believe, ain't it."

"That doesn't mean it isn't true."[96]

Later, Lila will come around to this vision of resurrection, believing that God in his grace will raise up loved ones like Doll simply because those who love them can't live without them. This reflects a theme throughout Robinson's writings. Characters hold onto those they love in memory "because they can't bear to be without them." That embrace somehow extends grace to them, similar to how Jesus forgave and healed the paralytic when he saw the faith of his friends who lowered him through the roof (Mk 2:5). Ames thinks of his brother Edward in these terms, just as Glory thinks of Jack: "If I or my father or any Boughton has ever stirred the Lord's compassion, then Jack will be all right. Because perdition for him would be perdition for every one of us."[97]

Throughout the story, Ames and Lila engage in apologetic conversations, talking about the problem of evil, heaven and hell, and supremely, "why things happen the way they do." But these conversations are more than just instructive for Lila. This is not just a story of Ames catechizing a seeker; he is enriched and challenged by her questions, forced to "reckon with her razor-edged experience."[98]

It takes time before Lila feels comfortable with Ames's vision of the world. At the end of the novel, she is still growing into her faith. Yet, what Lila gleans from inhabiting Ames's vision of the world is a centering truth: "things that happen mean something." She goes on: "Some man dies somewhere a long time ago and that means something. People eat a bit of bread and that means something."[99] This is tied up with Ames's fascination with the "mystery of existence." To Lila existence is wild and fierce, but Ames shows her it is also "remarkable."[100] What she is experiencing and coming to appreciate is a Christian imagination, in which everything

---

[96]Robinson, *Lila*, 142-43.

[97]Robinson, *Home*, 316.

[98]This is McGregor's phrase, and his analysis here is incisive: "Robinson would remind us that tradition needs untamed experience to keep it sharp, and community needs wild individuals to keep it alive." McGregor, "Sacred Loneliness and Sacred Comfort."

[99]Robinson, *Lila*, 34.

[100]Robinson, *Lila*, 112-13.

that happens means something, because a generous God intends it for us, even permitting us to suffer so that we would know the shock of grace when it comes.

Indeed, the central scene of the novel is Lila's baptism. After Ames baptizes her, Lila confesses how badly she hates herself for wanting anything at all: "I want you to marry me! I wish I didn't. It's just a misery for me. . . . I can't trust you. . . . I don't trust nobody. I can't stay nowhere. I can't get a minute of rest." Finally, she confesses her deepest secret:

"But don't you wonder why I don't even know my own name?"

"You'll tell me sometime, if you feel like it."

"I worked in a whorehouse in St. Louis. A whorehouse. You probably don't even know what that is. Oh! Why did I say that." She stepped away from him, and he gathered her back and pressed her head against his shoulder.

He said, "Lila Dahl, I just washed you in the waters of regeneration. As far as I'm concerned, you're a newborn babe."[101]

As we have seen, Lila will later try to wash off the regeneration, but as Ames assures her, it is not so easy to get rid of grace.

REIMAGINING APOLOGETICS AS BAPTISMAL BLESSING

If there is a common symbolic theme that runs through Robinson's novels that is relevant for reimagining apologetics, it is that of baptismal blessing. Water plays a significant role in each of the novels but takes on special significance in *Gilead*. As we have seen above, after an epiphany watching a young couple playing in the water, Ames opines that the primary purpose of water is for blessing and only secondarily for washing and watering. For Ames, creation is heavy with the water of divine blessing, like the branches of a tree after the rain, just waiting for someone to grab a bough so that the water can come pouring down. Another occasion, watching his little son and his friend playing in the water leads him to compare it to a baptismal scene:

---

[101]Robinson, *Lila*, 89-90.

> When I was in seminary I used to go sometimes to watch the Baptists down
> at the river. It was something to see the preacher lifting the one who was
> being baptized out of the water and the water pouring off the garments and
> the hair. It did look like a birth or a resurrection. . . . You two are dancing
> around in your iridescent little downpour, whooping and stomping as sane
> people ought to do when they encounter a thing so miraculous as water.[102]

In almost every one of these scenes, Ames uses words like *glistened* and
iridescent, drawing a connection between water and light, between
blessing and revelatory vision. We see this again in one of the most
epiphanic moments in the novel, when Ames recounts a dream, in which
his hardened old abolitionist grandfather appears from nowhere to
drench them in a deluge of water/blessing.

> I had a dream once that Boughton and I were down at the river looking
> around in the shallows for something or other—when we were boys it would
> have been tadpoles—and my grandfather stalked out of the trees in that
> furious way he had, scooped his hat full of water, and threw it, so a sheet of
> water came sailing towards us, billowing in the air like a veil, and fell down
> over us. Then he put his hat back on his head and stalked off into the trees
> again and left us standing there in that glistening river, amazed at ourselves
> and shining like the apostles. I mention this because it seems to me trans-
> formations just that abrupt do occur in this life, and they occur unsought
> and unawaited, and they beggar your hopes and your deserving.[103]

To say that water symbolizes divine blessing is to say too little. Though
he never uses the word, for Ames water is *sacramental*, an ordinary thing
that when intended to bless somehow exceeds itself with meaning and
grace.[104] To see God's gracious pleasure and blessing dripping from everywhere in creation means to feel the "shock of revelatory perception" and
then to participate in the posture of blessing. Ames tells his son that it

---

[102]Robinson, *Gilead*, 63.

[103]Robinson, *Gilead*, 203.

[104]Robinson does use this language in her essay on Bonhoeffer: "Two ideas are essential to Bonhoeffer's thinking: first, that the sacred can be inferred from the world in the experience of
goodness, beauty, and love; and second, that these things, and, more generally, the immanence
of God, are a real presence, not a symbol or a foreshadowing. They are fulfillment as well as
promise, like the sacrament, or the church." Robinson, *Death of Adam*, 121-22.

takes a God-given courage "to acknowledge that there is more beauty than our eyes can bear, that precious things have been put into our hands and to do nothing to honor them is to do great harm."[105] Only such prevenient courage, Ames writes, will enable us to be truly useful to the world, that is, to be generous in the face of such outrageous generosity.

Generosity—human participation in divine blessing—results in a particular orientation that acknowledges the sacredness of life, the created glory of all things. Ames recounts one occasion in his childhood when he and Boughton baptized some cats:

> We did respect the Sacraments, but we thought the whole world of those cats. . . . Everyone has petted a cat, but to touch one like that, with the pure intention of blessing it, is a very different thing. . . . There is a reality in blessing, which I take baptism to be, primarily. It doesn't enhance sacredness, but it acknowledges it, and there is a power in that. I have felt it pass through me, so to speak.[106]

Indeed, for Robinson, the root of sin is a failure to see the sacred, to discern God's presence in the world, and God's image in our neighbors. To live with a Christian imagination is fundamentally to acknowledge divine generosity and then to overflow with the same kind of generosity toward the other. As Robinson writes in one of her essays, "In this theater of God's glory we share with those strangers, our neighbors, love means awe, and awe means love."[107]

This is why the supreme triumph of grace in *Gilead* is when Ames humbly asks Jack for the opportunity to bless him. Jack agrees, closes his eyes and lowers his head:

> And I did bless him to the limit of my powers, whatever they are, repeating the benediction from Numbers, of course—"The Lord make his face to shine upon thee and be gracious unto thee: The Lord lift up His countenance upon thee, and give thee peace." Nothing could be more beautiful than that, or more expressive of my feelings, certainly, or more sufficient for that matter. Then, when he didn't open his eyes or lift up his head, I said,

---

[105]Robinson, *Gilead*, 246.
[106]Robinson, *Gilead*, 23.
[107]Robinson, *What Are We Doing Here?*, 36.

"Lord, bless John Ames Boughton, this beloved son and brother and husband and father." Then he sat back and looked at me as if he were waking out of a dream.[108]

All Ames can offer Jack, and the best that he can offer Jack, is not an argument for the truth of Christianity but a blessing. Here, perhaps, is a baptism without water, almost a baptism of desire.

It is important to remember that blessing, when extended, is never unidirectional. The act of blessing opens up the soul to the other, with a readiness to receive just as surely as a readiness to give. In an interview with Robinson, Rebecca Painter makes a connection between Ames's act of blessing and Robinson's larger intent in writing. Painter asks, "Can literature be a blessing to those unwilling to open themselves to religious experience?" Robinson responds that she doubts that literature can stand in for religion, having a human value all of its own. However, she reminds Painter that the blessing Ames gives Jack is "an act of recognition that blesses Ames, too. He is profoundly moved that he has had the occasion to do it, that Jack accepted it, wanted it." She continues by saying that all blessing is really mutual, and "that the moment of blessing is when people rise to the very beautiful seriousness of what they are."[109]

CONCLUSION

Robinson's apologetic strategy is not as systematic as MacDonald's. And yet my argument is that Robinson is doing for her readers what Ames does for Jack, not offering proofs but a posture of blessing, not offering arguments to evaluate but an imaginary to inhabit. This is the essence of reimagining apologetics: it blesses by embodying a Christian vision of the world—fallen, yet still created and loved by its creator, who has not abandoned it. Even when the vision is not embraced, the very act of blessing has the capacity to enlarge the imagination with a sense of what it feels like to inhabit such a world. Indeed, as Robinson points out in one of her essays, beauty disciplines. It trains our powers of perception, carving out

---

[108]Robinson, *What Are We Doing Here?*, 241.
[109]Painter, "Further Thoughts on a Prodigal Son," 490.

new categories, giving us new language to name and respond to what is "unconsciously and intimately known."[110]

Like MacDonald, Robinson invites us to rethink the parameters of apologetic witness. Although she sometimes resembles a traditional apologist in her invectives against the New Atheists, her primary apologetic contribution is the way that she blesses and baptizes the imagination of her reader by providing a visionary experience of the world. She offers a thick imaginative engagement in the age of authenticity, one that takes our felt experience of the world seriously. This thick engagement, which we see in both MacDonald and Robinson, shares not just a common method but a common theological ground: the conviction that the fallen world and the fallible soul remain flooded with divine presence. Drawing these two writers together, this theologically grounded apologetic posture is the subject I will explore in chapter six.

---

[110]Robinson, *What Are We Doing Here?*, 110.

– *six* –

Baptizing Imaginations
Learning from MacDonald and Robinson

There remains in all their work the ravishment, or the shock,

of revelatory perception. . . . Behind the aesthetics

and the metaphysics of classical American literature,

again and again we find the Calvinist soul,

universal in its singularity, and full of Calvinist wonder.

MARILYNNE ROBINSON, *JOHN CALVIN,*
STEWARD OF GOD'S COVENANT

ONCE UPON A TIME A MAN PICKED UP A BOOK at a train station. In the evening he began to read and found himself transfixed by the fantastic tale. He would later describe the experience of a "bright shadow coming out of the book into the real world and resting there, transforming all common things." The man was C. S. Lewis, and the book was George MacDonald's faerie romance *Phantastes*. Lewis described the encounter memorably: "In the depth of my disgraces, in the then invincible ignorance of my intellect, all this was given me without my asking, even without consent. That night my imagination was, in a certain sense, baptized; the rest of me, not unnaturally, took longer."[1] In MacDonald Lewis found the shock of revelatory perception.

His testimony exhibits the way that works of imagination can pull us in with a certain gravity, saturating us in unlooked-for aesthetic sensibilities. Perhaps we can all testify to having such an experience in reading, watching a movie, or listening to a piece of music. When we are fortunate, we hear Rilke's call: "You must change your life." Whether we do change our lives or remain the same, the "bright shadow" lingers in our imagination, hovering with (ah!) bright wings.

If MacDonald's fantasy baptized Lewis's imagination, Robinson's novels have continued that priestly ministry in our contemporary context. Indeed, in the previous chapter I noted the prevalence of baptismal imagery in Robinson's writings, suggesting that baptismal blessing is a fitting metaphor for her literary art. Robinson, like MacDonald seeks to touch the imagination "with the pure intention of blessing," naming the sacredness that is already there.[2]

Baptism, it should be remembered, is a sign and a seal of God's gracious promise. It acknowledges the reality of God's presence, attention, love, and blessing toward the world in general and toward the baptized person in particular. Calvin taught that the baptismal blessing should be united to the preaching of the gospel; without the word to explain the sign, the sacrament "hangs by a thread."[3] And yet, Calvin also argued that the signified promise is confined neither to the sacrament itself, nor to the time it is administered.[4] Thus, baptism may precede faith, and when faith dawns in the heart of the believer, it realizes the prior promise signified in

---

[1]C. S. Lewis, *Surprised by Joy: The Shape of My Early Life* (New York: Houghton Mifflin Harcourt, 1966), 181. Some readers might wonder why Lewis himself is not one of the models in this book. He well could be, since few writers have fused reason and imagination so seamlessly, especially in service of apologetic witness. Thankfully, that ground has been well-plowed by other writers. See especially Michael Ward, "The Good Serves the Better and the Best: C. S. Lewis on Imagination and Reason in Apologetics," in *Imaginative Apologetics* (Grand Rapids: Baker Academic, 2012), 59-78.

[2]Marilynne Robinson, *Gilead* (New York: Picador, 2006), 23.

[3]John Calvin, *Institutes of the Christian Religion*, ed. John T. McNeill, trans. Ford Lewis Battles (Louisville: Westminster John Knox, 2001) 4.16.1.

[4]This was a key point of debate between Calvin and Westphal. See John Calvin, *Treatises on the Sacraments, Tracts by John Calvin*, trans. Henry Beveridge. (Grand Rapids: Christian Focus, 2002), 341.

baptism. For this reason, Calvin did not see the need to rebaptize "converts" from Rome. He used his personal testimony to illustrate: "We reply that we indeed being blind and unbelieving, for a long time did not grasp the promise that had been given us in baptism; yet that promise, since it was of God, ever remained fixed and firm and trustworthy. . . . This promise was offered to us in baptism, therefore, let us embrace it by faith."[5]

The full benefits of baptism are realized only by those who embrace the promise of the gospel. And yet, the promise of baptism remains "fixed and trustworthy," notwithstanding human blindness and unbelief. It waits to be taken up and trusted, to be felt with all its force. Until that time, the bright shadow of blessing hovers over the baptized-but-yet-to-believe.

I take this digression into the theology of baptism because the project of apologetics in the age of authenticity may be less a matter of addressing intellects and more a matter of baptizing imaginations. Might it be possible that doubters and skeptics, those who find themselves unable to feel the truth of Christian claims, are nevertheless able to foretaste some of the benefits through works of art, as Lewis did when he read MacDonald? Might it be possible for those who find themselves unable to believe, upon encountering a capacious Christian imagination, at least find themselves able to suspend disbelief? This chapter highlights the way that literary artistry offers a model of the imaginative approach I am proposing.

Let us posit this baptismal posture of imaginative blessing as a common thread to draw MacDonald and Robinson together. I have described both writers as unconventional apologists, conversant with the preoccupations of their respective eras: MacDonald with the Victorian crisis of faith, Robinson with contemporary reductionism. But the larger frame, recognized by both writers, is the burgeoning value of authenticity in which one's felt experience of the world must be reckoned with as a matter of fundamental importance.

MacDonald and Robinson share more in common than this baptismal posture. Their literary imaginations are also funded by common theological source, a theological vision in which the world is drenched with

---

[5]Calvin, *Institutes* 4.15.17.

divine presence. To recall the earlier discussion, this denotes the conviction that all the good we find in the world or in ourselves is a divine gift. Likewise, if we find beauty or truth in human imaginings, we can look nowhere else for their source. This conviction is put quite beautifully by MacDonald in his novel *The Seaboard Parish:*

> Is not all the good in us his image? Imperfect and sinful as we are, is not all the foundation of our being his image? Is not the sin all ours, and the life in us all God's? We cannot be the creatures of God without partaking of his nature. Every motion of our conscience, every admiration of what is pure and noble, is a sign and a result of this. Is not every self-accusation a proof of the presence of his spirit?[6]

This theological vision yields a generative posture, one that seeks to recognize and participate in divine self-giving.

Two clarifications are necessary at this point. First, though I will explicitly connect this theological vision to Calvin, I am certainly not claiming that Calvinists alone can have such a capacious vision of the world. Experience alone testifies that other theological traditions have other resources for approximating if not exceeding what I am celebrating.[7] Rather, I am signaling the theological source of the apologetic method that I have imbibed in part from my two primary conversation partners. And I am suggesting that, contrary to popular caricature, Calvin has something other than "tulips" to offer the wider church.

Second, to be authentically Christian we must include antithesis as well as affirmation. There can be no blanket baptism of human imaginings if sin tilts the imagination toward idols. Indeed, Calvin himself is better known for saying things like this: "For as rashness and superficiality are joined to ignorance and darkness, scarcely a single person has ever been found who did not fashion for himself an idol or specter in place of God. Surely, just as waters boil up from a vast, full spring, so does an immense crowd of gods flow forth from the human mind."[8]

---

[6]George MacDonald, *The Seaboard Parish* (Whitethorn, CA: Johannesen, 1995), 172.
[7]Indeed, throughout this book I draw deeply from non-Reformed sources, including Charles Taylor, David Tracy, George Steiner, and Sarah Coakley.
[8]Calvin, *Institutes* 1.5.12.

Thus, we must not merely seek to recognize the lingering "signs of divinity" in humanity that "cannot be effaced."[9] We must also situate these signs in relationship to God's supreme revelation in Jesus Christ (Heb 1:3). In human imaginings, we find glimmers of glory but also egregious error. The gospel challenges all human imaginings, giving the clearest image of God in Christ.

To test my argument about the theological foundation of my project, I need first to demonstrate the common source of Robinson and MacDonald in a Calvinist visionary tradition and then to inquire whether their accounts of God's presence also provide the Christian antithesis. The conversation between Robinson and MacDonald will lead into a larger discussion on the limitations of an imaginative approach to apologetics. I will return to the question of whether the religious openness that we find in both authors leaves us with adequate theological substance. To put it plainly, do these authors' imaginative projects pull their readers toward creedal Christianity and the God who raised Jesus from the dead? Is their ministry mainly a matter of opening the imagination? Or do they also enjoin the imagination to *close* on something solid?[10] How far can or should reimagining apologetics take us? Where are the boundaries between apologetic preparation and evangelical witness? These are important questions. To answer them, I will proceed in reverse order, allowing Robinson's direct engagement with Calvin to prepare the way.

SURPRISED BY CALVIN: ROBINSON AND THE PROTESTANT IMAGINATION

Marilynne Robinson was not always conscious of her debt to Calvin. Yet as she chronicles her life, she recognizes that the Calvinist tradition was first imparted through her Presbyterian upbringing. It was then absorbed through her studies in nineteenth-century American literature.[11] But Robinson did

---

[9]Calvin, *Institutes* 1.5.5.

[10]So Chesterton: "The object of opening the mind, as of opening the mouth, is to shut it again on something solid." G. K. Chesterton, *The Autobiography of G. K. Chesterton* (San Francisco: Ignatius, 2006), 217.

[11]In an interview she says: "My family was pious and Presbyterian mainly because my grandfather was pious and Presbyterian, but that was more of an inherited intuition than an actual fact."

not fall in love with Calvin until around 1989. Her students at the University of Iowa had asked her to teach *Moby Dick*. Knowing the importance of Calvinist theology to Melville's work, she began to read Calvin's *Institutes*. She was startled by how the Calvin she encountered differed in every way from his popular reputation.[12] She has since made it her mission to combat the popular polemic against such a capacious thinker and tradition.[13]

Calvin's theology dazzled Robinson because it gave her a frame for her fascination with human perception. The desire for language that captures the mystery and miracle of perception predates her published work. She describes an experience from her sophomore year at Brown University, in which she stumbled onto a footnote about mirrors in a treatise by Jonathan Edwards. The footnote describes perception as grounded in theistic realism. In other words, perception is direct engagement with a world addressed to us by its Creator. It is possible because of God's intentional presence toward the world. This footnote, she writes, was her "first, best introduction to epistemology and ontology." She goes on: "Then, by grace of that footnote, I should think of God as present and intentional, and of reality as essentially addressed to human perception—perception being then as now my greatest interest and pleasure in life."[14] Upon reading Calvin himself, she found the roots of Edwards's metaphysical vision made plain. Here is her description of that vision: "God himself chooses to

---

Sarah Fay, "Marilynne Robinson, The Art of Fiction No. 198," *The Paris Review*, no. 186 (Fall 2008), www.theparisreview.org/interviews/5863/marilynne-robinson-the-art-of-fiction -no-198-marilynne-robinson.

[12]John Hesselink and Marilynne Robinson, "Hesselink and Robinson: An Exchange of Letters," *Perspectives*, March 1, 2001, 7.

[13]Her most substantive defense is found in her misleadingly titled essay "Marguerite de Navarre." Robinson admits the misdirection and defends it with the cheeky assertion that if it had been titled "John Calvin" no one would want to read it. She even avoids this popular surname to "free the discussion of the almost comically negative associations of 'John Calvin'": "My intention, my hope, is to revive interest in Jean Cauvin, the sixteenth-century French humanist and theologian." Marilynne Robinson, *The Death of Adam: Essays on Modern Thought* (New York: Picador, 2005), 174. Protestant theologians may quibble with this assessment of Calvin's reputation, yet Robinson's focus is the mainstream academy, and she cites numerous examples that bear out this prejudicial polemic. In any case, many theologians welcome Robinson as an unexpected ally; indeed, John Hesselink argues that *Gilead* "did more to awaken interest in Calvin in the general public than all of the fine studies by Calvin scholars published during the quincentennial celebration of Calvin's birth in 2009." John Hesselink, "Marilynne Robinson: Calvinian," *Perspectives Journal*, March 1, 2011, perspectivesjournal.org/blog/2011/03/01/marilynne-robinson-calvinian/.

[14]Marilynne Robinson, "Credo," *Harvard Divinity Bulletin* 36, no. 2 (Spring 2008): 26.

engage human consciousness thus intimately . . . to do so is his being toward us, and that to feel the presence and the meaning of his attention is our being toward him."[15] This, she realized, was the theological soil and the religious epistemology out of which her imaginative intuitions had grown.[16]

The centrality of perception became the common thread connecting her interest in Calvin to the nineteenth-century American authors that Robinson studied in her academic career. She was entranced by classical American literature and came to attribute its aesthetic to the Calvinist culture that nurtured its generation. In a preface to a collection of Calvin's writings, Robinson makes this plain, linking her favorite authors— Emerson, Thoreau, Dickinson, and Melville—to the Calvinist cultures that shaped their imaginations. She writes:

> Calvin's influence is so widespread as to elude description in this small space, but nowhere is it more evident than in the thought and writing of the early New Englanders, who were, through historical accident, the products of a substantially Calvinist culture. . . . there remains in all their work the ravishment, or the shock, of revelatory perception, whether of the sea, or of a slant of light, or of the floods of humanity crossing on the Brooklyn ferry. . . . Behind the aesthetics and the metaphysics of classical American literature, again and again we find the Calvinist soul, universal in its singularity, and full of Calvinist wonder."[17]

"Revelatory perception"—this is what Robinson came to believe the Calvinist imagination had to offer to a world addicted to materialistic reduction. In another place, she notes, "American culture is often said to be Calvinist. Maybe once it was, and maybe our once considerable generosity owed to the fact."[18]

Calvin's greatest contribution, Robinson claims, is the way that he places each person in such immediate relationship to God that ordinary

---

[15]Marilynne Robinson, *John Calvin: Steward of God's Covenant: Selected Writings*, ed. John F. Thornton (New York: Vintage, 2006),.

[16]Thus, while her later novels are explicitly religious (and Calvinist), her first novel *Housekeeping* is implicitly so.

[17]Robinson, *John Calvin*, xxvi-xxvii.

[18]Marilynne Robinson, *What Are We Doing Here? Essays* (New York: Farrar, Straus and Giroux, 2018), 251.

perception can become revelatory. She takes the priesthood of believers as a foundational metaphysical commitment: "The first assertion of Calvin's theology, both in order and in centrality, is the continuous, un-mediated character of the relationship between God and any human soul."[19] Against the Roman Church that insisted on mediating God's presence through the church, Calvin placed every soul before God (*coram deo*), unable to attain self-knowledge without knowledge of God. And though he rejected the use of iconography, Calvin opted instead for an iconic engagement with the larger world. This meant that even the unedu-cated could access the "great, continuous instruction in perception itself."[20] This iconic imaginative stance gives coherence to his thought. She writes,

> His theology is compelled and enthralled by an overwhelming awareness of the grandeur of God, and this is the source of the distinctive aesthetic coherency of his religious vision, *which is neither mysticism nor metaphysics, but mysticism as a method of rigorous inquiry, and metaphysics as an impas-sioned flight of the soul.* This vision . . . is the consequence of a poetic or imaginative stance.[21]

Most interpreters of Calvin agree that the "grandeur of God" is a central theme in Calvin. What makes Robinson's reading unique is her assessment of Calvin's theological method: "mysticism as a method of rigorous inquiry." Robinson is not using mysticism in the tradition of, say, the desert fathers: detachment and contemplation as a means to spiritual ascent. Rather, by mysticism she means an imaginative stance toward the world under the conviction that created reality is addressed to human consciousness, that it is "authored" for us, waiting to be taken up and read. Thus understood, we can draw from ordinary perception "the way a mystic draws from a vision."[22] Everyday experience can become divine encounter.

Robinson is stunned by this. She emphasizes that the adequacy of this perception is marred by sin, but for her this relates to the capacity of our

---

[19]Robinson, *John Calvin*, xvii.
[20]Robinson, *John Calvin*, xxiii.
[21]Robinson, *Death of Adam*, 188. Emphasis added.
[22]Sarah Fay, "Marilynne Robinson: The Art of Fiction No. 198."

perception. It does not remove God's nearness, which makes perception possible. She writes, "[Calvin's] esthetics, his ethics, his anthropology, and his ontology are all based on the faith that God is always present to us, waiting to be seen and known."[23] In fact, she proposes that there are really only two significant terms in Calvin's metaphysics: God and humanity. "Every other aspect of being," she argues, "is a revelation of God suited to human perception, or a form of comfort or sustenance provided to address human needs, or a test by which our understanding of God can be enlarged and deepened."[24] To her this is a stunning turn away from the static cosmologies of Aristotle and Plato. Calvin's cosmology is dynamic and relational, "something the pagan imagination could never have come up with."[25]

Indeed, for Robinson this relational orientation is the primary way the Christian antithesis is expressed. Although human depravity is pervasive, the human awareness of the divine is the deeper reality.[26] Robinson connects the sense of the divine to the image of God, writing that human participation in the divine nature is found in our "capacity for thought, perception, and intention, which are marvelous, clear signs of divinity, even in our condition of fallenness."[27] Since Robinson connects the image of God so closely to our capacity for perception, the essence of fallenness is that sin impairs and misdirects human consciousness so that our perception is grossly distorted. Conditioned by the limits of our understanding—which may be simply the fruit of finitude or the result of

[23]Marilynne Robinson, "Calvinism as Metaphysics," *Toronto Journal of Theology* 25, no. 2 (September 2009): 186.

[24]Robinson, "Calvinism as Metaphysics," 184.

[25]Scott Hoezee and Marilynne Robinson, "A World of Beautiful Souls: An Interview with Marilynne Robinson," *Perspectives Journal*, May 16, 2005, perspectivesjournal.org/blog/2005/05/16/a-world-of-beautiful-souls-an-interview-with-marilynne-robinson/.

[26]It is because of the common source in Calvin that Robinson's defense of the reliability of the human faculties shows remarkable affinity with Reformed epistemology, discussed in chapter two. Although Robinson shows no engagement with these thinkers, her arguments are strikingly similar, especially when discussing the *sensus divinitatis*. Compare, for example, how each describes their belief in God. Plantinga writes: "I am a theist; I believe that there is such a person as God; but I have never decided to hold this belief. It has always just seemed to me to be true. And it isn't as if I could rid myself of this belief by an act of will." Alvin Plantinga, *Knowledge and Christian Belief* (Grand Rapids: Eerdmans, 2015), 17. Robinson writes: "I felt God as a presence before I had a name for him, and long before I knew words like 'faith' or 'belief.' . . . I thought everyone else must be aware of it." Robinson, *Death of Adam*, 228.

[27]Robinson, "Calvinism as Metaphysics," 178.

rebellion—we have eyes but do not see; we have ears but do not hear.[28] In our fallen condition, we fail to perceive God's address in creation and God's image in those around us. Thus fallen, we have a "terrible privilege, a capacity for profound error and grave harm."[29] And yet, despite our blindness to the glory that surrounds us, God's active presence continues to make our acts of perception possible.

Robinson's reading of Calvin is brilliant yet also idiosyncratic; my purpose at the moment is to set forth her interpretation of Calvin without critique. I want to underline how Robinson's emphasis on the miracle of perception, grounded in Calvin's metaphysics, undergirds her imaginative approach. It is because God is present, engaging human consciousness, that human perception of the world is necessarily a relational encounter. Indeed, at times we can "feel the presence and meaning of his attention."[30] These moments are epiphanic; they are occasions when we experience the ravishment or shock of revelatory perception, the realization of a wider world. Robinson calls this the "metaphysics of encounter" and considers it Calvin's chief legacy.[31] And it is because she operates with the conviction that experience can be revelatory that she fills her stories with epiphanies of the ordinary, giving her readers a glimpse of a "Calvinist soul, universal in its singularity, and full of Calvinist wonder."

AN IMAGINATIVE MIRACLE? MACDONALD AND THE PROTESTANT IMAGINATION

Whereas Robinson makes her debt to Calvin explicit, the case of MacDonald is more complicated. Indeed, when it comes to MacDonald, the case is more difficult to make, since "Calvinism" is usually presented as the foil for MacDonald's imaginative work.[32] On this interpretation,

---

[28]Robinson fails to make a clear distinction between the concepts of finitude and fallenness, using them interchangeably.

[29]Robinson, *What Are We Doing Here?*, 49.

[30]Robinson, *John Calvin*, xxi.

[31]Intriguingly, this seems to be the Reformation thread picked up by Schleiermacher as well. Strangely, Robinson makes little if any mention of Schleiermacher, the father of modern liberal theology, though she is fascinated by his student Ludwig Feuerbach.

[32]I place "Calvinism" in scare quotes to represent the straw man against which many writers set MacDonald's work, in distinction from Calvinism, a complex and variegated phenomenon.

MacDonald's genius was commensurate to his ability to *escape* the strict "Calvinism" of his upbringing.[33] G. K. Chesterton was one of the earliest interpreters to set MacDonald and Calvinism in stark opposition, writing that MacDonald "evolved out of his own mystical meditations a completely alternative theology leading to a completely contrary mood." For Chesterton, MacDonald rediscovered his Celtic roots, and with it a sacramental vision of the world. He writes, "To have got back to it, or forward to it, at one bound of boyhood, out of the black Sabbath of a Calvinist town, was a miracle of imagination."[34] Already in Chesterton (himself a Roman Catholic) we see a cold assessment of "Calvinism," one that biographers have followed in narrating the deformative influence of "Calvinism" on MacDonald's childhood.[35] Underneath the narrative is the assumption that a Calvinist imagination must be thin and feeble when compared to Celtic, Romantic, or Roman Catholic alternatives. What are we to make of this? How can the same tradition that liberated Robinson also be the prison from which MacDonald needed to escape?

There is a real basis for the anti-Calvinist trope in MacDonald, even if it is ultimately a caricature. MacDonald's upbringing was immersed in Calvinist influences. His childhood was steeped in the Westminster Shorter Catechism, and his college education was undergirded by the weekly reflection on the Heidelberg Catechism.[36] Although the latter is barely mentioned in

---

[33]It has been fashionable in recent MacDonald studies to separate MacDonald's Christian faith from his literary work. The best discussion and refutation of this line of thinking is found in Kirstin Jeffrey Johnson, "Rooted in All Its Story, More Is Meant Than Meets the Ear: A Study of the Relational and Revelational Nature of George MacDonald's Mythopoeic Art" (PhD diss., University of St. Andrews, 2011), 22-62.

[34]Chesterton contrasts MacDonald with his contemporary Thomas Carlyle. Even after abandoning his faith, Chesterton argues, Carlyle always retained a touch of indignant bullying in his writing: "Carlyle never lost the Puritan mood even when he lost the whole of the Puritan theology." Chesterton's preface is found in Greville MacDonald, *George MacDonald and His Wife* (Whitethorn, CA: Johannesen), 12-14.

[35]This portrait of MacDonald's Calvinist childhood is anchored in the incident in which his Grandmother Isobel MacDonald burned his older brother Charles's violin, recapitulated with embellishment in *Robert Falconer*. Robert Wolff articulates the popular consensus when he writes of MacDonald's "brisk refutation" and "revulsion" against *Calvinism*. Robert Wolff, *Gains and Losses: Novels of Faith and Doubt in Victorian England* (New York: John Murray, 1977), 345-46.

[36]Rolland Hein, *George MacDonald: Victorian Mythmaker* (Whitethorn, CA: Johannesen, 1999), 47. There may be a reference to the first question of the Heidelberg Catechism in the closing lines of MacDonald's response to an unknown lady who has asked what he has "lost of the old faith": "To Him I belong heart and soul and body, and he may do with me as he will." George

MacDonald's works, Westminster makes more frequent appearances. In reference to its first question ("What is the chief end of man? To glorify God and to enjoy him forever"), MacDonald wryly notes, "I wish the spiritual engineers who constructed it had, after laying the grandest foundation-stone that truth could afford them, glorified God by going no further. Certainly many a man would have enjoyed Him sooner, if it had not been for their work."[37]

What was it about the rest of the catechism that MacDonald found so objectionable? His biographer Rolland Hein comments that it was not so much the content of the catechism that MacDonald despised as the way it was used "to crush the spirits of genuinely sensitive people."[38] Though MacDonald clearly resisted particular doctrines prized by the Westminster divines—especially penal substitution and eternal perdition—his greatest defiance was against applications of Calvinist theology that cast God as a narrow miser rather than a generous father. Greville MacDonald's statement that his father had "discarded all Calvinistic doctrine" is plainly incorrect.[39] MacDonald held resolutely to the doctrine of God's absolute sovereignty; indeed, there are few authors so convinced of the comprehensive providence of God.[40] Yet MacDonald also observes that these Calvinists "take up what their leader, urged by the necessity of the time, spoke loudest, never heeding what he loved most; and then work the former out to a logical perdition of everything belonging to the latter."[41] What MacDonald cherished was the grandeur of Calvin's God, and therefore he rejected the smallness and meanness of Calvin's followers.

MacDonald, *An Expression of Character: The Letters of George MacDonald*, ed. Glenn Edward Sadler (Grand Rapids: Eerdmans, 1994), 154.

[37]George MacDonald, *Alec Forbes of Howglen* (Whitethorn, CA: Johannesen, 1995), 41.

[38]Hein, *George MacDonald*, 13.

[39]Greville's brother Ronald gives a different interpretation: "his war was against the faithlessness of the officially faithful, and incidentally only, upon one or two Calvinist and Augustinian dogmas exaggerated out of all proportion to their service." Ronald MacDonald, *From a Northern Window: A Personal Remembrance of George MacDonald* (Eureka, CA: Sunrise, 1989), 88.

[40]Timothy Larsen notes in MacDonald's novels "the thunderous voice of John Knox echoing off the Scottish hills." Timothy Larsen, *George MacDonald in the Age of Miracles: Incarnation, Doubt, and Reenchantment* (Downers Grove, IL: IVP Academic, 2018), 103. To use categories popularized by George Marsden, we might say that MacDonald fits better with pietist than doctrinalist streams of Calvinism. George Marsden, "Reformed and American," in *Reformed Theology in America: A History of Its Modern Development*, ed. David F. Wells (Grand Rapids: Eerdmans, 2009).

[41]George MacDonald, *David Elginbrod* (Whitethorn, CA: Johannesen, 1995), 93.

Thus, while it is inappropriate to call MacDonald a Calvinist, his religious sensibilities were shaped, like Robinson's, by Calvin's epistemology. Indeed, this can be clearly seen as in his discussion of the imagination itself. In contrast to Romantic thinkers like Coleridge, MacDonald asserts a clear distinction between creator and creation. Though the imagination has creative power, we should not think that our imaginative work occurs on the same metaphysical plane as God's. *Poet* indeed means "maker," but MacDonald cautions,

> We must not forget . . . that between creator and poet lies the one unpassable gulf which distinguishes—far be it from us to say divides—all that is God's from all that is man's; a gulf teeming with infinite revelations, but a gulf over which no man can pass to find out God, although God needs not pass over it to find man; the gulf between that which calls, and that which is thus called into being; between that which makes in its own image and that which is made in that image. It is better to keep the word creation for that calling out of nothing which is the imagination of God.[42]

MacDonald makes it clear that he believes that human imagination is always metaphysically derivative: "In no primary sense is this faculty creative." Because of this he preferred to speak of imaginative work *finding*, not creating, since "the meanings are in the forms already" quite apart from human imagination.[43] *Finding* retains the posture of childlike wonder that MacDonald felt so necessary to virtue, in opposition to the image of man as the autonomous maker of his own destiny.[44]

If Romanticism transformed the imagination from mirror to lamp, MacDonald offers a mediating picture: a mirror that illuminates because of the image it reflects.[45] As divine light bounces off the mirror it lights

---

[42]MacDonald goes on to say that occasionally we may call "daring" works of symbolic expression truly creative, but even this is only because of the "likeness of man's work to the work of his maker." MacDonald, *Dish of Orts*, 2-3.

[43]George MacDonald, *A Dish of Orts* (Whitethorn, CA: Johannesen, 1996), 4-5.

[44]As MacDonald writes: "A little wonder is worth tons of knowledge." George MacDonald, *Home Again and The Elect Lady* (Whitethorn, CA: Johannesen, 1993), 42.

[45]"The meanings are in the forms already; else they could be no garment of unveiling. God has made the world that it should thus serve his creature, developing in the service that imagination whose necessity it meets. The man has but to light the lamp within the form: his imagination is the light, it is not the form." MacDonald, *Dish of Orts*, 5.

the wick of the lantern that already exists within the creation. Although entrusted with the light, the imagination is never the source of the light. It is always "God's candle." As MacDonald writes in *Paul Faber*: "It is God who gives thee thy mirror of imagination, and if though keep it clean, it will give thee back no shadow but of the truth."[46] God thus supplies the capacity (lamp) as well as the inspiration (light), and it is God's initiative, not human ingenuity, that is our hope:

> But God sits in that chamber of our being in which the candle of our consciousness goes out in darkness, and sends forth from thence wonderful gifts into the light of that understanding which is His candle. Our hope lies in no most perfect mechanism of the spirit, but in the wisdom wherein we live and move and have our being. Thence we hope for endless forms of beauty informed of truth. If the dark portion of our own being were the origin of our imaginations, we might well fear the apparition of such monsters as would be generated in the sickness of a decay which could never feel—only declare—a slow return towards primeval chaos. But the Maker is our Light.[47]

The work of the imagination is thus more than imitation but less than creation. It is a sort of creative discovery in which the human imagination is fueled by and responsive to the continual, creative self-giving love of God. As one of MacDonald's characters finds, "There must be truth in the scent of that pinewood: someone must mean it. There must be a glory in those heavens that depends not upon our imagination: some power greater than they must dwell in them."[48] For MacDonald as for Robinson, the "givenness of things"—grounded in divine self-giving—situates the source of meaning outside the human subject. Indeed, MacDonald writes, if a person can be said to have "a wise imagination," it signifies nothing less than the "presence of the spirit of God."[49]

Thus, to put MacDonald and Calvinism in simple antithesis, and to argue that MacDonald's work required a "wholly alternative theology" is

---

[46]George MacDonald, *Paul Faber, Surgeon* (Whitethorn, CA: Johannesen, 1992), 29.
[47]MacDonald, *Dish of Orts*, 25.
[48]George MacDonald, *Robert Falconer* (Whitethorn, CA: Johannesen, 1995), 123.
[49]MacDonald, *Dish of Orts*, 28.

a mistake.[50] *Exaggeration* is the word used by Ronald to describe the object of his father's belligerence: "his war was against the faithlessness of the officially faithful, and incidentally only, upon one or two Calvinist and Augustinian dogmas exaggerated out of all proportion to their service."[51] With Calvinism playing such a formative role in the "officially faithful," it makes sense that MacDonald paints portraits of narrow Calvinists in his novels. There is no shortage of religious characters in MacDonald's corpus who mistake doctrine for devotion.[52] But for MacDonald, there was no need to find a new epistemology in which to plant his love of God and wonder at God's world. Though it is true that some of MacDonald's Calvinist contemporaries emphasized doctrines that MacDonald despised, Calvin's God-entranced vision remained deeply resonant with MacDonald's Scottish sensibilities.[53]

If I am belaboring this point, it is because I want to distinguish Calvinism as a doctrinal system from a broader Calvinian imaginative

---

[50]To do so ignores the diversity within Calvinist thought, assumes that there were no counter-currents present in MacDonald's upbringing for resisting the excesses, and misses the modes of Calvinist theology that deeply shaped MacDonald's imagination. Johnson emphasizes that "Grandmother Isabella was an influence that they *visited*: George Sr., Uncle James, and their wives were the primary Christian influences of MacDonald's childhood, not Grandmother Isabella. . . . With [George Sr.'s] father a Catholic-born, fiddle-playing, Presbyterian elder, his mother an Independent church rebel, his first wife a sister to the Gaelic-speaking radical who became Moderator of the disrupting free church, and his second wife the daughter of an Episcopalian minister— merely using the tag "Calvinist" for his son's theological background is both simplistic and misleading." Johnson, "Rooted in All Its Story," 43-44. Oliver Crisp has argued that many of the ideas that were considered heterodox or heretical within particular Calvinist contexts (such as universal atonement) actually fit within the boundaries of the wider Calvinist tradition. See Oliver D. Crisp, *Deviant Calvinism: Broadening Reformed Theology* (Minneapolis: Fortress, 2014).

[51]MacDonald, *From a Northern Window*, 88.

[52]Even biographer Robert Wolff, who places MacDonald and Calvinism in sharp opposition, acknowledges that refutations of Calvinist doctrine are "accompanied by sympathetic and wholly convincing portrayals of individual Calvinists," like the stonemason Thomas Crann, who finds God's face within his Calvinism rather than apart from it. Wolff, *Gains and Losses*, 343.

[53]To attribute all that MacDonald loved to Celtic sources and all that he hated to Calvinist ones is a gross oversimplification. The two sources were deeply mingled, exerting a cumulative vision on the imaginations of Scotsmen like MacDonald. It could be argued that it was only when the Calvinists used their confession to replace rather than to fulfill the longings and legends of Celtic culture that Calvinism became toxic to the highlanders. One of the reasons why MacDonald was so drawn to his mentor A. J. Scott was the way that Scott saw "the Gospel was seen as fulfilling rather than destroying the old Celtic mythologies." J. Philip Newell, "A. J. Scott and His Circle" (PhD diss., Edinburgh University, 1981), 27. For more on the relationship between Scott and MacDonald, see Johnson to whom I am indebted for the source. Johnson, "Rooted in All Its Story," 63-122.

vision. Certainly, the two are connected. But it is possible for a thinker to reject points of Calvinist doctrine while remaining deeply gripped and shaped by something like Calvin's epistemology. As for the former, MacDonald refused to identify with Calvinism, even as he resisted any alternative, writing, "We are far too anxious to be definite and to have finished, well-polished, sharp-edged systems—forgetting that the more perfect a theory about the infinite, the surer it is to be wrong, the more impossible it is to be right. I am neither Arminian nor Calvinist. To no system would I subscribe."[54] Systems, he believed, could become idolatrous substitutes for piety, obscuring devotion to God and duty to neighbor. Nevertheless, I want to emphasize that MacDonald retains a deeply Calvinian apprehension of the world. To reverse Chesterton's conclusion, the miracle of imagination came *through* the Calvinian vision rather than apart from it. It was this Reformed corrective to the Romantic imagination that would fund MacDonald's response to the Victorian crisis, informing the apologetic thrust of his work. As Dearborn writes, "The priority given to God in all things held him fast against the full tide of Romanticism, and Cartesian self-assertion."[55] This theologically grounded vision results in a body of work that spoke powerfully to the felt narrowness of Victorian faith.

TESTING THE PROTESTANT IMAGINATION

I am aware that in contemporary times, Calvinism has many connotations besides the visionary element I have highlighted here. Thus, I am content to use a more neutral term and to speak of the Protestant imagination to prevent my readers from being pricked by Calvinism's "points." But for some, this may not be a significant advance. It is often claimed that a Protestant imagination will be necessarily impoverished. Protestants, the argument goes, are inhibited from producing quality art and literature

---

[54]MacDonald, *George MacDonald and His Wife*, 155. Yet already the year after his death a reviewer would write: "He was to his own age shockingly liberal, and to ours he is amazingly orthodox." Louise Collier Willcox, "A Neglected Novelist," *North American Review*, no. 183 (September 1906): 403. Cited in Kerry Dearborn, *Baptized Imagination: The Theology of George MacDonald* (Burlington, VT: Ashgate, 2006), 2.

[55]Dearborn, *Baptized Imagination*, 13.

because they lack a robust sacramental theology.[56] Writer Thomas Howard (who converted from Presbyterianism to Catholicism at age fifty) puts this pointedly, alleging that Protestants rarely produce quality literature. Noting that C. S. Lewis is an exception, he sources Lewis's genius in a high Anglican sacramentality because, as he writes, "You cannot ordinarily get literature like [Lewis] from the radically verbalist, propositionalist, discursive religion of the Reformation."[57]

MacDonald and Robinson offer a profound counterpoint to such an argument. The fact that Protestants have often been suspicious of aesthetics is undeniable, but this need not be the case.[58] The Protestant imagination experiences God's presence in the world, not as a matter of ontological constitution but as a continual, intentional address. To work from within this imaginative tradition is to inhabit the space carved out by Calvin himself in the introduction to his commentary on Genesis:

> We see, indeed, the world with our eyes, we tread the earth with our feet, we touch innumerable kinds of God's works with our hands, we inhale a sweet and pleasant fragrance from herbs and flowers, we enjoy boundless benefits; but in those very things of which we attain some knowledge, there dwells such an immensity of divine power, goodness, and wisdom, as absorbs all our senses.[59]

The Protestant imagination is equipped to recognize God's presence in the material world precisely because the world is the theater of God's glory. Calvin is, as Robinson points out, "intensely this-worldly . . . and sees the task of the soul as deep perception of the givenness of this world rather than as looking through or beyond it."[60] We may pervert God's gifts, but we can never escape the presence and address of their source.

---

[56]Such a diagnosis is made by Andrew Greeley: Greeley argues that while the Roman Catholic doctrine of "real presence" makes space for God to meet humanity in material things, Reformation theology is less equipped to recognize God's presence in the world, emphasizing instead the distance between God and Creation. Andrew Greeley, *The Catholic Imagination* (Berkeley: University of California Press, 2001).

[57]Thomas Howard, "The Cult of C. S. Lewis," *Crisis* 12, no. 7 (August 1994): 33.

[58]Richard J. Mouw, "Neo-Calvinism and 'The Catholic Imagination,'" in *Rerum Novarum: Neo-Calvinism and Roman Catholicism* (Third European Conference on Neo-Calvinism, Rome, Italy, 2014).

[59]Jean Calvin, *Commentary on Genesis*, ed. John King (Grand Rapids: Baker, 2003), 1.

[60]Marilynne Robinson, "Sacred Inwardness," *The Christian Century* 132, no. 14 (2015): 177.

As MacDonald reminds us, our deepest longings for beauty and goodness flow from a God whose reality "is deeper in us than our own life . . . the very centre and creative cause of that life which we call ours."[61] Creation and creativity alike invite our conscious attention, a "little willingness to see" the sparks of glory that surround us and move through us.

It is also the theological conviction of divine generosity, and the picture of God as the fountain of overflowing abundance, that fund both authors' hospitality to seekers and doubters. Both are fueled by the hope that grace will ultimately prove irresistible, "that the wanderers will find a way home."[62] If, as in the Calvinist understanding, every impulse toward beauty, goodness, and truth owes to God's grace, then, as MacDonald writes, "One better thought concerning [God], the poorest desire to draw near him, is an approach to him."[63] Thus they encourage us to hope that God is better and more beautiful than we have previously imagined. For when Lila says, "Well, but that's what you want to believe, ain't it," Ames responds, "That doesn't mean it isn't true."[64] Or as Wingfold says to Barbara, "Why . . . think anything too good to be true?"[65] To participate in this reimagined apologetic project is to follow MacDonald and Robinson in their posture of blessing, daring to hope that God is present and active in our felt experience of the world, as well as beyond it.

The limits of liberality: Is this theologically thick enough? The application and limits of divine generosity raises important questions. What are the limits to the theological openness that we find in both MacDonald and Robinson's apologetic art? To put it another way, are MacDonald or Robinson *consistently* theological thinkers in balancing affirmation with antithesis? As mentioned above, a Protestant imagination is not just iconic but also iconoclastic. It does not simply celebrate the sparks of God's glory but also sets the image of God in the face of Jesus Christ as the standard by which all of our imaginings must ultimately be judged.

---

[61]George MacDonald, *Salted with Fire* (Whitethorn, CA: Johannesen, 1996), 325.

[62]Marilynne Robinson, *Housekeeping* (New York: Picador, 1980), 195.

[63]George MacDonald, *There and Back* (Whitethorn, CA: Johannesen, 1991), 295.

[64]Robinson, *Lila* (New York: Picador, 2015), 143.

[65]MacDonald, *There and Back*, 196.

MacDonald's theology was considered liberal ("broad churchman") by many of the evangelicals of his day. His resistance to penal substitution (the idea that Christ is punished in our place) and eternal punishment was emblematic of a Victorian shift from emphasizing divine transcendence and human sinfulness to emphasizing divine immanence and fatherly love. Boyd Hilton describes this as a turn from "The Age of Atonement" to the "Age of Incarnation."[66] This is not to say that thinkers like MacDonald denied the necessity of Christ's death. It is rather that the incarnation is the lens through which the cross is understood.[67] For earlier evangelicals, the cross was the primary reason for the incarnation: Jesus was born so he could die. But for MacDonald and others like him, this reversed the order. "God with us" meant that both incarnation and atonement were bound together, demonstrating God's redeeming love, the lengths to which God will go to set humanity free.[68] MacDonald upheld a resolute view of divine justice, but he rejected the idea that it could be satisfied by punishment. Justice would not be satisfied, he believed, until we are comprehensively just, until like Jesus we love the Lord our God with all our heart, soul, mind, and strength and our neighbor as ourselves. It was for the sake of this sort of transformation that Christ came into the world, suffered, and was raised from the dead.

---

[66]See this argument in Boyd Hilton, *The Age of Atonement: The Influence of Evangelicalism on Social and Economic Thought, 1795-1865* (Oxford: Clarendon, 1988). Hilton's argument is developed with respect to MacDonald in Larsen, *George MacDonald in the Age of Miracles*, 12-13.

[67]As one of MacDonald's contemporaries put it, the Incarnation, "with all that it reveals concerning God, man, and the universe, concerning this life and the life to come, stands first." R. W. Dale, *The Old Evangelicalism and the New* (London: Hodder and Stoughton, 1889), 48-49. I am indebted to Larsen's book *George MacDonald in the Age of Miracles* for this source.

[68]MacDonald is reticent to give an explicit articulation of his own theory of atonement, in part because he was wary of the way that believers use theories about God to hide from God. In answer to those who ask him what theory he would substitute for penal substitution he writes, "In the name of the truth,' I answer, None. . . . Say if you will that I fear to show my opinion. Is the man a coward who will not fling his child to the wolves? What faith in this kind I have, I will have to myself before God, till I see better reason for uttering it than I do now." George MacDonald, *Unspoken Sermons: Series I, II, III in One Volume* (Whitethorn, CA: Johannesen, 1999), 532. This apophatic impulse is channeled by C. S. Lewis when Lewis writes, "The central belief is that Christ's death has somehow put us right with God and given us a fresh start. Theories as to how it did this are another matter: A good many different theories have been held as to how it works; what all Christians are agreed on is that it does work." C. S. Lewis, *Mere Christianity* (New York: Harper Collins, 2009), 57-58.

The inexorability of divine love in healing his beloved creation is the common thread in understanding MacDonald's resistance to the traditional doctrine of hell. It was not the idea of hell that MacDonald contested but its finality. The Spirit of God, he believed, would persistently pursue fallen humanity into the very depths of hell. The fires of hell would become purgative, meant to free humanity from their self-obsession and to draw humanity toward "the center of the life-giving fire, whose outer circles burn." No one who has read the agonizing struggle of Lilith to open her closed hand could think the process of purgation to be a pleasant experience. As Larsen points out, "It is a mistake to imagine that he opted for some kind of sentimental, fluffy view. His teaching on hell is, in a way, arguably more uncompromising than that of many traditionalists."[69] This is because MacDonald's God will not be satisfied with anything less than complete sanctification. This led MacDonald to hope for universal redemption, even while allowing the possibility of a final hell. In his final novel, he writes, "If at last it should prove possible for a created being to see good and evil as they are, and choose the evil, then, and only then, there would, I presume, be nothing left for God but to set His foot on him and crush him, as you crush a noxious insect. But God is deeper in us than our own life."[70] Notice that MacDonald grants the possibility of eternal destruction, even while resisting it, expressing, as Gwen Watkins puts it, "an intuitive conviction of its impossibility."[71] This intuition was grounded on his conviction of the inescapability of divine presence, that "God is deeper in us than our own life."

Whether we agree with MacDonald or not on the above doctrines, we can at least appreciate the theological substance and consistency of his imaginative vision. MacDonald not only celebrates the iconic nature of God's presence in the human soul and the wider world but also remains fiercely iconoclastic against human attempts to hide from God using anything else. This relates especially to the images we construct of our own

---

[69]Larsen, *George MacDonald in the Age of Miracles*, 113.
[70]MacDonald, *Salted with Fire*, 325.
[71]Gwen Watkins, "Two Notions of Hell," *North Wind: A Journal of George MacDonald Studies* 10 (1991): 6-7.

virtue, which obscure our sense of God. Dearborn puts it incisively: "MacDonald adopted wholeheartedly the confession's emphasis on God's gracious initiative, the radical distinction between Creator and creature, and the utter rejection of all idols, including the most insistent one—the self."[72] Despite his resistance to certain Calvinist doctrines, MacDonald's work evidences a fierce commitment to God's sovereignty, and his entire apologetic is grounded in the beauty of Jesus Christ as the one in whom the hope of all redemption and renewal is found.

The case of Robinson is more complex. Unlike MacDonald, she is uninterested in convincing or converting unbelievers. She writes, "While my thinking is Christian, it has led me to a kind of universalism that precludes any notion of proselytizing."[73] Unlike MacDonald, Robinson's audience is largely secular, people for whom the conclusions of the masters of suspicion (Freud, Marx, and Nietzsche) are largely taken for granted. While MacDonald challenges the idolatry of theological systems, Robinson's primary targets are contemporary ideologies, secular systems like Darwinism, Marxism, and Freudianism. She calls these systems "antibiotics of the intellect," for their tendency to exclude experiences that do not fit their explanatory filters. She notes a resemblance between our secular orthodoxies and the religious systems they attempt to replace: "these successor monisms modeled their claims on the old claims of religious orthodoxy." By contrast, she calls for a theology that would "embrace rather than exclude . . . a departure, not only from its own troublesome history but from the narrowness and aridity of the secular thinking that has displaced it."[74] Thus, for Robinson, what must be resisted are narrow visions of the world, whether they come in religious or secular guise.

In an article titled "Onward Christian Liberals," Robinson identifies the "great divide" in American Protestantism between those who insisted on the "being born again" and those who rejected "the idea that one could be securely persuaded of one's own salvation and could even apply a fairly objective standard to the state of other's souls." She places herself on the

---

[72]Dearborn, *Baptized Imagination*, 13.
[73]Robinson, *What Are We Doing Here?*, 206.
[74]Robinson, *What Are We Doing Here?*, 36-37.

"liberal side" of the great divide, believing this to be indicative of "a return to Calvinism and its insistence on the utter freedom of God."[75] Notice that Robinson appeals to Calvinism's conception of divine freedom in support of her own liberalism, against what she sees as a novel and narrow enclosure of God's grace. She proudly claims the title of "liberal Protestant," if for no other reason than to distinguish her variety of Christian faith from the religious right.

But what Robinson has principally in mind in using the word *liberal* has less to do with ideological content and more to do with intellectual posture. She even argues that the root of modern liberalism, which is characterized by a generosity of spirit, has its sources in the Old Testament. It is the commitment to this kind of liberalism that results in openness to all varieties of religious experience. Once again, she sources this view in Calvin: "Liberal that I am, I would not presume to doubt the authenticity of the religious experience of anyone at all. Calvinism encourages a robust sense of human fallibility, in particular forbidding the idea that human beings can set any limits to God's grace."[76] Fallibility necessitates openness to being wrong, which entails a generosity of spirit toward competing interpretations. This is why Robinson reserves her harshest words for fundamentalist atheists and Christians who, to her mind, shut down the dialogue between God and the human soul with their claims of certainty. If one already knows all the answers, there is no need to keep the conversation going.

This liberalism, which she elsewhere describes as a religious commitment to "intellectual openness, leads to an ambivalence towards traditional creeds and confessions."[77] She cites Bonhoeffer's concept of "religionless Christianity," noting that while creeds "stabilize the intense speculations" of religion, they also limit "the very things they enable." Like

---

[75]Marilynne Robinson, "Onward, Christian Liberals: Faith Is Not About Piety or Personal Salvation, but About Helping Those in Need," *The American Scholar* 75, no. 2 (2006): 44.

[76]Robinson, "Onward, Christian Liberals," 47. The word *liberal* is fraught with definitional difficulty, since it could refer to Robinson's political commitment, theological beliefs, or methodological starting point (religious experience, rather than Scripture or creed). Robinson fits at least two of the three, though she takes Calvin rather than Schleiermacher as her source for her method.

[77]Robinson, "Credo," 27.

any other systematic exposition of the truth, creeds fail to account sufficiently for the complexity of faith in its lived experience.[78]

What then is the center and substance of Robinson's theological project? It is what she calls "sacred inwardness," the conviction that every human being is engaged in an individual encounter with God that plays itself out in human consciousness.[79] So personal is the nature of this encounter that "no one else is in a position to understand or to judge."[80] And yet the fact that each and every human being shares in this inwardness provides a common ground both for dignity and for ethical action. The fact that humans are *souls,* so brilliantly creative and destructive, entails that each individual person has "absolute dignity," and that all of our thoughts, actions, and even dreams are invested with eternal significance.[81]

As a general truth, the conviction that human beings are sacred does not require one to become a Christian faith to share it.[82] Nevertheless, for Robinson, Christ remains the ontological condition of this truth. This position strikes me as inclusivist rather than pluralist, and her rationale for rejecting an exclusivistic soteriology is her refusal to "set any limits to God's grace." Thus, she feels no need to specify how doubters like Jack and Doll will find a place in the kingdom apart from personal faith. She simply

---

[78]Marilynne Robinson, "That Highest Candle," *Poetry* 190, no. 2 (May 2007): 130.

[79]Robinson writes, "If the fate of souls is at the center of the cosmic drama, is it difficult to imagine that it will unfold, so to speak, in a place set apart, a holy of holies—that is, a human consciousness? Where better might an encounter with God take place? If God is attentive to us individually, as Jesus' saying about the fall of a sparrow certainly implies, then would his history with us be the same in every case, articulable and verifiable, manifest in behaviors that square with expectations?" Marilynne Robinson, "Sacred Inwardness," *The Christian Century* 132, no. 14 (2015): 24.

[80]In an interview, she expresses it this way: "I feel very deeply—very deeply—that faith is a conversation between God and the individual soul that no one else is in a position to understand or to judge." S. L. Mariotti and J. H. Lane, eds., *A Political Companion to Marilynne Robinson* (Lexington: University of Kentucky Press, 2016), 299.

[81]Robinson, *What Are We Doing Here?*, 212.

[82]So Robinson affirms the Apostles' Creed, even as she qualifies it to avoid exclusivism: "I have spent all this time clearing the ground, so that I can say, and be understood to mean, without reservation, that I believe in a divine Creation, and in the Incarnation, the Crucifixion, the Resurrection, the Holy Spirit, and the life to come. I take the Christian mythos to be a special revelation of a general truth, that truth being the ontological centrality of humankind in the created order, with its theological corollary, the profound and unique sacredness of human beings." Marilynne Robinson, *The Givenness of Things: Essays* (New York: Farrar, Straus and Giroux, 2018), 222.

expresses a hopeful confidence that it will be the case, grounding this hope in the specificity of the Christian story:

> John says, God is love. At best, hope is an intuition that this could be true, with the kind of essential truth affirmed in eternity, in the Being of God. . . . Say that in our indifference from everything else we and God are like each other—creative, knowing, efficacious, deeply capable of loyalty. Say that in his healing and feeding and teaching, Jesus let us see that the good that matters to us mortals matters also to eternal God. Then we have every reason to hope.[83]

For Robinson as for MacDonald, hope is grounded in the being of God and manifested in God's human face, Jesus Christ.

It is curious that Robinson mentions the "healing and feeding and teaching" of Jesus but not also his "death and resurrection." Is this omission a legacy of the triumph of the incarnation over the atonement in the nineteenth century? Of course, this is a false choice. Yet, despite her enthusiastic celebration of Calvin, Robinson's reading of the Reformer does seem top-heavy. That is, she makes much of book one of the *Institutes* concerning God the creator but seems reticent to speak of the particularity of God as redeemer. Claiming a high Christology, she argues that her reticence to speak of Christ apart from God the Father is a reflection of her commitment to the inseparability of divine operations.[84] Yet although Calvin clearly does not divide the work of the members of the Trinity, he certainly distinguishes between them in doctrinal particularity. Given Robinson's point on the primacy of perception, it would be worthwhile to ask about the relationship between union with Christ and human perception. Does being united to Christ by the Spirit make *any* difference in our power of perception? Indeed, the Spirit is scarcely mentioned by Robinson; what role might the Spirit play with respect to sacred inwardness, fallen perception, and redeemed imagination? Finally, with her emphasis on the reliability of the individual consciousness, she seems to have little to say about how our individual sense of reality might be

---

[83]Robinson, *What Are We Doing Here?*, 237.
[84]Robinson, *Givenness of Things*, 209.

situated, sharpened, and critiqued in relationship to perceptual traditions such as those found in a denomination or a church.[85] Surely God alone is the ultimate judge of answerable humans in the great conversation. But that does not necessarily rule out prudential and provisional judgments of orthodoxy, orthopathy, and orthopraxy in the meantime.

Robinson's work seems to burst the apologetic box even as we try to place it inside. For whom and to whom is Robinson speaking? She writes that she is more interested in making space for outsiders, in standing in the gap for the sake of the hungry souls "who yearn for a meaningful church" all over the secular map. She wants to emphasize that a loss of doctrine need not necessitate a loss of faith: "Doctrine and practice can shore up belief, even stand in the place of it, when the deeper leanings of the soul tend not to sustain it. This must mean that there is also a deeper faith behind the seeming lack or loss of faith."[86] Her intent is to dignify this deeper faith and somehow situate it within a Christian account of theistic realism.

To return to a figure from earlier in the book, we find in Robinson an apologetic sensitivity reminiscent of Schleiermacher himself. Schleiermacher wrote for a Romantic audience rapidly moving away from religious language. He hoped to awaken them to the divine reality present in life by using language more familiar to their sensitivities. So too Robinson, when pressed to express her convictions with more Trinitarian nuance or christocentric particularity, responds that her audience is primarily secular, and she is "a Christian apologist for the secular world rather than to it."[87] She stands as a provocative bridge-builder, with the stated goal of "reauthorizing experience, felt reality, as one important testimony to the

---

[85]She does write that the "contingency of relationship" requires the continuous "negotiation of your sense of reality with somebody else's sense of reality" but does not elaborate about what this might look like in the context of a religious institution like a local church. Thomas Gardner, *A Door Ajar: Contemporary Writers and Emily Dickinson* (Oxford: Oxford University Press, 2006), 56.

[86]Robinson, *What Are We Doing Here?*, 213.

[87]Quoted in Hesselink, "Marilynne Robinson: Calvinian." This qualification notwithstanding, it would be better to say that Robinson is both: an apologist for the secular world, and an apologist to it. Indeed, she elsewhere writes that the word "secular has no real meaning" since God is present everywhere. Robinson, "Sacred Inwardness."

nature of reality itself."[88] Here is an apologetic for the age of authenticity, but an apologetic that cuts both ways. It refuses to let Christians exclude religious experiences that occur outside the walls of the church, even as it refuses to let atheists exclude the category altogether.

This is why Robinson's work, like Schleiermacher's, represents a salutary start for reimagining apologetics even if it is unsatisfying as a comprehensive theological scheme.[89] Calvinist thinkers will want to continue reading Calvin's later books, to coordinate the work of God the creator with the work of Christ the redeemer, as well as with the Spirit as renewer. But perhaps Robinson offers the "shock therapy" that the contemporary cultured despisers of religion need. Indeed, apologetics need not articulate a complete theology, even if it is implicitly funded by one. Apologetics rather serves to prepare the way for faith, or even to leave the door of faith slightly ajar. Imaginative engagement of the sort we see in Robinson's fiction creates such an opening. It allows the seeker to see and feel what it might mean to live a life of faith, situating their felt experience of the world within the active presence of God.

Apologetics need not *begin* by naming this active presence as the Holy Spirit. But the Spirit testifies to the revelation of God in Jesus Christ. His story limits the imagination with scandalous particularity. But it also sets the imagination free in generous participation, or to use the word MacDonald used, obedience. As he writes, "Your theory is not your faith, nor anything like it. Your faith is your obedience; your theory I know not what."[90] The Christian story is not theory but theodrama, and we affirm divine presence fundamentally by our faithful response.

The limits of the literary: Is this really apologetics? This brings us to the methodological question. Does the literary exploration we see in MacDonald and Robinson strain the limits of what is called apologetics? I have already discussed the danger of subsuming literary work under the heading of apologetics: it runs the risk of instrumentalizing storytelling

---

[88]Robinson, *What Are We Doing Here?*, 103.

[89]Though I find the explicitly Calvinist metaphysic that funds Robinson's imaginative universe to be significantly thicker than the version that we find in Schleiermacher, I wonder how Robinson might fill out the picture in relationship to other theological loci.

[90]George MacDonald, *Unspoken Sermons*, 532.

as a means to some other end. Like MacDonald, Robinson would resist the reduction of her art to apologetics and the identification with what commonly goes by that name.

MacDonald's apologetic intent is much easier to demonstrate; indeed, the case of Ruskin shows that he often had the doubts of particular individuals in mind as he crafted his characters. It is less clear whether Robinson has any particular persons in mind as she writes her novels. Accordingly, at least one commentator explicitly rejects the idea of Robinson's fiction being taken as a "straightforward polemic for religion, a kind of literary apologetics."[91] The world of *Gilead*, he argues, is too morally complex, suggesting that the attempt to draw apologetic wisdom from Robinson's fiction is doomed to fail.

But much depends on what we mean by apologetics. Must apologetics demonstrate the necessity of belief (epistemic obligation), or may apologetics merely show the possibility of belief (epistemic permission)? If the latter is acceptable, then apologetics need not be "straightforward," and it can work by means of any numbers of provocations, suppositions, and explorations. What I have been calling a reimagined apologetic is only polemical to the degree that the Protestant imagination calls for an expansion of reductive ways of envisioning the world. It is consistent with what Robinson describes as "a religious belief in intellectual openness."[92]

In arguing that artists may be our greatest apologists in the age of authenticity, I am not arguing that artists should restrict the scope of their art to the narrow aims of traditional apologetics. Rather, I am arguing that apologetics be widened and reimagined to include the faithful imaginings of believing artists and writers. These artists offer an unprecedented gift to the wider world: the opportunity to see with Christian eyes, to experience Christian sensibilities, to feel the way into faith.

---

[91]Engebretson, "Dear Ordinary," 141.

[92]She writes: "I am not of the school of thought that finds adherence to doctrine synonymous with firmness of faith. On the contrary, I believe that faith in God is a liberation of thought, because thought is an ongoing instruction in things that pertain to God. To test this belief is my fictional practice, the basis for the style and substance of my two novels and the motive behind my nonfiction. This might seem to some people to be paradoxical, a religious belief in intellectual openness." Robinson, "Credo," 26-27.

OBJECTIONS TO REIMAGINED APOLOGETICS:
SIN AND SUBJECTIVISM

Let me depart from the specific cases of MacDonald and Robinson to deal with general objections to the approach I am commending. The first objection is that in seeking beauty, goodness, and truth in human imaginings, we may underestimate the profundity of human depravity. In other words, we cannot merely consider the "passions that move people to act, build, and create"[93] because these are also the passions that move people to tear down and destroy. James K. A. Smith puts this objection poignantly: "Our disordered longings [don't] merely fall short; they are aimed in the wrong direction. What makes these religious is not that they are almost Christian, but rather that they are idolatrous."[94] Alluding to Calvin's diagnosis of the human heart as a factory of idols, Smith warns us that the call to imaginative engagement may sound like a call to continue in evil imaginations.

My response advances along three lines. First, although the imagination shares in the totality of human depravity, we should not consider the imagination to be somehow more fallen than the intellect. Both are thoroughly contaminated by sin, and both must be renewed if we are to accurately grasp the world. Neither human imaginings nor human intellect is the deepest ground of faith; the deepest ground is revelation. Revelation is the condition of all human knowledge, and this means that there is a sense in which God is always graciously meeting humanity in our depravity and enabling us dimly to see, notwithstanding our rebellious hearts.

Second, God's sovereignty and the wider work of the Holy Spirit are the grounds of this expectation rather than human ability. Exactly how the Holy Spirit engages human imagination outside the walls of the church is mysterious; the Spirit's wider work does not allow us to make blanket affirmations of human imaginings. And yet God's image lies

---

[93]William A. Dyrness, *Poetic Theology: God and the Poetics of Everyday Life* (Grand Rapids: Eerdmans, 2011), 5.

[94]James K.A. Smith, "Erotic Theology," *Image Journal* 69, accessed March 29, 2017, www.imagejournal.org/article/erotic-theology/.

beneath our imaginings, and the impulse to affirm the human faculty is an impulse to identify the work of God within the movements of the heart. Recall MacDonald's questions: "Imperfect and sinful as we are, is not all the foundation of our being his image? Is not the sin all ours, and the life in us all God's? . . . Is not every self-accusation a proof of the presence of his spirit?"[95] Insofar as the Protestant imagination chooses to attribute the source of all beauty, goodness, and truth to God, we should anticipate God's presence in surprising places.

Third, the idolatrous drift of the human heart does not disqualify all human desires. Idolatry always overvalues some creational good, and the fact that our desires are tilted toward idolatry does not mean that they are fundamentally idolatrous. Human desires are not monolithic. Our passions themselves are at war with one another (Jas 4:1); they are a "fragmented ensemble of contradicting drives."[96] The cumulative direction of fallen human desires pull us away from God, but beneath multivalent desires are creational structures that can be more fully oriented toward God by the Spirit's power.

The second objection is that accepting the postromantic value of authenticity places human desires, needs, and imaginings at the theological center instead of God. This is a danger for almost any apologetic approach; indeed, the accusation of its human center has led many to reject the very idea of apologetics. Herman Bavinck voices this critique when discussing methods that seek to ground Christian faith in the satisfaction of the human heart and conscience: "The often-repeated claim that Christianity corresponds to human needs brings with it the very real danger that the truth is tailored to suit human nature. The thesis that the truth is authentically human because it is so intensely divine so easily turns into its opposite . . . that it is only divine because it is human."[97] If this is a legitimate danger of any method that seeks to show the existential satisfactions of faith, it is even more pronounced for a method that seeks such satisfaction

---

[95]George MacDonald, *The Seaboard Parish* (Whitethorn, CA: Johannesen, 1995), 172.

[96]Bernard Van den Toren, *Christian Apologetics: Religious Witness as Cross-Cultural Dialogue* (London: T&T Clark, 2011), 216.

[97]Herman Bavinck, *Reformed Dogmatics, Vol. 1: Prolegomena*, ed. John Bolt and John Vriend (Grand Rapids: Baker Academic, 2003), 1:552-53.

on the basis of a "felt" sense! My desire to work within the parameters of the age of authenticity, rather than merely denouncing expressive individualism, opens me up to this critique: I want to begin with human imaginings, and this is an anthropological starting point.

My response is simply to say that such a starting point is unavoidable, and to remind my readers that one's starting point is not the same as the ground. It is because the world belongs to God that we can begin almost anywhere in moving toward him. Faith itself is a subjective starting point, but it is grounded on the prior, objective action of God toward us. Bavinck acknowledges this when arguing for faith as the "internal principle" of the Christian religion: "By making this statement Christian theology indeed takes its starting point in the human subject. The accusation of subjectivism immediately launched against this position, however, is unwarranted and in any case premature. . . . All that is objective exists for us only by means of a subjective consciousness; without consciousness the whole world is dead to us." The problem, Bavinck goes on to write, is when we mistake the starting point for the source: "Thinking is not the source of the idea . . . representation is not the cause of the thing."[98] We think, imagine, and feel our way into faith because we are responding to the active, felt presence of God, who graciously accommodates himself not only to our weakness but also to the way that we have been shaped to grasp for meaning in the world.[99] Like Taylor, I do not wish to repeal the postromantic age but to affirm the basic impulse to authenticity and then to offer the thickest possible version.

CONCLUSION: THEODRAMA
AND THE APOLOGETIC MOODS

A thick version of authenticity requires a larger horizon of meaning. For Christians this is the biblical theodrama, the expansive story of God and

---

[98]Bavinck, *Reformed Dogmatics*, 1:564. Cornelius van der Kooi criticizes Bavinck's starting point as too rooted in the individual subject as opposed to the corporate experience of the church, which is a version of the church corrective discussed in chapter two. Cornelius van der Kooi, "The Appeal to the Inner Testimony of the Spirit, especially in H. Bavinck," *Journal of Reformed Theology* 2 (2008): 103-112.

[99]Charles Partee, *The Theology of John Calvin* (Louisville: Westminster John Knox, 2010), 154-57.

humanity, centered in the story of Israel and Jesus. This story comes to us in many harmonious voices, embodying multiple "moods" of faith. British theologian David Ford writes, "One caricature of theology is as a neat, unquestioning package of dogma in which there are affirmations that say 'Believe this!' and commands that say 'Do this!' That is theology in what grammarians call the indicative and imperative moods."[100] Ford goes on to say that although affirmations and imperatives are essential for the life of faith, a more dynamic understanding of theology recognizes the presence of other theological moods, such as the optative (hoping):

> The biblical theodrama, from creation to the "last things," with the Christian climax coming in the story of Jesus Christ, shows why the indicative cannot be the embracing mood of Christian theology. This is an unfinished story; final affirmations cannot be made yet; all are provisional until the consummation. The promises embedded in biblical testimonies kindle the desire for God's future, and this openness is reflected in a theology led by this desire and alert for possibilities and surprises. So the optative of desire and longing repeatedly challenges both the neat packages, which already have past, present, and future wrapped up, and the opposite tendencies toward lack of definiteness and direction.

Ford calls us to attend to "complex interplay of moods across a range of biblical books," leading us to reject both "neat packages and amorphous fragmentations."[101] Thick theological investigation sits between two extremes: rigid religious systems that limit exploration, and religious formulations so fluid that they are unable to offer substantive food for the soul. Ford argues that wise theological thinking and living involves finding the right mix of the theological moods, a "wise balance of questions, explorations, affirmations, commands, and desires."[102]

Ford's categories offer us promising postures when considering the practice of reimagining apologetics.[103] Using his categories, imaginative apologetics might be considered a series of engagements in irrealis moods,

---

[100]David F. Ford, *The Future of Christian Theology* (Oxford: Wiley-Blackwell, 2011), 68.
[101]Ford, *Future of Christian Theology*, 71
[102]Ford, *Future of Christian Theology*, 70.
[103]Although Ford does not develop this grammatical scheme in an apologetic direction, he does note the stake in relating to other religions and the rest of society.

such as the subjunctive, the mood of experiment and possibility. The indicative affirmations and imperative exhortations of the Christian faith must still be reckoned with: Scripture makes claims and gives commands with illocutionary force. But the subjunctive mood also makes space for mystery, accommodates imaginative exploration, and avoids shutting down the conversation with premature pronouncements about reality. The consideration of possibilities in the subjunctive mood is in constant dialogue with the indicative and imperative moods, which call our vision of reality into question, opening up space for the interrogative mood. This includes articulating the questions we have for God, as well considering the questions that God has us: "Where are you?" (Gen 3:9); "What do you want?" (Jn 1:38); and "Who do you say I am?" (Mt 16:15).

Although the subjunctive mood is the operative posture of reimagining apologetics, it is not the goal of apologetic dialogue. Rather, the goal is that the subjunctive mood would be directed toward the optative. The optative mood represents hope, longing, and desire; it says, "May it be so!" The optative mood is the mood of hope as well as blessing. In casting a capacious vision of Christian faith, imaginative apologetics seeks to arouse confidence that the object of our hope is attainable, instantiating that hope in the blessing itself. This is why the best apologists tell stories that are able to baptize the imagination. They gift the eyes of the heart with the blessing of eschatological sight, arousing us to seek God's kingdom. Indeed, one of the reasons why we find such generative apologetic models among storytellers is because "narrative hosts all the moods, and the interplay between them is critical for the shape and thrust of a theology."[104] To practice imaginative apologetics is to get caught up in the story itself, and the story is taking us somewhere: further up and further in toward the light of the glory that shines from the face of Christ.

Both MacDonald and Robinson challenge the habit of closed minds and open the imagination to a larger vision of the world. Consider the testimony of journalist Mark O'Connell, who reviewed Gilead for the New Yorker: "She makes an atheist reader like myself capable of identifying

---

[104]Ford, *Future of Christian Theology*, 72.

with the sense of a fallen world that is filled with pain and sadness but also suffused with divine grace."[105] To be confronted with this vision is to open oneself up to the new possibilities for life in this world. This opens the door for faith, conceived not as an act of the will, but as an openness to divine address that may be met with the shock of the revelation that always precedes it.

But few will write novels; and fewer still will have the scope of influence as MacDonald and Robinson. What could reimagining apologetics look like for the rest of us? The time has come to draw these streams together. This is the task of my conclusion, in which I will articulate the contours of a reimagined apologetic, which proceeds from the felt sense of the goodness of creation and human creativity, provoking the hope of divine renewal.

---

[105]Mark O'Connell, "The First Church of Marilynne Robinson," May 30, 2012, www.newyorker .com/books/page-turner/the-first-church-of-marilynne-robinson.

Sowing in Hope

The Apologetics of Culture Care

What are you seeking? Because if these arguments simply add up
to a range of arid, abstract possibilities, then they are not grabbing you
existentially in the way that they would if you were prepared
to put your life on the line in terms of practices.

SARAH COAKLEY, "WHY BELIEVE IN GOD?"

SPELLS, SOIL, AND SOCIAL IMAGINARIES

I opened this book with the story of an emerging adult whose crisis of faith sent me in search of "stronger spells." I wanted to know why my sermons had power on Sundays but not on Mondays. Or to move from a magical to an agricultural metaphor, why did the seeds I was planting as a pastor so often fall on shallow soil (Mt 13:3-8)? The latter metaphor captures something of the environmental factors of belief, the space in which faith flourishes or fades. I have found it helpful to follow Charles Taylor, who names this background for belief our social imaginary.[1]

---

[1]This background for belief has been given other names, which share a family resemblance: paradigm (Kuhn), *épistémè* (Foucault), and plausibility structure (Berger). Thomas S. Kuhn, *The*

A social imaginary is an unarticulated and often unexamined sense of the world and our place in it. It consists of habitual ways of experiencing the world, worked in and worked out by the rhythms of our common life. It is carried around and carried on through practices, stories, and cultural artifacts, which are often profoundly dissonant with what we say we believe.

Let me give an example. As a Christian, I believe that food is God's good gift, meant to be cultivated responsibly, enjoyed gratefully, and shared freely. Yet my social and cultural world is arranged to shape my relationship with food in conflicting ways. Within this sociocultural matrix, I have developed habits of consumption that continually reinforce this relationship. Where I live food is widely available and easily accessible, produced and distributed on a massive scale. It comes to my table with little direct effort on my part. I am presented with a myriad of eating options and commercial jingles that train me to "have it my way," prioritizing convenience and personal satisfaction, obscuring my awareness of those who pick, process, and prepare the food, or others for whom healthy options are not so easily accessible. A cultural commitment to "getting my money's worth," combined with excessive portion size, habituate me to stretch my enjoyment to overindulgence, or to waste my leftovers, deterring me from responsible enjoyment. Addiction to busyness, short lunch breaks, and ubiquitous drive-through windows conspire to facilitate meals that are quick if not "on the go," undermining my commitment to receive my food with thanksgiving. I could go on. The point is that I may say that I believe in grateful, responsible, and generous eating. But my context privileges visions of eating that are resistant to my beliefs. Like the parabolic seed, my theology of eating finds itself on rocky soil.

So, what happens to my beliefs when they are so situated? If I continue to prize them, they may begin to function as superficial identity markers.

Structure of Scientific Revolutions (Chicago: University of Chicago Press, 1996); Michel Foucault, *The Order of Things: An Archaeology of the Human Sciences* (New York: Vintage, 1994); Peter L. Berger, *The Sacred Canopy: Elements of a Sociological Theory of Religion* (Garden City: Doubleday, 1967). I have avoided the term *worldview* since that term can be mistakenly focused on the beliefs themselves. See this critique in James K. A. Smith, *Desiring the Kingdom: Worship, Worldview, and Cultural Formation* (Grand Rapids: Baker Academic, 2009).

In other words, they are meant to reassure myself and others that I hold a "biblical" view of food. I may still mutter hasty prayers before meals, only vaguely aware of the incongruity between the vision of eating that I profess and the one that my actions endorse. Alternatively, I may decide that the Christian vision of eating is idealistic and naive, and that food is nothing more than functional fuel for everyday life or comfort for my creaturely cravings. The point is that my relationship with food—what I actually do with food—is shaped less by articulated beliefs and more by my intuitively felt and constantly reinforced sense of my place in the world and the options available to me. This is my social imaginary.

I often say that I went back to school in search of better answers, but instead I found better questions. It struck me that while much of my ministry was aimed at what people believe, I had not adequately considered the imaginative context that situates belief. These two emphases are not mutually exclusive. It is certainly essential to articulate what the Christian faith compels us to believe. But how does one address the unarticulated background of belief, grounded as it is in the structures and stories of a society, and in our deeply ingrained habits of experience?[2] Related to this, I wondered: If I could only do so much to affect the larger social imaginary, might it be fruitful to address the imagination itself? Could that be done? What might it mean to disciple the imaginations of those I was called to serve? And what might it mean to address the imaginings of those outside the walls of the church? These are the questions I've tried to explore in this book, questions that continue to orient my professional and pastoral work.

Let me briefly review where we've been before giving a sketch of how I will attempt to bring the threads together. In part one I demonstrated the need for a reimagined apologetic method by considering the imaginative crisis in Western secularity, the absence of imagination in contemporary apologetic method, and what a constructive account of the imagination might entail. In part two I offered two models of imaginative apologetics,

---

[2] I have been helped along enormously by the work of James K. A. Smith, whose Cultural Liturgies project first caused me to ask this question. See James K. A. Smith, *Imagining the Kingdom: How Worship Works* (Grand Rapids: Baker Academic, 2013).

sourcing their shared approach in a theological vision that discerns God's active presence in the midst of everyday life. In these final pages I want to offer some parameters to guide a reinvigorated approach. Earlier, I drew a contrast between the apologetics of hope and the apologetics of despair. Here I want to draw a second contrast between the apologetics of culture care and the apologetics of culture war.

THE APOLOGETICS OF CULTURE CARE

I have noted the suspicion with which many younger Christians experience the word apologetics. Part of the problem with using the word is that in our contemporary context apologetics (already associated with "defending the faith") is further wrapped in militaristic metaphors and leveraged as part of the culture war. This defensive mentality can even find its way into the work of even the most winsome apologists. Holly Ordway, who also advocates an imaginative approach to apologetics, writes that we should avoid "the militaristic idea that apologetics is a battle that can somehow be 'won' against an unbeliever."[3] And yet despite this wise counsel for interpersonal witness, the metaphor returns with reference toward the larger culture. She argues that the need for imaginative apologetics is strategic: if we "rely *only* on propositional argument, then we will lose the battle for *meaning* in the wider culture."[4]

Are Christians enjoined to engage in a battle for meaning in the wider culture? The question of the relationship of the church to the culture in which we make our way is a complicated one.[5] But with others I am convinced that using military metaphors (fight, war, battle) for the church's engagement with culture betrays the character of that engagement.[6] Most apologists would agree that treating an interpersonal conversation as a battle is dehumanizing. So too treating our cultural task as a

---

[3]Holly Ordway, *Apologetics and Christian Imagination: An Integrated Approach to Defending the Faith.* (Steubenville, OH: Emmaus Road, 2017), 169.

[4]Ordway, *Apologetics and Christian Imagination*, 158. Emphasis original.

[5]See the classic work by H. Richard Niebuhr, *Christ and Culture* (San Francisco: Harper & Row, 1975).

[6]James Davison Hunter, *Culture Wars: The Struggle to Control the Family, Art, Education, Law, and Politics in America* (Memphis: Basic Books, 1992); Andy Crouch, *Culture Making: Recovering Our Creative Calling* (Downers Grove, IL: InterVarsity Press, 2008).

battle is secularizing: it grants the assumption of secularity that there is a contested, neutral space that can be won or lost through ideological conquest and institutional affiliation.[7] The culture war can only proceed on the assumption that there is such a thing as a space where God is not present. But if the world remains saturated with God's presence and address, despite our attempts to deny or shut it out, Christian engagement with culture becomes more a matter of discernment than defense.

"Culture care" is a term used by artist and writer Makoto Fujimura, which he proposes as an alternative model in our polarized environment. He writes, "After many years of culture wars, no one can claim victory. We have all been further dehumanized, fragmented, and exiled from genuine conversation. Culture at large is a polluted, overcommoditized system that has failed us." The solution, he writes, will not be found in taking up ever-more-incisive weapons. Rather, we must recover a biblical understanding of culture in which "culture is not a territory to be won or lost but a resource we are called to steward with care. Culture is a garden to be cultivated."[8] We must learn to care for the larger culture the same way that we would care for a polluted ecosystem or a traumatized soul. We must make space and reconnect with beauty, cultivating a generative environment where the creative spirit of our culture can be healed and unleashed. Beauty, Fujimura writes, is a recognition of the gratuity of being, of the God who "created a world he did not need because he is an artist." Beauty may not be necessary to our survival. But it is essential for our flourishing.[9] And it is essential for the church's mission in the world.

The answer in our polarizing climate is not armed resistance but cultural renewal: telling better stories, painting more beautiful pictures,

---

[7]As Robinson puts it: "Is secularism on the march as we are told so often? Is the word secularism actually descriptive or useful? The old Protestantism I have invoked believed that God was continuously attentive to every human mind and soul. Is there another doctrine among us now?" Timothy Larsen and Keith L. Johnson, eds., *Balm in Gilead: A Theological Dialogue with Marilynne Robinson* (Downers Grove, IL: IVP Academic, 2019), 174. See an excellent parallel discussion in Andrew Root, *Faith Formation in a Secular Age: Responding to the Church's Obsession with Youthfulness* (Grand Rapids: Baker Academic, 2017), 106-9.

[8]Makoto Fujimura, *Culture Care: Reconnecting with Beauty for Our Common Life* (Downers Grove, IL: InterVarsity Press, 2017), 40.

[9]Fujimura, *Culture Care*, 51.

making connections that were previously unimagined. Artists are uniquely equipped to lead the way in moving from culture war to culture care. Fujimura notes how artists tend to be "border-stalkers," moving on the margins, comfortable with ambiguity, but uncomfortable with homogeneity. It is this liminal position that makes them ideal mediators between "warring tribes": "The generosity of an artist in this sense can mean mediation in the culture wars, beginning by overcoming caricatures and injecting diversity, nuance, and even paradox into the nature of the conversation, and then moving on to teach society a language of empathy and reconciliation. Grounded artists can provide rallying points around which reconciliation begins."[10]

Fujimura is onto something important here. It is because of the hope of reconciliation that I have selected two "grounded artists" as my models for reimagining apologetics. In our postromantic context aesthetic artifacts carry more weight in imparting the felt sense of the truth of Christian faith than analytical treatises. To return to an earlier distinction, if Uppercase Apologetics is the default mode of the apologetics of culture war, then perhaps a reimagined approach might play a contrasting role in the larger task of culture care. Perhaps imaginative apologists can join artists in their aim "to surprise our jaded culture with delight and remind others of what we humans truly long for."[11] Perhaps we can join MacDonald when he writes: "I will try to show what we might be, may be, must be, shall be—and something of the struggle to gain it."[12]

THREE ESSENTIAL ELEMENTS FOR REIMAGINING APOLOGETICS

What, then, are the essential characteristics of a reimagined approach? In an earlier chapter I distinguished between three dimensions of imagining: sensing (where a world of meaning impresses itself on the imagination), seeing (where the imagination expresses itself toward the world), and shaping (where space is made to negotiate sense and sight). If apologetics

---

[10]Fujimura, *Culture Care*, 61.
[11]Fujimura, *Culture Care*, 56.
[12]Rolland Hein, *George MacDonald: Victorian Mythmaker* (Whitethorn, CA: Johannesen, 1999), 22.

is to engage the imagination, it must take into account at least one of these aspects, and the more aspects that are engaged, the more potent the imaginative force. Below I offer three essential elements, corresponding to these three dimensions.[13]

Element one: Aesthetic sense. Reimagining apologetics gives methodological priority to the aesthetic dimension. The aesthetic dimension is the dimension in which our felt sense is essential to what is meaningful.[14] Thus imaginative apologetics begins by orienting itself around the question, "What would make belief beautiful and believable for this person?" or alternatively, "What makes belief ugly and unbelievable?" In order to answer these questions adequately, we must pay attention to the ecosystems in which belief withers or thrives. These social, cultural, and relational contexts shape the contours of what is beautiful and believable; they are the soil in which beliefs take root. They constitute the aesthetic dimension of a person's life: her lived, felt sense of the world, especially as it relates to the possibilities that orient her existence.

To make this concrete, let us examine the case of a contemporary skeptic, from the 2006 comedy *Nacho Libre*. In the film, the main character Nacho has a conversation about faith with his friend Esqueleto:

Nacho: I'm a little concerned right now. About your salvation and stuff. How come you have not been baptized?

Esqueleto: Because I never got around to it ok? I dunno why you always have to be judging me because I only believe in science.[15]

The scene is comedic, and shortly thereafter Nacho sneaks up on and forcibly baptizes scientific Esqueleto. Witness the violence of modern apologetics!

---

[13]Whereas in chapter three I discussed them in logical order (seeing, sensing, shaping), in this chapter I will discuss them in phenomenological order (sensing, seeing, shaping), reflecting our usual imaginative experience of the world.

[14]Note David Morgan's definition of the aesthetic: "the sensuous, imagined, or more broadly speaking, the embodied experience of meaning, whose significance is measured in feeling no less than in intellectual content." David Morgan, "Protestant Visual Piety and the Aesthetics of American Mass Culture," in *Mediating Religion: Studies in Media, Religion, and Culture*, ed. Jolyon P. Mitchell and Sophia Marriage (London: T&T Clark, 2003), 107.

[15]Jared Hess, Jack Black, David Klawans, Julia Pistor, Mike White, Jerusha Hess, and Peter Stormare, *Nacho Libre* (Paramount Pictures, 2006).

But in all seriousness, what would it mean to "baptize" Esqueleto's imagination? It would begin with exploring what he means when he says, "I only believe in science." Is "science" a belief system in the same way that Christianity is a belief system? What is it about science that *feels* more capacious than Christianity? How does each way of seeing the world limit our life in the world? What do these limits make possible?

In our postromantic situation, this aesthetic dimension is most decisive, and the first question is not, "Is it true?" but rather "How does it move Esqueleto?" or "How does it resonate with Esqueleto?" If it does resonate with him, if it connects to his desires or generates new possibilities for navigating the world, then it has the ring of authenticity, and he may be motivated to inquire as to its truth.

Accordingly, an imaginative approach aims at drawing out the desire through the imagination. This has two components. First, it means surfacing and naming the desires that are already orienting Esqueleto's life: the things in which he is invested, the things that have already captured his imagination. What is it about science that he finds such security? What else resonates deeply with him? What is beautiful to him? In what arenas of life does he seek fullness? Next, it means rethinking the way that the gospel of Jesus Christ might address and makes sense of Esqueleto's desires and directions. This follows the apologetic counsel of Pascal to "make good men wish it were true,"[16] and of Cardinal Cesar de La Luzerne: "Our goal is less to make you see how true religion is than to make you feel how beautiful it is."[17] MacDonald's counsel through Wingfold on how to address Richard's unbelief also hits close to the mark: "Make his thoughts dwell on such a God as he must feel would be worth having. Wake the notion of a God such as will draw him to wish there were such a God . . . and he will go and look if haply such a God may be found."[18] We must discern what a person might wish to be true, what sort of a God would be worth having, and what kind of faith they would feel is worthy of further consideration. Or, if a person is not yet

---

[16]Blaise Pascal, *Pensées*, trans. A. J. Krailsheimer (London: Penguin, 1995), 4.
[17]César De la Luzerne, *Instruction Pastorale Sur L'excellence de La Religion* (Langres, 1786), 5.
[18]George MacDonald, *There and Back* (Whitethorn, CA: Johannesen, 1991), 226-27.

ready to consider these suppositions, perhaps they can start with something like Ames's counsel to his son: "There is more beauty than our eyes can bear . . . precious things have been put into our hands and to do nothing to honor them is to do great harm."[19] To contextualize this counsel for contemporary seekers, we must first have a sense of what precious things have been put into a person's hands (the loves in which they are invested) and what it would look like to honor them. Imaginative apologetics appeals to the beauty of faith. But for the beauty of the Christian faith to be felt, we must first explore what a person *would* find resonant, what *would* strike them as beautiful, and what *would* capture their imagination. Then we must inquire in what way the gospel might speak to those desires, reorienting them, or creating a larger context in which they might be transfigured.

This does not mean altering the gospel for the sake of disordered desire. It means showing how the gospel offers something deeper than, but not discontinuous with, human longing. Just as Bible translators seek to give a faithful translation of the Christian Scriptures in the "heart language" of a people group, so too imaginative apologists seek a telling of the Christian story that resonates with the movements of a person's heart. It is because the apologist has confidence that the Holy Spirit is already at work within human longings that she orients her presentation there. Imaginative apologetics starts with human meaning making. But it aims to draw out desire toward something not of our making: the God who moves toward creation in love.

Recognition of God's active presence requires us to grow in receptivity. Receptivity requires humility. To explore our imaginative hopes without humility too quickly leads to hubris. But humility reverses the trajectory of desire from self-assertion to longing. It opens up space for surprise, the unexpected, the un-looked-for.[20] The cultivation of humble receptivity is no mere human achievement but part of the Spirit's work provoking the human imagination to reach toward another world.

---

[19]Marilynne Robinson, *Gilead* (New York: Picador, 2006), 246.
[20]I am indebted to my colleague Mark Tazelaar both for articulating this point about humility and surprise, and for modeling it.

Humility cuts both ways: it requires openness to surprise on the part of the believer as well as the seeker, as connections are sought between her story and the Christian story of reality. Even when the openness does not appear to be present, addressing the imagination, either through imaginative works (story) or imaginative exploration (supposition), can offer an immersive experience of the logic of faith, where more is caught than taught. Awakened desire means that reasons for belief may begin to engage the seeker in new ways. Exploring desire, cultivating an aesthetic sense of what is possible, can enable a second essential element: sight.

Element two: Orienting vision. Reimagining apologetics invites exploration of a larger vision of the world. Insofar as the apologist seeks not just to defend but also to commend the Christian faith, it requires that human desire be resituated in terms of the theodrama in which we are all participants. Accordingly, imaginative apologetics seeks to impart a vicarious Christian vision, inviting outsiders to view the world through Christian eyes. Whereas the previous movement asks, "What would resonate?," this movement asks, "What would it be like to see the world through eyes of faith?" Robinson is a wonderful model of this. She takes up an imaginative stance shocked by the glory of creation, helping us to see the world through eyes filled with wonder. If God's active presence means that ordinary perception can become revelatory, then we must offer imaginative spaces *in which* and *from which* this new way of seeing is possible.

If the previous essential element requires the cultivation of humbled hope, this element requires the cultivation of empathetic vision. This, too, is generative in both directions: it invites empathy from outsiders, and it cultivates empathy for outsiders. It seeks empathy because it asks others to take on the Christian perspective and experience the world of Christian meaning. In doing so, it commends the Christian vision, but on imaginative grounds rather than merely intellectual ones. It is not yet asking anyone to affirm the Christian creed. Rather, it is showing what it would be like to experience the world through the filter of the Christian faith. In some cases, this will mean shepherding the observer into the thick world of story, as MacDonald and Robinson both show us, though it can also mean offering micronarratives embedded in personal testimony. When

I tell someone my story, when I explain how faith has opened up the world for me, I hope that our shared humanity will open the door for my story to be received with hospitality.

But in inviting an empathic gaze, the story I tell requires empathy for outsiders. Asking someone to try on the spectacles of faith means recognizing just how different the world looks to someone on the outside. To invite another person to explore the Christian way of seeing means meeting them where they are, clearing a space for mutual understanding, and showing hospitality toward their doubt and unbelief. In *Gilead*, Robinson reminds us that even John Ames's capacious vision is still fraught with finitude: Ames does not see his godson Jack clearly for most of his memoir. Even at the end of the story, in the absence of mutual understanding, the best Ames can offer his godson is blessing. Blessing, the posture of the imaginative apologist, requires an act of mutual recognition. It assumes the active presence of the God in whom all live and move and have their being. Like Robinson and MacDonald, we must be careful to carve out an imaginative space large enough for the longings and losses of outsiders who have not yet found their way in. As MacDonald writes to his doubting contemporaries, "But do not think that God is angry with you because you find it hard to believe. It is not so; that is not like God; God is all that you can honestly wish Him to be, and infinitely more."[21] For both these authors, it is divine generosity that makes space for the authentic human search. This space is important because what we are really after is not primarily a pronouncement on the details of eschatological renewal (how and when and by what means God will heal creation). What we are called to is a posture of blessing that generates hope and empathy for the other, warning and inviting, in imitation of God.[22]

Here the imaginative resources of the Christian faith are not simply its intrinsic attractiveness but also in its empathic generativity. There is a

---

[21]George MacDonald, *God's Words to His Children: Sermons Spoken and Unspoken* (New York: Funk & Wagnalls, 1887), 116.

[22]On divine empathy see Richard Mouw, *He Shines in All That's Fair: Culture and Common Grace* (Grand Rapids: Eerdmans, 2002), 39.

burgeoning body of literature on the role of the imagination in cultivating empathy. Philosopher Karsten Steuber summarizes the basic starting point of the research as the assumption that "our ability to empathize with another person is based on or activated through our ability to imaginatively take up that person's perspective."[23] Yet even as our shared human experience creates a common ground for empathic imagining, sociocultural differences create gaps that set limits for understanding. The political polarization of our current moment bears this out: next-door neighbors may inhabit in entirely different imaginative universes. This is because different sources are fueling our imaginations, stirring up disparate desires.[24] For empathetic understanding to take place, it is not enough to be sensitive to the differences.[25] What is needed when sharing the Christian vision is not merely the willingness to share—in expectation that it will be well received—but the willingness to translate that vision into an accessible form.

We need not look outside of our Christian tradition to find resources to do this. Indeed, missiologist Lamin Sanneh has called Christianity a "vernacular translation movement."[26] What he means by this is that the Christian movement has always sought to retell the Christian story in language and logic that makes sense to the cultures it encounters. Indeed, from the gift of the Spirit at Pentecost we see the dignity that is given to human language and culture (Acts 2). When people from many nations hear the Word of God in their own language, we learn that the Spirit has something to say to these people too.

---

[23]Karsten R. Steuber, "Empathy and the Imagination," in *The Routledge Handbook of Philosophy of Imagination*, ed. Amy Kind (London: Routledge, 2016), 368. Indeed a widely used assessment tool for measuring empathy uses *fantasy* as a subscale, understood as "the tendency to imaginatively transpose oneself into fictional situations." Mark H. Davis, "A Multidimensional Approach to Individual Differences in Empathy," *JSAS Catalog of Selected Documents In Psychology* 10 (1980): 85-104.

[24]As Steuber writes, "The greater the difference between individuals and the greater the cultural gap between them, particularly regarding well-entrenched cognitive habits and value commitments, the harder it becomes to reenact them and to appropriately quarantine our attitudes from the imaginative engagement with another person's perspective." Steuber, "Empathy and the Imagination," 375.

[25]Steuber, "Empathy and the Imagination," 377.

[26]Lamin Sanneh, *Translating the Message: The Missionary Impact on Culture* (Maryknoll: Orbis, 1989), 7.

This is because what is being narrated is not an abstract truth but a particular story that happened (and is still happening) in history. Outsiders are invited into the story of God, not just *my* story, or my tribe's story. God's story, a theodrama, embraces these smaller stories, but it does so by catching them up and transfiguring them. As Willie Jennings argues, with respect to this story all non-Jews are outsiders who have been invited in. Every new act of translation requires an act of joining, which enriches the story itself as it unfolds in new ways, as well as the storyteller.[27] True Christian translation is "loving, caring, intimate joining . . . a sharing in the pain plight, and life of another."[28] We know that translation has occurred when the longings and laments of outsiders have been taken seriously enough to break open our own world in the encounter.

Translation is usually reserved for communication across cultural and linguistic gaps. But insofar as this strategy is entailed by the Christian story itself, translation is also the model for apologetic communication. Imaginative apologetics aims to open up a uniquely generative space for negotiating difference and imparting understanding. Here our experience of imaginative artifacts can shed fresh light on biblical truth, even as the spectacles of Scripture reorient the vision of all. What we are really after is an experience of seeing the world in all its particularities through the lens of the Christian story: creation, fall, and redemption. This brings us to our third essential element.

Element three: Poetic participation. *Reimagining apologetics situates human projects within the redemptive project of God.* It is in the space carved out by imaginative vision, which explores new possibilities that the third aspect of imagining plays its part. If in the first movement we

---

[27]To speak the Christian story in a new language assumes, as Jennings writes "a life lived in submersion and submission to another's cultural realities." Willie James Jennings, *The Christian Imagination: Theology and the Origins of Race* (New Haven: Yale University Press, 2010), 266. To use Paul Ricoeur's language, imaginative translation of the Christian vision necessitates not just a refiguration in the world of the recipient but also the reciprocal refiguration in the world of the messenger in response to the agency of the audience. Paul Ricoeur, *Time and Narrative* (Chicago: University of Chicago Press, 2012), 76.

[28]This, Jennings argues, is the true work of Christian translation: "The story of Israel connected to Jesus can crack open a life so that others, strangers, even colonized strangers begin to seep inside and create cultural alienation for the translator and even more, deep desire for those who speak native words." Jennings, *Christian Imagination*, 165-66

explore desire, asking, "What kind of faith would resonate?," and in the second movement we inhabit vision, asking, "What would faith feel like?," in the third movement we seek the negotiation of the two. Here we explore the question, "What new possibilities would faith facilitate?"

All humans are hungry for meaning; we cannot live without it. Meaning is experienced as a sense and depth of connection to the world. And yet the meaning we feel in our work, in our relationships, in our loves and losses, always exists against the larger horizon of God's redemptive project. It is precisely because God's imagination is the source material for human imagination that there is a surplus of meaning in all our making. As MacDonald writes, "A genuine work of art must mean many things; the truer its art the more things it will mean."[29] He goes on:

> One difference between God's work and man's is, that, while God's work cannot mean more than he meant, man's must mean more than he meant. For in everything God has made, there is layer upon layer of ascending significance; also he expresses the same thought in higher and higher kinds of thought: it is God's things, his embodied thoughts, which alone a man has to use, modified and adapted to his own purposes, for the expression of his thoughts; therefore he cannot help his words and figures falling into such combinations in the mind of another as he had himself not foreseen, so many are the thoughts allied to every other thought, so many are the relations involved in every figure, so many the facts hinted in every symbol.[30]

This does not mean that any interpretation is valid; it means that there will always be *more* meaning in our projects than we can foresee, because it owes to "a larger origin than man alone . . . the inspiration of the Almighty shaped its ends."[31] This creates profound space for human creative projects to be situated in the larger creative work of God. Yet the imaginative reframing of a person's projects and pursuits should never be a violent imposition that ignores the agency of a seeker to reinterpret her own life. The Christian narrative cannot be simply painted over her pursuits. What reimagination offers is a more capacious and liberating

---

[29]George MacDonald, *A Dish of Orts* (Whitethorn, CA: Johannesen, 1996), 317.
[30]MacDonald, *Dish of Orts*, 320.
[31]MacDonald, *Dish of Orts*, 25.

possibility for interpreting reality that must be taken up by the seeker in her own time and her own way. Thus, imaginative apologetics proceeds by way of provocation. Faith provides, as Robinson writes, "a language of orientation that presents itself as a series of questions."[32] What if the universe is not empty, but full? What if there is more meaning than you imagine? What if culture is not reducible to power? What if the claims of Christ were true? What would that mean? Rather than saying, "Here is why you should believe," imaginative apologetics says, "Here is how faith could reframe your quest" (see fig. 2).[33]

We have seen this kind of reframing on a larger scale, such as in Augustine's *City of God*. But the strategy of retelling the Christian story in such a way that it offers a larger frame for particular human desires is an imaginative strategy that can be taken up by everyday apologists as well.[34] This involves discerning how the creative projects of doubters may actually already be moving within the grooves of creation. MacDonald was particularly attuned to the Victorian longing for moral order: to be good and to do good. He sought to resituate the Victorian quest for virtue as a quest for God, showing how virtue opens the way for imaginative vision.[35] In our own setting the quest is for authenticity,

---

[32]Sarah Fay, "The Art of Fiction No. 198," *The Paris Review*, no. 186 (Fall 2008), www.theparisreview.org/interviews/5863/marilynne-robinson-the-art-of-fiction-no-198-marilynne-robinson.

[33]I understand reimagining apologetics as an extension of what William Dyrness calls "poetic theology," which seeks to make sense of the way that "human longing for a good (even beautiful) life inclines people inevitably to shape poetic practices . . . to find a way to flourish beyond what is given in life." The poetic approach seeks to discern the theological significance of these poetic practices—"those projects that embody the desires and dreams around which people orient their lives"—and hopes to reorient the quest for beauty, goodness, and meaning within the project of God, what God is making of humanity and the world. I might have called the project pursued in this book *poetic* apologetics, insofar as it seeks to reshape apologetic methodology with poetic theology. Nevertheless, I also want to emphasize the earlier two dimensions as well: the paradigmatic power of imaginative vision and the dynamic power of desire. Both of these aspects of imagining situate the poetic space in which a person pursues a meaningful and beautiful life. Dyrness himself situates his work as a kind of "apologetic theology," reflecting "on the presence and purposes of God in relation to cultural patterns and trends." William Dyrness, *Poetic Theology: God and the Poetics of Everyday Life* (Grand Rapids: Eerdmans, 2011), 6.

[34]See an exposition of this in Curtis Chang, *Engaging Unbelief: A Captivating Strategy from Augustine and Aquinas* (Eugene, OR: Wipf and Stock, 2007).

[35]Waking the conscience wakes the imagination, and in both spaces MacDonald wants to show how the Spirit of God draws the seeker to behold the good and beautiful God: "He that will do the will of THE POET, shall behold the Beautiful." MacDonald, *Dish of Orts*, 36.

and imaginative apologetics will involve helping the seeker to discern how the search for a beautiful, resonant life connects to the active presence of God.

Figure 2: Apologetic Desiderata

Aspect of Imagining	Sensing: imagination as aesthetic sense	Seeing: imagination as orienting vision	Shaping: imagination as poetic participation
Operative Question	What is worth pursuing?	Where are we?	What will we do?
Kind's Taxonomy	Sensory Imagining World → Mind	Propositional Imagining Mind → World	Creative Imagining Intermediate Space
Apologetic Desiderata	Gives methodological primacy to the aesthetic dimension	Invites exploration of a more capacious vision of the world.	Situates human projects within the larger project of God.
Orienting Question	What kind of faith would resonate?	What would faith feel like?	What new possibilities would faith facilitate?

This larger horizon, God's redemptive project, requires us to reevaluate what it means to make a beautiful life. The classical understanding of beauty has to do with proportion, balance, and symmetry: things properly ordered, arranged as they should be. But the Christian understanding of beauty centers on the cross of Jesus Christ. Here is the most unique contribution of Christianity to human imagination. As Fleming Rutledge reminds us: "Until the gospel of Jesus Christ burst upon the Mediterranean world, no one in the history of human imagination had conceived of such a thing as the worship of a crucified man."[36] An instrument of torture, humiliation, and death, the cross reminds us that imaginative passion leads people not just to build and create but also to tear down and destroy. The cross forces us to recognize the ugliness and brutality of the world, and our complicity in it. It forces us to come to terms with how severely we fail to live up to our highest imagination. Celebration of the imagination, apart from a consideration of the cross, can lead only to an apologetics of glory. But it will be a lesser glory, one limited by our best imaginings. If the human imagination

---

[36]Fleming Rutledge, *The Crucifixion: Understanding the Death of Jesus Christ* (Grand Rapids: Eerdmans, 2015), 1.

is never confronted and humbled by the cross, then it will be unable to imagine the deep hope that only the cross can provide.

For once the cross has humbled us, it offers us hope, precisely at the moment we least expect it and least deserve it. Indeed, in the gospel, this symbol of the worst that humans can do has been reimagined as a sign of the best that God can do.[37] Whenever we place the cross on our tombstones, we do so in hope that what happened at the cross will make some difference for those who lie buried beneath the ground. The cross invites us to reimagine beauty and a beautiful life in cruciform terms. Like the Japanese art of *kinsukori*, it repairs our shattered hopes with gold, opening up all the possibilities of redemption. Faith in Christ does not change the past, but it can change the meaning of the past. Christian faith opens up the most capacious possible life, because it tells us that even death will be swallowed up in the end.

BEAUTIFUL, BELIEVABLE, BELIEVED

But perhaps this exploration of the beauty of faith does not go far enough. Ordway, in proposing her own imaginative method, notes where such a project runs into problems. She writes,

> A challenge for imaginative apologists in the modern era, however, is that people often have difficulty moving to the next step. It is entirely possible, in this culture, that people will find the Christian faith interesting, even meaningful, yet not be interested in the question of whether or not it is *true*. Or, less noticeably, people may (and often do) accept Christianity only insofar as they, personally find it to be acceptable: each doctrinal point weighed and possibly rejected. Someone who accepts Christian teaching on the basis that it is beautiful and meaningful has come far, but has not come quite far enough unless he also accepts it as *true*—independent of his own preferences and views, even contrary to his own preferences and views. . . . We must offer a meaningful, compelling story, yes. But we must also bring people to realize that they must decide whether they believe the story also to be true.[38]

---

[37]This turn of phrase is from Malcolm Guite: "In a daring and beautiful creative reversal, God takes the worst we can do to him and turns it into the very best he can do for us." Malcolm Guite, *The Word in the Wilderness* (London: Canterbury Press, 2014), 8.

[38]Ordway, *Apologetics and the Christian Imagination*, 152-55.

There is a common-sense, analytical clarity that Ordway's distinction brings to the discussion. Finding a story beautiful is not the same as finding it believable, still less actually believing it in a way that makes a meaningful difference. When the film ends, after all, the willing suspension of disbelief is broken, and we go about our business in the "real world." A similar danger exists for imaginative apologetics: that once the spell is broken, we go about our business having been entertained or engaged but not challenged or transformed.

And yet putting things so starkly oversimplifies the complex dynamic of what it means to believe. The line between what is beautiful and what is believable is quite porous. Beauty itself trains our sensibilities to recognize its own inner logic. Beauty is, as Robinson writes, "a conversation between humankind and reality, and we are an essential part of it, bringing to it our singular gifts of reflection and creation."[39] Indeed, to feel grasped by beauty is in some sense to assent to its truth, to allow ourselves to be touched by its goodness. Furthermore, the move from recognizing beauty and affirming truth is not a straightforwardly cognitive act. If the Christian faith is not simply a set of truths to affirm but more fundamentally a way of seeing the world (as the theater of God's glory), then it has to do with more than convincing our intellect. It also has to do with exercising our imaginations and cultivating imaginative dispositions.[40]

We have already seen one of these dispositions, humility. Let us consider another: patience. God is unspeakably patient with his creation, and so we too must learn to wait and hope. Theologian Tomas Halik provocatively suggests that perhaps atheists are simply those who have grown tired of waiting for God. They want to resolve the apparent absence of God by slamming the door of belief instead of enduring it. But believers also wrestle with God's apparent silence, inaction, and delay; when you live with faith, it

---

[39]Marilynne Robinson, *What Are We Doing Here?: Essays* (New York: Farrar, Straus and Giroux, 2018), 217.

[40]Penner writes that Christianity is a hermeneutical paradigm: "The reason I accept Christian faith, then, is it enables me to interpret my life fruitfully and the world meaningfully through the practices, categories, and language of Christian faith, so that I have a more authentic understanding of myself and a sense of wholeness to my life." Myron Penner, *The End of Apologetics: Christian Witness in a Postmodern Context* (Grand Rapids: Baker Academic, 2013), 76.

does not do away with the experience of absence. Rather, faith changes *how* you experience it. Faith, Halik writes, is patience with God, grounded on the conviction that the experience of absence is not the deepest reality.[41]

How is such patience, the willingness to hold the door ajar, cultivated? Only through practices, and secondarily through their approximation in imaginative immersion. Faith, after all, is not just being convinced of propositions but being committed to practices, in which I put my life on the line trusting that the cosmos is really meaningful, authored by a God who is present and active, who wrote himself into the story in the person of Christ. Believers pray to this God, even if we do not always sense God's presence, and the practice itself is an instantiation of our faith. Mature believers will testify to the continuing experience of doubt, of struggles to believe from one day to the next. Yet the struggle has integrity because it happens in the posture of faith, where believing and wanting to believe may be difficult to distinguish. Ordway is right: we cannot suspend disbelief forever. The Christian story, and the cross at its center, makes a claim on all who encounter it. But helping people to make the leap from agnosticism to faith will not be aided by discounting the imagination. Indeed, the move toward meaningful practice is essentially a leap of the imagination.[42]

TWO MORE MODELS

Everyday imaginative apologetics. For Christians, these questions are lived realities, and many believers address them with winsomeness and warmth. My wife works for a health care management company based just outside of a major city. Her irreligious coworkers find her Christian faith quaint or exotic but respect her enough to express interest. On one occasion, a coworker ventured to ask why we would indoctrinate our children with Christianity rather than allowing them to choose a religion for themselves. Melissa understood that a frame had been placed on faith; for this coworker, faith is opposed to freedom and thus should always be consciously chosen.

---

[41]Tomas Halik, *Patience with God: The Story of Zacchaeus Continuing in Us*, trans. Gerald Turner (New York: Doubleday, 2009).
[42]I found this lovely phrase in Rupert Shortt, "Review Article: How Christianity Invented Modernity," *Times Literary Supplement*, December 14, 2016, www.the-tls.co.uk/articles/public/at-the-prow-of-history/.

Underneath the objection is the ethic of authenticity: people should believe what feels right to them rather than being told what to believe. Melissa's response was to sketch an alternative picture. "That's not really the way faith works for us," she said. "For us, faith is the most liberating thing we have ever experienced. We feel like it is this amazing gift that we get to pass on to our children." The coworker was stunned: "I've never thought of it that way." She had never imagined that faith could feel so generative.

What Melissa had offered this friend was a glimpse of what faith feels like from the inside. The invitation to see the world through the eyes of faith affirms the value of authenticity but situates it in terms of the Christian imaginative vision, asking, "What if faith can actually set you free? What if the open space that you are looking for can actually be found in living with faith?" Melissa's short testimony prompted her friend to reconsider what it means to live an authentic life, embodied in her concrete person. Another coworker, who describes himself as "religiously apathetic," recently told her that her faith is "the one thing about you that doesn't make sense." What I think he means is that she is generous, funny, and intelligent, and this does not fit with his picture of people of faith. The cognitive dissonance created by a beautiful life is itself an imaginative provocation. It is an apologetic opening that challenges the habits of too-quickly-closed minds. The provocation invites, if not yet belief, at least the suspension of disbelief. It invites the observer to hit pause on their incredulity and to take a look.[43] It invites the imaginative leap of imagination that may be already the first movement of faith.

Extended imaginative apologetics. I want to offer one more model of an imaginative approach in a traditional apologetic setting. Robert Lawrence Kuhn hosts the PBS series *Closer to the Truth*, which boasts the tagline, "The world's greatest thinkers exploring humanity's deepest questions." In the eleventh season, Kuhn interviews Anglican priest and theologian Sarah Coakley on the question, "Why believe?"[44] Kuhn begins the

---

[43]This is Coleridge's phrase for describing "poetic faith." Samuel Taylor Coleridge, *Biographia Literaria, or, Biographical Sketches of My Literary Life and Opinions*, ed. James Engell and Walter Jackson Bate (London: Routledge, 1983), 174.

[44]All quotes in this section are from this interview for the "Why Believe in God?" episode of the public program *Closer to the Truth*, which was released on July 14, 2015.

interview by admitting two things: that he would like to believe in God, but that he does not. So why should he believe?

Instead of turning to rational argumentation, Coakley presses him on his inclination to believe, because as she says, the arguments for God's existence will strike him differently depending on his motivation. Coakley notes that she values such arguments but that they must be situated in terms a person's desire. For some, the classical arguments will be necessary; for others, not so much. Arguments will not take root unless a person's will is in some way "turned towards the reality that might lie behind them." So instead she begins by asking Kuhn the question asked of monks upon entering the monastery: *Quid petis?* "What do you seek?" In other words, what is needed before the demonstration of the rationality of Christian belief is the provocation of the impulse to take the demonstration seriously. What is needed is an exploration of the desires that *would* draw out belief, and this is the move that Coakley makes: "Let's say that God is reaching out to you in some way to work on this niggle that you have, that you would like to believe in God, and let's say that there are some arenas of your life which have a sort of element of vulnerability in them, of love, of desire, of pain, where God could get in, under what conditions do you think that might lead to something?"

Two things are of note here. First, in addressing Kuhn's question, "Why should I believe?" Coakley operates in the subjunctive mood throughout her response. She uses phrases like, "Let's say," and "I would ask you," instead of directly confronting and asking him. If Kuhn chooses to engage her suppositions, he must join her in the realm of possibility. She explores the contours of a hypothetical conversation, because for them to have a real conversation Kuhn would need to acknowledge the way that he is already invested in faith and doubt.

Also, in keeping with our first essential element, Coakley is beginning with the aesthetic dimension, suggesting that it is in the spaces of longings and losses that God may be reaching out to him. But this is precisely the point of Kuhn's resistance, and Kuhn answers that he has elements of vulnerability in all of these arenas, and this is the thing that concerns him:

> I would love to believe in God because that would give meaning to the
> universe and to my life. It would give at least the only possible hope of a
> life after death. So I have every reason to want to believe in God and would
> like to believe in God but that's exactly why I am concerned, because I have
> the desire, that the end product of that would be generated by my desire
> rather than by reality and the last thing I want to do is to fool myself.

Notice that Kuhn is resisting the impulse of authenticity from fear of
embracing something that might be inauthentic! The same desire that
draws out the inclination to believe also seems to disqualify that inclination. He is concerned that *wanting* to believe would be tantamount
to fooling himself were he to give in. Coakley reminds him that this
"rather abstract and arid view of the intellectual life" is not really accurate, because no one lives in a space uncontaminated by desire. He is
also operating from the standpoint, as Coakley points out, in which he
is remote and solely responsible for what he chooses to believe. But
rather than further deconstructing Kuhn's standpoint (which would
follow an apologetic of despair), she instead moves in the direction of
hope. She surfaces his desire for authenticity by reframing his *Closer to
the Truth* programs as a spiritual quest: "So your quest for the deep
reality of life, which seems to animate these programs, seems to me to
have some spiritual dimension to it. It may not find its place in any
practice of religion at the moment, but it clearly is an itch. You wouldn't
be making all these programs if you didn't find this an ultimately
fascinating question."

In calling the program a "quest for the deep reality of life," Coakley
gives spiritual legitimacy to Kuhn's projects and resituates them in the
larger possibility that just as Kuhn reaches out to reality, that reality is also
reaching out to him. This is a wonderful illustration of the third essential
element, which shows how the very act of questioning joins the conversation that God is already having with creation.

It is at this point that Coakley says that she would bring in rational
arguments, though she does not do so directly in the interview. Her point
is that the arguments for God would not matter until the desire is engaged
and oriented toward the possibility of God. She says she would be "very

happy to lay out a range of arguments why it seems to me very rational to believe in God, including profoundly experiential reasons." But after laying out these arguments, she says that she would return to the existential question that frames the entire quest:

> Then I would ask you the big existential question, which is "where are true joys to be found?" Which is to circle back to that question, what are you seeking? Because if these arguments simply add up to a range of arid, abstract possibilities, then they are not grabbing you existentially in the way that they would if you were prepared to put your life on the line in terms of practices. Because I as a priest, as a believer, find that it is in silent waiting on God that ultimate, transcendent reality impinges on me. And every time I do that I think of it as a sort of rehearsal for the moment when I have to give over control, which will be the moment I die. And as a priest I think that rehearsing for death is one of the most important things we do as humans, because when we're no longer afraid of death, we're no longer afraid of life.

And here Coakley fulfills the second essential element, inviting Kuhn to glimpse the world through her eyes. She invites him to *see*: "as a priest, as a believer," here is what I find. Since he is unable or unwilling to put his "life on the line in terms of practices," she allows him to vicariously experience the presence and solace that she feels in surrendering to God. The invitation itself is a series of imaginative provocations. What if in silent waiting you could experience God's presence? What if you could rehearse for death by surrendering every day? What if freedom from the fear of death could lead to a more liberated life?

Coakley offers an example of what imaginative apologetics looks like even with an interlocutor that is resistant to the provocations of desire. She begins and ends with the aesthetic dimension that situates his unbelief, reframes his creative projects in terms of a spiritual quest, and offers a vision of life through the eyes of faith. Insofar as she operates in the subjunctive mood, she does not force her vision of reality upon him. Rather she offers the generative possibility of belief, which has the power to shift the paradigms of doubt. She makes space for the classical arguments, but she begins and ends with the aesthetic dimension, asking the question, "What do you seek"? For it is only once this question is becoming clear that the practices and professions of Christian faith will begin to have purchase. The provocations of desire lead to a consideration of the new possibilities that faith facilitates, which in turn invites the seeker to put her life on the line and take the leap.

CONCLUSION: IMAGINATION, MYSTERY, AND HOPE

Opportunities to sketch such a comprehensive response to the question, "Why believe?" may not come as frequently for the rest of us as for Coakley. And yet all believers are called to "give the reason for the hope that [we] have . . . with gentleness and respect" (1 Pet 3:15). Notice that it is Christian hope—the confidence in a not-yet-realized future reality breaking into the present—we are answering for, not just extracted Christian truths. Certainly, the conviction that "these things happened" grounds Christian hope (1 Pet 1:3). But the starting point of answering for our hope is not proving its ground. It is showing the way that hope generates a fully authentic life. Indeed, the apostle assumes that embodied Christian witness is always already generating the kind of dissonance that challenges perceptions and leads to questions.

But apologetic theology, like all theology, is not primarily about giving answers, even if that is an important part of the pedagogy of faith. Theology is, as Thomas Weinandy puts it, less about solving problems than discerning mysteries.[45] Theology is grounded in our exploration of mysteries that are open secrets: the mystery of God's work in Christ (1 Tim 3:16), the mystery of our inclusion in Israel's story (Eph 3:6), and the mystery of the gospel (Eph 6:19). These things are mysteries, not because we know nothing about them, but because we are just beginning to explore the ways that God's plan to renew all of creation opens up new possibilities for life in God's world. To extend this exploration in the direction of apologetics means to move toward the world with faith seeking understanding. It means discerning the surprising presence of God's Spirit at work within

---

[45]Thomas G. Weinandy, "Doing Christian Systematic Theology: Faith, Problems, and Mysteries," *Logos: A Journal of Catholic Thought and Culture* 5, no. 1 (2002): 120-38. I am thankful to Rich Mouw for alerting me to Weinandy's distinction.

and among the imaginative impulses of human beings who have been made in God's image.

Taking the imagination seriously has great promise for the contemporary apologetic task. Insofar as it casts an inhabitable vision, cultivates empathic understanding, and creates space for negotiating difference, reimagining apologetics offers a salutary resource for bridging gaps in apologetic communication. A life of faith, after all, is less like an intellectual achievement and more like a work of art—a work of imagination. As such, it requires a sense of receptivity and a sense of responsibility. Such a work remains rooted in reality. We find ourselves hurled onto a stage we did not make, confronted by the givenness of things. But we must also take authentic ownership of our lives, making something that is attuned to the beauty, goodness, and truth that we find. In a certain sense authoring some sort of imaginative project is unavoidable. So too the call of reimagining apologetics is not just to tell beautiful stories but, by God's grace, to cultivate beautiful lives. Such lives may give a sense of something greater, offering resonance for smaller stories to be taken up in the story of God.

Hope, after all, has a definite object. The goal of a story is not just to take the characters on a journey but ultimately to arrive with them at a more spacious place. For Lewis as well, the baptism of his imagination was only the beginning. As his character John finds in *The Pilgrim's Regress*, "For this end I made your senses and for this end your imagination, that you might see my face and live."[46] If there is some other end for a reimagined apologetic, surely it is penultimate to this one.

---

[46]C. S. Lewis, *The Pilgrim's Regress* (Grand Rapids: Eerdmans, 2014), 196.

Bibliography

Abrams, Meyer H. *The Mirror and the Lamp: Romantic Theory and the Critical Tradition.* New York: Oxford University Press, 1971.

Alston, William P. *A Realist Conception of Truth.* Ithaca, N.Y.: Cornell University Press, 1996.

Appleyard, Bryan. "He Is Risen." *The Sunday Times*, November 2, 2014. www.thetimes.co.uk/article/he-is-risen-2t9hsgl7gv9.

Bailey, Justin. "The Body in Cyberspace: Lanier, Merleau-Ponty, and the Norms of Embodiment." *Christian Scholar's Review* 45, no. 3 (2016): 211-28.

———. "In Search of Stronger Spells." *Inheritance Magazine* 53 (March 2017): 7-10. www.inheritancemag.com/stories/in-search-of-stronger-spells.

———. "The Theodramatic Imagination: Spirit and Imagination in the Work of Kevin Vanhoozer." International Journal of Public Theology: 12 (2018), 455–470.

Baker, Deane-Peter. *Tayloring Reformed Epistemology: The Challenge to Christian Belief.* London: SCM, 2008.

Balthasar, Hans Urs von. *The Glory of the Lord, Vol. 1.* Edited by John Riches. New York: Ignatius, 2009.

———. *Theo-Logic: Theological Logical Theory: The Truth of the World, Vol. 1.* San Francisco: Ignatius, 2001.

Barbour, John D. *Versions of Deconversion: Autobiography and the Loss of Faith.* Charlottesville: University of Virginia Press, 1994.

Barfield, Owen. *Poetic Diction: A Study in Meaning.* 3rd ed. Philosophy & Literature, no. 626. Middletown, CT: Wesleyan University Press, 1973.

Barfield, Raymond. *The Ancient Quarrel Between Philosophy and Poetry.* Cambridge: Cambridge University Press, 2014.

Barth, Karl. *Church Dogmatics: The Doctrine of the Word of God, Volume 1, Part 2: The Revelation of God; Holy Scripture: The Proclamation of the Church.* London: T&T Clark, 2004.

———. *The Theology of Schleiermacher: Lectures at Gottingen, Winter Semester of 1923-24.* Grand Rapids: Eerdmans, 1982.

Bavinck, Herman. "Common Grace." *Calvin Theological Journal* 24, no. 1 (1989): 35-65.

———. *Reformed Dogmatics, Vol. 1: Prolegomena.* Edited by John Bolt and John Vriend. Grand Rapids: Baker Academic, 2003.

———. *The Philosophy of Revelation.* Grand Rapids: Baker, 1979.

Bazzell, Pascal Daniel. "Toward a Creational Perspective on Poverty." In *Genesis and Christian Theology*, edited by Nathan MacDonald, Mark W. Elliott, and Grant Macaskill, 228-41. Grand Rapids: Eerdmans, 2012.

Berger, Peter L. *Homeless Mind: Modernization and Consciousness.* New York: Vintage, 1974.

———. *The Sacred Canopy; Elements of a Sociological Theory of Religion.* Garden City: Doubleday, 1967.

Billings, J. Todd. *Calvin, Participation, and the Gift: The Activity of Believers in Union with Christ.* Oxford: Oxford University Press, 2007.

Bradley, James E., and Dale Van Kley, eds. *Religion and Politics in Enlightenment Europe.* Notre Dame: University of Notre Dame Press, 2001.

Bromhead, Helen. *The Reign of Truth and Faith: Epistemic Expressions in 16th and 17th Century English.* Berlin: Walter de Gruyter, 2009.

Brown, Callum. "The Secularisation Decade: What the 1960s Have Done to the Study of Religious History." In *The Decline of Christendom in Western Europe, 1750-2000*, edited by Hugh McLeod and Werner Ustorf, 29-46. Cambridge: Cambridge University Press, 2011.

Budd, Susan. *Varieties of Unbelief: Atheists and Agnostics in English Society, 1850-1960.* London: Heinemann, 1977.

Bundy, Murray Wright. *The Theory of Imagination in Classical and Mediaeval Thought.* Urbana, IL: University of Illinois Press, 1927.

Calvin, John. *Commentary on Genesis.* Edited by John King. Grand Rapids: Baker, 2003.

———. *Institutes of the Christian Religion.* Edited by John T. McNeill. Translated by Ford Lewis Battles. Louisville: Westminster John Knox, 2001.

———. *Treatises on the Sacraments: Tracts by John Calvin.* Translated by Henry Beveridge. Grand Rapids: Christian Focus, 2002.

Calvin, John, and Marilynne Robinson. *John Calvin: Steward of God's Covenant: Selected Writings.* Edited by John F. Thornton. New York: Vintage, 2006.

Chang, Curtis. *Engaging Unbelief: A Captivating Strategy from Augustine and Aquinas.* Eugene, OR: Wipf and Stock, 2007.

Chesterton, G. K. *The Autobiography of G. K. Chesterton.* San Francisco: Ignatius, 2006.

———. *The Annotated Thursday: G. K. Chesterton's Masterpiece, The Man Who Was Thursday.* San Francisco: Ignatius, 1999.

Clydesdale, Tim, and Kathleen Garces-Foley. *The Twentysomething Soul: Understanding the Religious and Secular Lives of American Young Adults.* New York: Oxford University Press, 2019.

Coakley, Sarah, ed. *Faith, Rationality and the Passions*. Malden, MA: Wiley-Blackwell, 2012.

Cockshut, A. O. J. *The Art of Autobiography in 19th and 20th Century England*. New Haven: Yale University Press, 1984.

Coleridge, Samuel Taylor. *Biographia Literaria, or, Biographical Sketches of My Literary Life and Opinions*. Edited by James Engell and Walter Jackson Bate. London: Routledge, 1983.

Comte, Auguste. *A General View of Positivism*. Translated by J. H. Bridges. Ithaca: Cornell University Library, 2009.

Conyers, A. J. *The Eclipse of Heaven: The Loss of Transcendence and Its Effect on Modern Life*. South Bend, IN: St. Augustine's Press, 1999.

Cowan, Stephen, ed. *Five Views on Apologetics*. Grand Rapids: Zondervan, 2010.

Craig, William Lane. *Reasonable Faith: Christian Truth and Apologetics*. Wheaton, IL: Crossway, 2008.

———. "Response to Kelly James Clark." In *Five Views on Apologetics*, edited by Stephen Cowan, 285-90. Grand Rapids: Zondervan, 2010.

———. "You've Ruined My Life, Professor Craig!" ReasonableFaith.org. Accessed February 28, 2017. www.reasonablefaith.org/you-have-ruined-my-life-professor-craig.

Crisp, Oliver D. *Deviant Calvinism: Broadening Reformed Theology*. Minneapolis: Fortress Press, 2014.

Crouch, Andy. *Culture Making: Recovering Our Creative Calling*. Downers Grove, IL: InterVarsity Press, 2008.

Currie, Gregory, and Ian Ravenscroft. *Recreative Minds: Imagination in Philosophy and Psychology*. Oxford: Clarendon, 2003.

Dale, R. W. *The Old Evangelicalism and the New*. London: Hodder and Stoughton, 1889.

Dalferth, Ingolf U. *Creatures of Possibility: The Theological Basis of Human Freedom*. Translated by Jo Bennett. Grand Rapids: Baker Academic, 2016.

Davis, Mark H. "A Multidimensional Approach to Individual Differences in Empathy." *JSAS Catalog of Selected Documents In Psychology* 10 (1980): 85-104.

Davis, Philip. *The Oxford English Literary History, 1830-1880: The Victorians*. Oxford: Oxford University Press, 2002.

Davison, Andrew. "Christian Reason and Christian Community." In *Imaginative Apologetics: Theology, Philosophy, and the Catholic Tradition*, edited by Andrew Davison, 12-28. Grand Rapids: Baker Academic, 2012.

Dawkins, Richard. *The God Delusion*. New York: Houghton Mifflin, 2008.

De la Luzerne, César. *Instruction Pastorale sur l'excellence de la Religion*. Langres, 1786.

De Wit, Willem J. *On the Way to the Living God*. Amsterdam: VU University Press, 2011.

Dearborn, Kerry. *Baptized Imagination: The Theology of George MacDonald*. Burlington, VT: Ashgate, 2006.

Dennett, Daniel C. *Breaking the Spell: Religion as a Natural Phenomenon.* New York: Penguin, 2007.

Desmond, William. *Is There a Sabbath for Thought? Between Religion and Philosophy.* New York: Fordham University Press, 2005.

Dobbelaere, Karel. *Secularization: An Analysis at Three Levels.* New York: Peter Lang, 2002.

Dreyfus, Hubert L. *Skillful Coping: Essays on the Phenomenology of Everyday Perception and Action.* Oxford: Oxford University Press, 2014.

Dulles, Avery Cardinal. *A History of Apologetics.* San Francisco: Ignatius, 2005.

———. *The Survival of Dogma.* New York: Crossroad, 1982.

Durkheim, Émile. *The Elementary Forms of Religious Life.* Translated by Karen E. Fields. New York: Free Press, 1995.

Dyer, John. "The New Novelist." In *The Penn Monthly.* Philadelphia: University Press Company, 1870.

Dyrness, William A. "Is There a Reformed Aesthetic?" Presented at The Reformed Institute of Metropolitan Washington, Washington, DC, January 25, 2014.

———. *Poetic Theology: God and the Poetics of Everyday Life.* Grand Rapids: Eerdmans, 2011.

———. "Poised Between Life and Death: The Imago Dei After Eden." In *The Image of God in an Image Driven Age: Explorations in Theological Anthropology,* edited by Beth Felker Jones and Jeffrey W. Barbeau, 47-65. Downers Grove: IVP Academic, 2016.

———. *Reformed Theology and Visual Culture: The Protestant Imagination from Calvin to Edwards.* Cambridge University Press, 2004.

———. *The Earth Is God's: A Theology of American Culture.* Maryknoll, NY: Orbis, 1997.

Eisenstadt, Shmuel N., ed. *Multiple Modernities.* New Brunswick: Transaction, 2002.

Engebretson, Alexander John. "'The Dear Ordinary': The Novels of Marilynne Robinson." PhD diss., City University of New York, 2013.

Fay, Sarah. "Marilynne Robinson, The Art of Fiction No. 198." *The Paris Review,* no. 186 (Fall 2008). www.theparisreview.org/interviews/5863/marilynne-robinson-the-art-of-fiction-no-198-marilynne-robinson.

Feuerbach, Ludwig. *The Essence of Christianity.* Translated by George Eliot. Buffalo: Prometheus, 1989.

Fiddes, Paul S. *Freedom and Limit: A Dialogue Between Literature and Christian Doctrine.* New York: St. Martin's, 1991.

Ford, David F. *The Future of Christian Theology.* Oxford: Wiley-Blackwell, 2011.

Foucault, Michel. *The Order of Things: An Archaeology of the Human Sciences.* New York: Vintage, 1994.

Fujimura, Makoto. *Culture Care: Reconnecting with Beauty for Our Common Life.* Downers Grove, IL: InterVarsity Press, 2017.

Gans, Herbert. *Popular Culture and High Culture: An Analysis and Evaluation Of Taste.* New York: Basic Books, 1999.

Gardner, Thomas. *A Door Ajar: Contemporary Writers and Emily Dickinson.* Oxford: Oxford University Press, 2006.

Geertz, Clifford. *The Interpretation of Cultures.* New York: Basic Books, 2017.

Geisler, Norman L. *Christian Apologetics.* Grand Rapids: Baker Academic, 1988.

Gerrish, B. A. *A Prince of the Church: Schleiermacher and the Beginnings of Modern Theology.* Eugene, OR: Wipf and Stock, 2001.

Gibbs, Jeremiah. *Apologetics After Lindbeck: Faith, Reason, and the Cultural-Linguistic Turn.* Eugene, OR: Pickwick, 2015.

Gorski, Philip S., and Ates Altinordu. "After Secularization?" *Annual Review of Sociology* 34 (2008): 55-85.

Goudzwaard, Robert. *Capitalism and Progress: A Diagnosis of Western Society.* Translated by Josina Van Nuis Zylstra. Carlisle: Paternoster, 1997.

Graham, Elaine. *Between a Rock and a Hard Place: Public Theology in a Post-Secular Age.* London: SCM, 2013.

Greeley, Andrew. *The Catholic Imagination.* Berkeley: University of California Press, 2001.

Green, Garrett. *Imagining God: Theology and the Religious Imagination.* Grand Rapids: Eerdmans, 1998.

Griffiths, Paul. "An Apology for Apologetics." *Faith and Philosophy* 5, no. 4 (October 1998).

Groothuis, Douglas R. *Christian Apologetics: A Comprehensive Case for Biblical Faith.* Downers Grove, IL: IVP Academic, 2011.

Guite, Malcolm. *The Word in the Wilderness.* London: Canterbury Press, 2014.

Gunton, Colin E. *The Triune Creator: A Historical and Systematic Study.* Grand Rapids: Eerdmans, 1998.

Hadden, Jeffrey K. "Toward Desacralizing Secularization Theory." *Social Forces* 65, no. 3 (1987): 587-611.

Halik, Tomas. *Patience with God: The Story of Zacchaeus Continuing in Us.* Translated by Gerald Turner. New York: Doubleday, 2009.

Hansen, Lesley Alan. "The Frightful Reformation: Victorian Doubt and the Personal Novel of Religious Unconversion." PhD diss., Columbia University, 1984.

Hardy, Lee. "The Apologetics of Despair." Unpublished syllabus, Calvin Theological Seminary. Fall 2007.

Harris, Sam. *The End of Faith: Religion, Terror, and the Future of Reason.* New York: W. W. Norton, 2005.

Hart, Trevor. *Between the Image and the Word: Theological Engagements with Imagination, Language and Literature.* Burlington, VT: Ashgate, 2013.

———. "Imagining Evangelical Theology." In *Evangelical Futures: A Conversation on Theological Method,* edited by John G. Stackhouse, 191-200. Grand Rapids: Baker, 2000.

Hein, Rolland. *George MacDonald: Victorian Mythmaker.* Whitethorn, CA: Johannesen, 1999.

Hesselink, John. "Marilynne Robinson: Calvinian." *Perspectives Journal* (blog), March 1, 2011. perspectivesjournal.org/blog/2011/03/01/marilynne-robinson-calvinian/.

Hesselink, John, and Marilynne Robinson. "Hesselink and Robinson: An Exchange of Letters." *Perspectives*, March 1, 2001.

Hilton, Boyd. *The Age of Atonement: The Influence of Evangelicalism on Social and Economic Thought, 1795-1865.* Oxford: Clarendon, 1988.

Hitchens, Christopher. *God Is Not Great: How Religion Poisons Everything.* New York: Twelve, 2009.

Hoezee, Scott, and Marilynne Robinson. "A World of Beautiful Souls: An Interview with Marilynne Robinson." *Perspectives Journal* (blog), May 16, 2005. perspectivesjournal .org/blog/2005/05/16/a-world-of-beautiful-souls-an-interview-with-marilynne -robinson/.

Howard, Thomas. "The Cult of C. S. Lewis." *Crisis* 12, no. 7 (August 1994): 33.

Hübenthal, Christoph. "Apologetic Communication." *International Journal of Public Theology* 10 (2016): 7-27.

Hughes, John. "Proofs and Arguments." In *Imaginative Apologetics: Theology, Philosophy, and the Catholic Tradition,* edited by Andrew Davison, 3-11. Grand Rapids: Baker Academic, 2012.

Hume, David. *A Treatise of Human Nature.* Edited by David Fate Norton and Mary J. Norton. Oxford: Oxford University Press, 2000.

Hungerford, Amy. *Postmodern Belief: American Literature and Religion Since 1960.* Princeton: Princeton University Press, 2010.

———. *The American Novel Since 1945: Lecture 16—Marilynne Robinson, Housekeeping.* Open Yale Courses, 2012. oyc.yale.edu/english/engl-291/lecture-16.

Hunter, James Davison. *Culture Wars: The Struggle to Control the Family, Art, Education, Law, and Politics In America.* Memphis: Basic Books, 1992.

Husserl, Edmund. *Ideas Pertaining to a Pure Phenomenology and to a Phenomenological Philosophy.* Translated by F. Kersten. The Hague: Nijhoff, 2001.

———. *Logical Investigations.* Edited by Dermot Moran. London: Routledge, 2001.

Jager, Colin. "This Detail, This History: Charles Taylor's Romanticism." In *Varieties of Secularism in a Secular Age,* edited by Michael Warner, Jonathan VanAntwerpen, and Craig Calhoun, 166-92. Cambridge: Harvard University Press, 2010.

Jansen, Julia. "Husserl." In *The Routledge Handbook of Philosophy of Imagination,* edited by Amy Kind, 69-81. London: Routledge, 2016.

Jennings, Willie James. *The Christian Imagination: Theology and the Origins of Race.* New Haven: Yale University Press, 2010.

Jenson, Robert W. *Systematic Theology: The Triune God.* Oxford: Oxford University Press, 2001.

Johnson, Joseph. *George MacDonald: A Biographical and Critical Appreciation.* London: Pitman, 1906.

Johnson, Kirstin Jeffrey. "Rooted in All Its Story, More Is Meant Than Meets the Ear: A Study of the Relational and Revelational Nature of George MacDonald's Mythopoeic Art." PhD diss., University of St. Andrews, 2011.

Johnston, Robert K. *God's Wider Presence: Reconsidering General Revelation*. Grand Rapids: Baker Academic, 2014.

Jordan, Pamela Lee. "Clergy in Crisis: Three Victorian Portrayals of Anglican Clergymen Forced to Redefine Their Faith." PhD diss., Ball State University, 1997.

Joustra, Robert, and Alissa Wilkinson. *How to Survive the Apocalypse: Zombies, Cylons, Faith, and Politics at the End of the World*. Grand Rapids: Eerdmans, 2016.

Kant, Immanuel. *Critique of Pure Reason*. Edited by Paul Guyer and Allen W. Wood. Cambridge: Cambridge University Press, 1999.

Kearney, Richard. *The Wake of Imagination: Toward a Postmodern Culture*. Minneapolis: University of Minnesota Press, 1988.

Kind, Amy. "Introduction: Exploring Imagination." In *The Routledge Handbook of Philosophy of Imagination*, edited by Amy Kind, 1-11. London: Routledge, 2016.

Koukl, Gregory. *Tactics: A Game Plan for Discussing Your Christian Convictions*. Grand Rapids: Zondervan, 2009.

Kuhn, Thomas S. *The Structure of Scientific Revolutions*. Chicago: University of Chicago Press, 1996.

Kuipers, Ronald A. "Religious Belonging in an 'Age of Authenticity': A Conversation with Charles Taylor (Part Two of Three)." *The Other Journal*, June 23, 2008. theotherjournal.com/2008/06/23/religious-belonging-in-an-age-of-authenticity-a-conversation-with-charles-taylor-part-two-of-three/.

Larsen, Timothy. *Crisis of Doubt: Honest Faith in Nineteenth-Century England*. Oxford: Oxford University Press, 2009.

———. *George MacDonald in the Age of Miracles: Incarnation, Doubt, and Reenchantment*. Comprehensive ed. Downers Grove, IL: IVP Academic, 2018.

Larsen, Timothy, and Keith L. Johnson, eds. *Balm in Gilead: A Theological Dialogue with Marilynne Robinson*. Downers Grove, IL: IVP Academic, 2019.

Leon, Derrick. *Ruskin, the Great Victorian*. Hamden, CT: Archon, 1969.

Lewis, C. S. "Bluspels and Flalansferes: A Semantic Nightmare." In *Selected Literary Essays*, edited by Walter Hooper. Cambridge: Cambridge University Press, 2013.

———. *George MacDonald: An Anthology*. New York: Macmillan, 1947.

———. *God in the Dock: Essays on Theology and Ethics*. Grand Rapids: Eerdmans, 1972.

———. *Mere Christianity*. New York: Harper Collins, 2009.

———. *Surprised by Joy: The Shape of My Early Life*. New York: Houghton Mifflin Harcourt, 1966.

———. *The Pilgrim's Regress*. Grand Rapids: Eerdmans, 2014.

———. *The Silver Chair*. New York: HarperCollins, 2002.

———. *The Weight of Glory*. New York: Macmillan, 1949.

Lindbeck, George A. *The Nature of Doctrine: Religion and Theology in a Postliberal Age.* Philadelphia: Westminster, 1984.

Lovejoy, Arthur O. "On the Discrimination of Romanticisms." *PMLA* 39, no. 2 (1924): 229-53.

Lundin, Roger. *Believing Again: Doubt and Faith in a Secular Age.* Grand Rapids: Eerdmans, 2009.

MacDonald, George. *A Dish of Orts.* Whitethorn, CA: Johannesen, 1996.

———. *Alec Forbes of Howglen.* Whitethorn, CA: Johannesen, 1995.

———. *An Expression of Character: The Letters of George MacDonald.* Edited by Glenn Edward Sadler. Grand Rapids: Eerdmans, 1994.

———. *Annals of a Quiet Neighborhood.* Whitethorn, CA: Johannesen, 2004.

———. *David Elginbrod.* Whitethorn, CA: Johannesen, 1995.

———. *The Gifts of the Child Christ and Other Stories and Fairy Tales.* Edited by Glen Edward Sadler. Grand Rapids: Eerdmans,1996.

———. *God's Words to His Children: Sermons Spoken and Unspoken.* New York: Funk & Wagnalls, 1887.

———. *Home Again and The Elect Lady.* Whitethorn, CA: Johannesen, 1993.

———. *Lilith: First and Final.* Whitehorn, CA: Johannesen, 1998.

———. *Paul Faber, Surgeon.* Whitethorn, CA: Johannesen, 1992.

———. *Robert Falconer.* Whitethorn, CA: Johannesen, 1995.

———. *Salted with Fire.* Whitethorn, CA: Johannesen, 1996.

———. *The Princess and Curdie.* Whitethorn, CA: Johannesen, 2000.

———. *The Seaboard Parish.* Whitethorn, CA: Johannesen, 1995.

———. *There and Back.* Whitethorn, CA: Johannesen, 1991.

———. *Thomas Wingfold, Curate.* Whitethorn, CA: Johannesen, 1997.

———. *Unspoken Sermons: Series I, II, III in One Volume.* Whitethorn, CA: Johannesen, 1999.

MacDonald, Greville. *George MacDonald and His Wife.* Whitethorn, CA: Johannesen, 1998.

MacDonald, Ronald. *From a Northern Window: A Personal Remembrance of George MacDonald.* Eureka, CA: Sunrise, 1989.

MacIntyre, Alasdair. *Whose Justice? Which Rationality?* London: Bloomsbury, 2013.

Marion, Jean-Luc. *In Excess: Studies of Saturated Phenomena.* New York: Fordham University Press, 2002.

Mariotti, S. L., and J. H. Lane, eds. *A Political Companion to Marilynne Robinson.* Lexington: University of Kentucky Press, 2016.

Marsden, George. "Reformed and American." In *Reformed Theology in America: A History of Its Modern Development*, edited by David F. Wells. Grand Rapids: Eerdmans, 2009.

Mascord, Keith A. *Alvin Plantinga and Christian Apologetics.* Eugene, OR: Wipf and Stock, 2007.

McGregor, Jonathan D. "Sacred Loneliness and Sacred Comfort: A Review of Marilynne Robinson's 'Lila.'" Mere Orthodoxy, December 2, 2014. mereorthodoxy.com/sacred-loneliness-sacred-comfort-review-marilynne-robinsons-lila/.

McIntyre, John. Faith, Theology, and Imagination. Edinburgh: Handsel, 1987.

McLeod, Hugh. The Religious Crisis of the 1960s. Oxford: Oxford University Press, 2010.

Mellon, James G. "The Secular and the Sacred: Reflections on Charles Taylor's A Secular Age." Religion, State and Society 44, no. 1 (January 2, 2016): 75–91.

Merleau-Ponty, Maurice. Phenomenology of Perception. Translated by Colin Smith. London: Kegan Paul, 1962.

———. Phenomenology of Perception. Translated by Donald A. Landes. London: Routledge, 2012.

———. The World of Perception. London: Routledge, 2004.

Milbank, Alison. "Apologetics and the Imagination: Making Strange." In Imaginative Apologetics, 31-45. Grand Rapids: Baker Academic, 2012.

Milbank, John. Theology and Social Theory: Beyond Secular Reason. Oxford: Blackwell, 2006.

Miyazono, Kengo, and Shen-yi Liao. "The Cognitive Architecture of Imaginative Resistance." In The Routledge Handbook of Philosophy of Imagination, edited by Amy Kind, 368-79. London: Routledge, 2016.

Montgomery, John Warwick. Faith Founded on Fact: Essays in Evidential Apologetics. Nashville: Thomas Nelson, 1978.

Morgan, David. "Protestant Visual Piety and the Aesthetics of American Mass Culture." In Mediating Religion: Studies in Media, Religion, and Culture, edited by Jolyon P. Mitchell and Sophia Marriage. London: T&T Clark, 2003.

Mouw, Richard J. Adventures in Evangelical Civility: A Lifelong Quest for Common Ground. Grand Rapids: Brazos, 2016.

———. He Shines in All That's Fair: Culture and Common Grace. Grand Rapids: Eerdmans, 2002.

———. "Neo-Calvinism and 'The Catholic Imagination.'" In Rerum Novarum: Neo-Calvinism and Roman Catholicism. Rome, 2014.

Newell, J. Philip. "A. J. Scott and His Circle." PhD diss., Edinburgh University, 1981.

Niebuhr, H. Richard. Christ and Culture. San Francisco: Harper & Row, 1975.

Noble, Alan. Disruptive Witness: Speaking Truth in a Distracted Age. Downers Grove, IL: InterVarsity Press, 2018.

Oliphint, K. Scott, and William Edgar. Covenantal Apologetics: Principles and Practice in Defense of Our Faith. Wheaton, IL: Crossway, 2013.

Ordway, Holly. Apologetics and the Christian Imagination: An Integrated Approach to Defending the Faith. Steubenville, OH: Emmaus Road, 2017.

Painter, Rebecca M. "Further Thoughts on a Prodigal Son Who Cannot Come Home, on Loneliness and Grace: An Interview with Marilynne Robinson." Christianity & Literature 58, no. 3 (2009): 485-92.

Partee, Charles. *The Theology of John Calvin*. Louisville: Westminster John Knox, 2010.

Pascal, Blaise. *Pensées*. Translated by A. J. Krailsheimer. London: Penguin, 1995.

Penner, Myron B. *The End of Apologetics: Christian Witness in a Postmodern Context*. Grand Rapids: Baker Academic, 2013.

Pennington, John. "A 'Wolff' in Sheep's Clothing: The George MacDonald Industry and the Difficult Rehabilitation of a Reputation." In *George MacDonald: Literary Heritage and Heirs*, 239-55. Wayne, PA: Zossima, 2008.

Phillips, Timothy R., and Dennis L. Okholm, eds. *The Nature of Confession: Evangelicals and Postliberals in Conversation*. Downers Grove, IL: InterVarsity Press, 1996.

Plantinga, Alvin. *Knowledge and Christian Belief*. Grand Rapids: Eerdmans, 2015.

———. *Warranted Christian Belief*. New York: Oxford University Press, 1999.

Plato. *The Republic*. Translated by Allan Bloom. New York: Basic Books, 2016.

Reardon, Bernard M. G. *Religious Thought in the Victorian Age: A Survey from Coleridge to Gore*. London: Routledge, 2014.

Reid, Thomas. *Essays on the Intellectual Powers of Man*. Edited by James Walker. Cambridge: John Bartlett, 1852.

———. *Thomas Reid's Inquiry and Essays*. Edited by Ronald E. Beanblossom and Keith Lehrer. Indianapolis, IN: Hackett, 1983.

Richards, E. Randolph, and Brandon J. O'Brien. *Misreading Scripture with Western Eyes: Removing Cultural Blinders to Better Understand the Bible*. Downers Grove, IL: InterVarsity Press, 2012.

Ricoeur, Paul. *Time and Narrative*. Chicago: University of Chicago Press, 2012.

Robinson, Marilynne. *Absence of Mind: The Dispelling of Inwardness from the Modern Myth of the Self*. New Haven: Yale University Press, 2011.

———. "Calvinism as Metaphysics." *Toronto Journal of Theology* 25, no. 2 (2009): 175-86.

———. "Credo." *Harvard Divinity Bulletin* 36, no. 2 (2008).

———. *Gilead*. New York: Picador, 2006.

———. *Home*. New York: Picador, 2009.

———. *Housekeeping*. New York: Picador, 1980.

———. "Hysterical Scientism—the Ecstasy of Richard Dawkins." *Harper's Magazine*, November 2006, 81.

———. *John Calvin: Steward of God's Covenant: Selected Writings*. Edited by John F. Thornton. New York: Vintage, 2006.

———. *Jack*. New York: Picador, 2020.

———. *Lila*. New York: Picador, 2015.

———. "Onward, Christian Liberals: Faith Is Not About Piety or Personal Salvation, but About Helping Those in Need." *The American Scholar* 75, no. 2 (2006): 42-51.

———. "Religion and the Arts Award Lecture." Atlanta, 2015.

———. "Sacred Inwardness." *The Christian Century* 132, no. 14 (2015): 24-25.

———. "That Highest Candle." *Poetry* 190, no. 2 (May 2007): 130-39.

———. *The Death of Adam: Essays on Modern Thought*. New York: Picador, 2005.

———. *The Givenness of Things: Essays*. New York: Farrar, Straus and Giroux, 2015.

———. *What Are We Doing Here?: Essays*. New York: Farrar, Straus and Giroux, 2018.

———. "What Unitarians Know (and Sam Harris Doesn't)." *Wall Street Journal—Eastern Edition* 256, no. 79, October 2, 2010, C5.

———. *When I Was a Child I Read Books: Essays*. Picador, 2013.

———. "Writers and the Nostalgic Fallacy." *The New York Times*, October 13, 1985. www.nytimes.com/1985/10/13/books/writers-and-the-nostalgic-fallacy.html.

Root, Andrew. *Faith Formation in a Secular Age: Responding to the Church's Obsession with Youthfulness*. Grand Rapids: Baker Academic, 2017.

Ruskin, John. *Fors Clavigera: Letters, to the Workmen and Labourers of Great Britain*. Vol. 4. 4 vols. New York: Greenwood, 1968.

———. *Praeterita*. Edited by Francis O'Gorman. Oxford: Oxford University Press, 2012.

Ruskin, John, and Charles Eliot Norton. *The Correspondence of John Ruskin and Charles Eliot Norton*. Edited by John Lewis Bradley and Ian Ousby. Cambridge: Cambridge University Press, 1987.

Rutledge, Fleming. *The Crucifixion: Understanding the Death of Jesus Christ*. Grand Rapids: Eerdmans, 2015.

Ryken, Leland, James C. Wilhoit, and Tremper Longman III, eds. "Heart." In *Dictionary of Biblical Imagery*, 368-69. Downers Grove, IL: InterVarsity Press, 1998.

Sanneh, Lamin. *Translating the Message: The Missionary Impact on Culture*. Maryknoll: Orbis, 1989.

Schleiermacher, Friedrich. *Brief Outline of Theology as a Field of Study: Revised Translation of the 1811 and 1830 Editions*. Translated by Terrence N. Tice. Louisville: Westminster John Knox Press, 2011.

———. *On Religion: Speeches to Its Cultured Despisers*. Translated by John Oman. New York: Harper & Row, 1958.

———. *The Christian Faith*. Edited by H. R Mackintosh and James S Stewart. Edinburgh: T&T Clark, 1999.

Searle, Alison. *"The Eyes of Your Heart": Literary and Theological Trajectories of Imagining Biblically*. Colorado Springs, CO: Paternoster, 2008.

Seerveld, Calvin. *Rainbows for the Fallen World: Aesthetic Life and Artistic Task*. Toronto: Tuppence, 1980.

Shelley, Percy Bysshe. *A Defence of Poetry*. Indianapolis: Bobbs-Merrill, 1904.

Shortt, Rupert. *God Is No Thing: Coherent Christianity*. London: Hurst, 2016.

Slepyan, Jocelyne. "'With All Sorts of Doubts I Am Familiar': George MacDonald's Literary Response to John Ruskin's Struggles with Epistemology." In *Rethinking George MacDonald: Contexts and Contemporaries*. Glasgow: Scottish Literature International, 2013.

Smith, James K. A. *Desiring the Kingdom: Worship, Worldview, and Cultural Formation*. Grand Rapids: Baker Academic, 2009.

———. *How (Not) to Be Secular: Reading Charles Taylor*. Grand Rapids: Eerdmans, 2014.

———. *Imagining the Kingdom: How Worship Works*. Grand Rapids: Baker Academic, 2013.

———. "Marilynne Robinson's Apologia Gloriae." *Comment Magazine*, March 1, 2018. www.cardus.ca/comment/article/marilynne-robinsons-apologia-gloriae/.

Spina, Girogio. "The Influence of Dante on George MacDonald." Translated by Paul Priest. *North Wind* 9 (1990): 15-36.

Stark, Rodney. "Secularization, RIP." *Sociology of Religion* 60, no. 3 (1999): 249-73.

Steiner, George. *Real Presences*. Chicago: University of Chicago Press, 1989.

Steuber, Karsten R. "Empathy and the Imagination." In *The Routledge Handbook of Philosophy of Imagination*, edited by Amy Kind, 368-79. London: Routledge, 2016.

Stevenson, Leslie. "Twelve Conceptions of Imagination." *British Journal of Aesthetics* 43, no. 3 (July 2003): 238-59.

Sutanto, Nathaniel Gray. "Neo-Calvinism on General Revelation: A Dogmatic Sketch," *International Journal of Systematic Theology* 20, no. 4 (2018): 495–516.

Tanner, Kathryn. *Theories of Culture: A New Agenda for Theology*. Minneapolis: Fortress, 1997.

Tanner, Laura E. "'Looking Back from the Grave': Sensory Perception and the Anticipation of Absence in Marilynne Robinson's 'Gilead.'" *Contemporary Literature* 48, no. 2 (2007): 227-52.

Taylor, Charles. *A Secular Age*. Cambridge: Harvard University Press, 2007.

———. "Afterword: Apologia pro Libro Suo." In *Varieties of Secularism in a Secular Age*, edited by Michael Warner, Jonathan VanAntwerpen, and Craig Calhoun, 300-321. Cambridge: Harvard University Press, 2010.

———. "Disenchantment-Reenchantment." In *Dilemmas and Connections: Selected Essays*, 287–302. Cambridge, MA: Harvard University Press, 2011.

———. "Merleau-Ponty and the Epistemological Picture." In *The Cambridge Companion to Merleau-Ponty*, 26-49. New York: Cambridge University Press, 2005.

———. *Modern Social Imaginaries*. Durham: Duke University Press, 2004.

———. "Self-Interpreting Animals." In *Philosophical Papers*, 1:45-76. Cambridge: Cambridge University Press, 1985.

———. *Sources of the Self: The Making of the Modern Identity*. Cambridge: Harvard University Press, 1992.

———. *The Ethics of Authenticity*. Cambridge: Harvard University Press, 1992.

Thiselton, Anthony C. *The Hermeneutics of Doctrine*. Grand Rapids: Eerdmans, 2007.

Tolkien, John Ronald Reuel. *Tree and Leaf; Smith of Wootton Major; the Homecoming of Beorhtnoth, Beorhthelm's Son*. London: Unwin, 1975.

Tracy, David. *Blessed Rage for Order: The New Pluralism in Theology*. Chicago: University of Chicago Press, 1996.

———. *The Analogical Imagination: Christian Theology and the Culture of Pluralism*. New York: Crossroad, 1998.

Trexler, Robert. "George MacDonald: Merging Myth and Method." *The Bulletin of the New York C. S. Lewis Society* 34, no. 4 (August 2003): 1-13.

Tyson, Paul. *Seven Brief Lessons on Magic*. Eugene, OR: Cascade, 2019.

Van den Toren, Bernard. *Christian Apologetics: Religious Witness as Cross-Cultural Dialogue*. London: T&T Clark, 2011.

Van der Kooi, Cornelius. *As in a Mirror: John Calvin and Karl Barth On Knowing God*. Leiden: Brill, 2005.

———. "The Appeal to the Inner Testimony of the Spirit, especially in H. Bavinck," *Journal of Reformed Theology 2* (2008): 103-112.

Van Leeuwen, Neil. "The Imaginative Agent." In *Knowledge Through Imagination*, edited by Amy Kind and Peter Kung, 85-109. Oxford: Oxford University Press, 2016.

Van Til, Cornelius. *Christian Apologetics*. Edited by William Edgar. Phillipsburg, NJ: P&R, 2003.

Vanhoozer, Kevin J. *The Drama of Doctrine: A Canonical-Linguistic Approach to Christian Theology*. Louisville: Westminster John Knox Press, 2005.

Walton, Kendall L. *Mimesis as Make-Believe: On the Foundations of the Representational Arts*. Cambridge, MA: Harvard University Press, 1990.

Ward, Graham. *Unbelievable: Why We Believe and Why We Don't*. London: I. B. Tauris, 2014.

Ward, Michael. "The Good Serves the Better and the Best: C. S. Lewis on Imagination and Reason in Apologetics." In *Imaginative Apologetics*, 59-78. Grand Rapids: Baker Academic, 2012.

Warnock, Mary. *Imagination*. Berkeley: University of California Press, 1976.

Watkins, Gwen. "Two Notions of Hell." *North Wind* 10 (1991).

Weinandy, Thomas G. "Doing Christian Systematic Theology: Faith, Problems, and Mysteries." *Logos: A Journal of Catholic Thought and Culture* 5, no. 1 (2002): 120-38.

Werpehowski, William. "Ad Hoc Apologetics." *The Journal of Religion* 66, no. 3 (1986): 282-301.

Westermann, Claus. *Genesis 1-11: A Continental Commentary*. Minneapolis: Fortress, 1994.

"Why Believe in God?" *Closer to the Truth*, July 14, 2015. www.closertotruth.com /episodes/why-believe-god.

Willcox, Louise Collier. "A Neglected Novelist." *North American Review*, no. 183 (1906).

Wittgenstein, Ludwig. *Philosophical Investigations*. Translated by G. E. M. Anscombe. 3rd ed. Englewood Cliffs, NJ: Pearson, 1973.

Wolff, Robert. *Gains and Losses: Novels of Faith and Doubt in Victorian England*. New York: John Murray, 1977.

Yamaguchi, Miho. "Poor Doubting Christian: An Exploration of Salvation, Love, and Eternity in MacDonald's Wingfold Trilogy." *North Wind* 23 (2004): 1-12.

Yong, Amos. *The Spirit Poured Out on All Flesh: Pentecostalism and the Possibility of Global Theology*. Grand Rapids: Baker Academic, 2005.

Author Index

Scripture Index